DISCOVERING Hebrews

DISCOVERING Hebrews

an exposition

Jerry Vines

Free Church Press

Copyright © 2024 by Jerry Vines

All rights reserved. No part of this book may be reproduced in any manner whatsoever without written permission except in the case of brief quotations embodied in critical articles and reviews.

First Printing, 2024 by Free Church Press
ISBN: 978-1-939283-15-3

Formerly published as *The Believer's Guide to Hebrews* © 1993 by Jerry Vines by Loizeaux Brothers, Inc.

Unless otherwise indicated, Scripture quotations are taken from the King James version of the Bible.

Quotation from The Living Bible © 1971 is used by permission of Tyndale House Publishers, Inc., Wheaton, IL 60189. All rights reserved.

Scripture quotations taken from The Holy Bible, New International Version® NIV®
Copyright © 1973, 1978, 1984, 2011 by Biblica, Inc.
Used with permission. All rights reserved worldwide.

freechurchpress.com

CONTENTS

	Preface	1
1	Oh, What a Savior! Hebrews 1:1-14	3
2	It's Just Too Good to Miss Hebrews 2:1-4	11
3	Believers' Destination: Glory! Hebrews 2:5-13	19
4	Why Jesus Became a Man Hebrews 2:14-18	27
5	Where on Earth Does God Live? Hebrews 3:1-6	35
6	The Deadly Danger of Disbelief Hebrews 3:7-4:11	43
7	Why is the Bible so Special? Hebrews 4:12-13	51
8	Jesus, Our Great High Priest Hebrews 4:14-16	59
9	Our Heavenly High Priest Hebrews 5:1-7	67

CONTENTS

10 | Let's Talk About Our Salvation Hebrews 5:8-10 73

11 | Let Us Go On Hebrews 5:11-6:3 79

12 | Tragedy of a Backslidden Life Hebrews 6:4-9 87

13 | Dancing on the Promises Hebrews 6:10-15 95

14 | My Anchor Will Forever Hold Hebrews 6:16-20 101

15 | The Mystery of Melchizedek Hebrews 7:1-28 107

16 | The New and Better Covenant Hebrews 8:1-13 115

17 | Our Great Tabernacle Revealed Hebrews 9:1-14 121

18 | Christ's Last Will and Testament Hebrews 9:15-28 129

19 | One Sacrifice Offered Forever Hebrews 10:1-18 137

20 | Come On In! Hebrews 10:19-25 143

21 | Can Christians Get by with Sin? Hebrews 10:26-31 149

CONTENTS

22 | When There's No Turning Back Hebrews 10:32-39 157

23 | Christians Live Only by Faith Hebrews 11:1-7 163

24 | Abraham: Looking for a City Hebrews 11:8-10 171

25 | A Tested Faith is a True Faith Hebrews 11:11-19 177

26 | Dying in Faith Hebrews 11:20-22 185

27 | Moses: Seeing the Invisible God Hebrews 11:23-27 193

28 | Faith is Forever the Victory Hebrews 11:28-31 199

29 | Always Striving to be Faithful Hebrews 11:32-40 205

30 | Ready...Set...Go for the Gold! Hebrews 12:1-3 213

31 | God's Loving Chastisement Hebrews 12:4-13 221

32 | Missing the Grace of God Hebrews 12:14-17 229

33 | Where We Have Now Come Hebrews 12:18-24 237

CONTENTS

34 | Things Unshakable That Remain
Hebrews 12:25-29 245

35 | We Can Build a Better Life Hebrews 13:1-8,17,24 253

36 | It Just Keeps Getting Better! Hebrews 13:9-16 261

37 | Pay Attention to This Letter Hebrews 13:18-23,25 269

ABOUT THE AUTHOR 277

Preface

DISCOVERING Hebrews: an exposition is the first volume published in a proposed multi-volume series entitled *DISCOVERING the Bible* by Jerry Vines. Among other titles scheduled for 2024 are *DISCOVERING Revelation: an exposition* and *DISCOVERING the Pastorals: an exposition of 1 & 2 Timothy and Titus*. I'm very excited about *DISCOVERING the Bible* series that, by God's sweet grace, will initially cover the entire New Testament. As God blesses our work, we prayerfully hope to begin on the Old Testament once the New Testament is complete.

DISCOVERING Hebrews: an exposition is a reprint of my original *The Believer's Guide to Hebrews* published in 1993. Only minor changes have been made. The original has been out of print for several years. Jerry Vines Ministries gets so many requests for it that the decision was made to publish it first.

As you will read in the original preface below, preaching through Hebrews was a rich, blessed experience for me. I pray this exposition will be an encouragement and help for those who will preach or teach or study through this marvelous book.

Jerry Vines, 2024

Original Preface

Someone has well said that the book of Hebrews begins like a treatise, proceeds like a sermon, and ends like a letter. All of these elements are certainly seen in this masterpiece of Christian literature. Hebrews begins with a beautiful presentation of the person and work of our Lord Jesus, proceeds with a clear discussion of the fulfillment of Old Testament typology in our Savior, and closes like the other doctrinal letters with appeals and exhortations.

Actually, I approached Hebrews in my own preaching with some sense of apprehension. First, the length of the book was a concern. I preach to a modern, mobile people and many of my listeners are in the city and out before I get an extended opportunity to share the Word with them. The average American moves about every five years. Further, I wondered how a discussion of the Old Testament sacrifices and ceremonies would be received by people who are not as biblically literate as congregations used to be.

My concerns were unwarranted. As I started into my messages in Hebrews I was delighted that each sermon could be so presented that it stood alone. Also I found my people were very interested to see how Old and New Testament truths fit together, the New flowing from the Old. My enthusiasm for the series grew each week and the response of the people was correspondingly positive. As it turned out, I enjoyed my journey through Hebrews as much as my study of any other Bible book I have tackled, and the congregation indicated that the series helped them as much as any other messages I have shared with them.

I should have known there was no need to be concerned. *The key to Hebrews is that Jesus is better.* In Jesus we have a *better* Savior, a *better* sacrifice, a *better* priest, *better* promises, a *better* destiny—a *better* everything! One never goes wrong preaching about Jesus.

I have not prepared these studies in Hebrews for scholars. I am no scholar myself. I have prepared them for believers like myself who earnestly want to know what God has to say in His Word about how to live for Him, serve Him, and lead others to Him.

Jerry Vines, 1993

1

Oh, What a Savior! Hebrews 1:1-14

Mr. and Mrs. Klepfish are Christian believers in the state of Maryland. When they applied for their license plates one year they wanted to put something on their tags that would be a Christian testimony, so they requested that their license plates read: GOD IS. They could never have imagined the furor they started. Evidently some people who saw those two words complained. The motor vehicle administration of the state of Maryland recalled their tags and told them they could not put those words on their license plates. When they appealed the case, the head of the Maryland department of transportation overruled the opinion of the motor vehicle administration. The Klepfishes could use those words.

Whether the government allows that affirmation to be made or not, God is. The Bible everywhere assumes the reality of God. "In the beginning God . . . ." Hebrews begins with the statement that God spoke in times past and now has also spoken in His Son. There is no attempt in the Bible to prove the existence of God.

We study Hebrews for several reasons. One reason is to encourage ourselves as believers. This book is called a word of exhortation—or a word of encouragement (13:22).

Another reason is to examine our faith to see if what we have is the real thing. The greatest reason we ought to study Hebrews is that there is no other place in all of the Bible where the Lord Jesus Christ is so exalted and magnified. If you love Him, you will love to study Hebrews.

All through this book we see the writer saying that Jesus is better. In Jesus we have a better priest, a better sacrifice, a better resurrection, a better destiny.

I. HE OUTSPEAKS THE PROPHETS (1:1-3)

Jesus is better because He outspeaks the prophets. In Hebrews 1:1 an assumption is made, the assumption that God is, that God exists, that God is real. A second assumption immediately follows: God has spoken (1:2).

Religion is man's attempt to find the supernatural God. Salvation is God's entry into human existence to reveal Himself. John MacArthur illustrated the difference between religion and salvation by raising and answering this question: How can human beings who are enclosed by time and space in a natural box make contact with the supernatural God who is outside the box? Two possible answers arise. Either man can attempt to chip a hole in a corner of the box, or God can come down into that box and reveal Himself in an understandable way. Religion is my reaching up trying to make contact with God. Salvation is God's reaching down into my existence and contacting me. That is the substance of Hebrews 1:1-2. God has spoken.

A. His Partial Word (1:1)

God has spoken primarily in two ways. First God spoke through the prophets. "God, who at sundry times"—we can translate that "in many pieces." Here a little, there a little. "And in divers manners"—we can translate that "in many ways." The writer was referring to the Old Testament. He was saying that it isn't God's full and final word. The Old Testament is God's partial word.

The Old Testament was composed over a span of approximately fifteen hundred years and written by more than forty authors on several different continents. Each one received bits and pieces of revelation. This is progressive revelation, a progressive unfolding of God's truth. Each prophet seemed to be given a little additional piece, but always there was more. To some prophets God spoke in visions and dreams; to others He spoke with a still small voice or a literal voice as loud as thunder.

One of the key features of the Old Testament is the unfolding of prophecy concerning the coming of the Lord Jesus Christ. Moses in Genesis said He would be the seed of the woman (Gen 3:15), yet there was more to be said. Micah said He would be born in Bethlehem (Mi 5:2; cp. Mt 2:6), but there was more to be said. Isaiah said He would be born of a virgin (Isa 7:14) and would be a suffering servant who would die for mankind's sin (Isa 53). Yes, but there was more to be said. First Peter 1:10 says that the prophets inquired and searched diligently. They were puzzled by the pieces that they examined because they were aware that a key piece was missing. They couldn't get the total picture until God spoke His final word. Always they were looking for greater fulfillment. The Bible says that to Him, that is to Jesus, all the prophets gave witness.

B. His Final Word (1:2-3)

The writer of Hebrews said that God "hath in these last days spoken unto us by his Son" (1:2). In other words, Jesus is God's total word to man. Then the writer laid before us seven magnificent statements about Christ.

Jesus Christ is the "heir of all things." When God created Adam and Eve and placed them in the garden of Eden, God said He would give them dominion over everything. When sin entered Eden, they lost dominion. When Jesus came, not only did He save us from our sins, but He also inherited the right to be Lord of all things. We don't see all things under His feet right now, but ultimately this entire universe is going to bow before the Lord Jesus Christ.

Sometimes heirs are selfish. When they inherit something they keep it for themselves. But Jesus wasn't that kind of heir. The Bible says that if you will come to Him and let Him save you, He'll make you an heir too. Romans 8:17 says we are "joint-heirs with Christ." Everything Jesus owns, I own. We own all the trees on all the continents on this earth. In Jesus the meek shall inherit the earth.

"By whom also he made the worlds." Jesus Christ created the universe and everything it takes to keep that universe in operation. Colossians 1:16 says that "all things were created by him, and for him." Jesus Christ made it all.

How do you account for the existence of this universe? Several years ago a scientist said that the chance of intelligent life on the earth coming about by a series of accidental occurrences is about 400,000 trillion trillion to one. The most incredible thing he said is that though it will never happen again, that's how it all came about! By accident. (I would say a guy like that is about a quart low!).

Think of the heart that's pumping right now in your body. If you live a normal lifetime, your will pump an estimated eight hundred million times. Is all of that a colossal accident? John 1:3 says, "All things were made by him; and without him was not any thing made that was made."

"Who being the brightness of his glory"—that is, the outshining of His glory. Jesus Christ the Son reveals God the Father. The rays of the sun express the sun. Jesus Christ expresses the Father. In Jesus we behold the glory of God. Jesus is the brightness, the effulgence, of the glory of God.

He is the "express image of his person," His nature, His substance. Jesus Christ is the exact reproduction of the nature of God. When an imprint is stamped on a seal, whatever the imprint is, the seal is. If you want to know what God is like, look at Jesus Christ. If you want to know what God would say, listen to Jesus. Jesus said, "He that hath seen me hath seen the Father" (Jn 14:9).

"Upholding all things by the word of his power." The writer of Hebrews was not talking about Jesus as some Atlas holding up the world. The picture here is of maintaining and sustaining all things. Colossians 1:17 says, "By him all things consist." All things hold together. He keeps this universe from going to pieces. We depend on a universe that operates on the basis of natural laws that are under His control. One of these days the Lord Jesus is going to take His hands off this universe and the whole thing is going to come apart; then Jesus is going to make a new heaven and a new earth.

If Jesus is able to sustain this universe, don't you think He can sustain you and me? I like that little spiritual, "He's Got the Whole World in His Hands." It says, "He's got the little, tiny baby in His hands. He's got you and me, brother, in His hands."

"When he had by himself purged our sins." The Hebrews author moved from creation to Calvary. It's not enough for us to know that Jesus Christ created this universe. The good news of God's final word to us is that Jesus Christ paid the price that cleansed us from our sins.

That phrase "our sins" contains volumes of heartaches; much of the sorrow that you and I experience is there. That's the problem—*our sins*. We all are sinners who need a Savior.

"Sat down on the right hand of the Majesty on high." Jesus paid for the sins of the world. Although they buried Him in h a tomb, three days later He burst its doors and came out in resurrected life. After many post-resurrection appearances, He ascended to the Father. He sat down at the right hand of the Father reigning as Lord of lords and King of kings this very moment. That's God's final word.

Jesus came all the way from the bosom of the Father to the bosom of a woman. In infancy, He frightened a king. In boyhood, He confounded scholars. In manhood, He ruled nature. In death He conquered sin. In resurrection, He conquered death. He is the rock of geology. He is the star of astronomy. He is the lamb of zoology. He is the Lord of history, and He is the God of eternity. Jesus outspeaks the prophets!

IL HE OUTRANKS THE ANGELS (1:4-9,13-14)

In the rest of the chapter, the inspired author gave us seven Old Testament quotations to prove that Jesus outranks the angels. In New Testament times people probably made too much of angels. Probably in our time we make too little of angels. There is a balance in the Bible. The Bible teaches the existence of angels. Angels are referred to 105 times in the Old Testament and 165 times in the New Testament. Angels exist!

According to Scripture, angels go on errands for God. Gabriel went on an errand for God and appeared to a young oman named Mary. God's message to Mary was that He had chosen her to be the human vehicle through whom His final word would come. Years later, when Simon Peter was in jail, God sent one of his earthquake angels to shake up the jail and open its doors. Angels were present at the birth of the Lord Jesus and at His resurrection. They will be present when He comes again.

A. Excellent Name (1:4-8)

But in spite of all the wonderful things the Bible says about angels, Jesus outranks them. He has a "more excellent name" (1:4). While angels are merely servants of God, Jesus is the Son of God. The Father says, "Let all the angels of God worship him" (1:6), "but unto the Son he saith, Thy throne, O God, is for ever and ever" (1:8). As angels serve before the throne of God, Jesus the Son sits on the throne of God.

B. Exalted Nature (1:9,13-14)

The Son also has a more exalted nature. Because He loved righteousness and hated iniquity, Jesus was anointed with the oil of gladness above His fellows (1:9). We can picture Jesus leaping for joy in glory. We can also picture Jesus being given the place of honor and power at God's right hand (1:13). Ultimately all will recognize the Son's exalted nature, and even His enemies will be under His feet. Angels, being of lesser rank, are sent forth to minister (1:14). All in the universe will be in subjection to the Son, but no such rule is given to angels.

III. HE OUTLASTS THE UNIVERSE (1:10-12)

"Thou, Lord, in the beginning hast laid the foundation of the earth; and the heavens are the works of thine hands" (1:10). Jesus created the universe, and He is still in the creation business today. "If any man be in Christ, he is a new creature: old things are passed away; behold, all things are become new" (2 Cor 5:17).

A. Creation Will Collapse (l:10-12a)

This creation is collapsing. "They shall perish . . . they all shall wax old as doth a garment; And as a vesture shalt thou fold them up, and they shall be changed" (1:11-12). We have confirmed in science what God has already told us in His Bible; namely, this whole universe is winding down. The sun is winding down, burning out at a rate of 4.2 million tons per second. There will come a time when the stars will burn out like sparks in a fireplace.

Ever have a tire start wobbling on your car? The first car I ever had, I had it nine months and had eight flat tires. When I brought that flivver home after my final exams in college, those tires collapsed! Think of that brand-new car you are so proud of, the car you shine every week. There is already a little nick on it. That's just the beginning of the end. It's just a matter of time, and that car is going to rust away. That new dress you bought you should look at it closely. There is a hole in it already. That little hole is going to get bigger and eventually you will have to discard the dress. Everything in the universe is going to fold up. Don't pin your hopes on something that is collapsing.

B. Christ Will Continue (1:12b)

"They shall perish; but thou remainest." Jesus outlasts the universe. I'm glad I have a Savior who will live forever and ever. "They shall be changed: but thou art the same" (1:12). A billion, billion, billion years from now, Jesus Christ will still be on His throne. He will be the same and will still love and care for us.

When Abraham Lincoln died, Edwin Stanton, the secretary of war rose from his chair, went to the window, pulled the blinds, looked back at the lifeless form, and said, "Now, he belongs to the ages." That was only relatively true. The One who belongs to the ages is the One to whom the ages belong—our Lord Jesus Christ.

2

It's Just Too Good to Miss
Hebrews 2:1-4

Once upon a time there was a young man named William. One day his father and elder brother said, "William, we are going to give you a magnificent farm with thousands of acres of land. We want you to take this farm and make it everything it possibly can be." The farm had exceptionally fertile soil. All William had to do was plow the fields and plant the seeds, and he would have an abundant, luscious crop. All William had to do was prune the tree sand pick the fruit. If he drilled, he would find oil. If he dug, he would find gold.

His father and brother not only gave him that wonderful farm; they also provided him with all the necessary farm tools. They said, "William, to help you make your farm all that it ought to be, we have written a book for you. In this book are all the directions you will ever need, and there are warnings to tell you what to avoid. Just follow the directions. After a while we are going to come back and see what kind of job you have done."

At the beginning, everything went quite well. William cultivated the soil and produced great crops. He gathered fruit from the trees and grapes from the vines. He dug for gold. He drilled for oil. But after a while William began to be careless and neglectful. Because of his indifference, his farm became unproductive. When his father and elder brother came to inspect the farm, they didn't take it away from William. It was still his possession, but the blessings and benefits that were possible were not his.

The story is imaginary, but the situation is real. It is what Hebrews 2:1-4 is about. These verses of Scripture were written to believers to admonish them to take the wonderful salvation provided by the heavenly Father in the person of the Lord Jesus and make it everything it can possibly be.

I. GREATNESS OF OUR SALVATION (2:3-4)

The center of this passage is a word in 2:3: *salvation*. "How shall we escape, if we neglect so great salvation." *Salvation* is an inclusive word, encompassing everything God does for us and intends for us when He saves us. Salvation involves regeneration; that happens the moment of our new birth. Salvation involves sanctification —our progressive growth in righteousness. Salvation includes glorification—our final state of being what God intended us to be when He saved us.

"Therefore we ought to give the more earnest heed to the things which we have heard, lest at anytime we should let them slip" (2:1). "How shall we escape, if we neglect so great salvation; which at the first began to be spoken by the Lord, and was confirmed unto us by them that heard him" (2:3). Notice the use of personal pronouns. The writer is talking here not primarily to lost people but to saved people. He is talking about neglecting salvation, not rejecting salvation.

Moving from that center, we can move outward to the cautions and encouragements that God has for us in these verses. This Scripture portion is the first of a series of five passages in the book of Hebrews that contain warnings or exhortations. This first warning passage is an admonition that believers not fail to receive and enjoy everything that salvation includes; we must not miss the greatness of our salvation.

A. Method (2:3)

There is greatness in the method of salvation. Look at how this salvation was brought to us. This salvation originated with the Lord Jesus. It was first "spoken by the Lord."

This salvation was *substantiated* by the apostles. It "was confirmed unto us by them that heard him." Jesus spoke the gospel to men who confirmed that what Jesus said was true. Look at the people Jesus chose to be His apostles. He took a cursing fisherman and made him a great gospel preacher. He took John, a son of thunder, and made him the apostle of love.

This salvation was *authenticated* by God the Father: "God also bearing them witness" (2:4). During the time when the apostles were preaching the gospel, God authenticated their message as being accurate and from Heaven. He bore them witness with "signs and wonders." That was for the benefit of the Jews. Then there were "divers miracles," which authenticated their message to the Gentiles. And there were "gifts" or distributions of the Holy Spirit. That authenticated their message to the church.

B. Meaning (2:4)

There is also greatness in the meaning of this salvation. "How shall we escape, if we neglect so great salvation." See that little word *so*. What does it mean?

This salvation of ours was planned by God. Suppose you called all the wise men of all the ages to one immense convocation and said to them, "Now you work out a plan that can adequately deal with sin and at the same time forgive the sinner." If they worked on the problem for an eternity, they would never come up with an adequate plan. But our salvation is more than adequate. It is so great because it was planned by God the Father Himself.

Our salvation is also great in its price. You and I may know that salvation is free, but that doesn't mean it is cheap. Salvation cost the blood of the Lord Jesus Christ. The Bible says, "Unto him that loved us, and washed us from our sins in his own blood" (Rev 1:5).

Salvation is great in its scope. It takes care of our past, it takes care of our present, and it takes care of our future. I have been saved, I am being saved, and I am going to be saved. Salvation takes care of every part of the personality. Salvation takes care of the spirit; I received a brand-new spirit when I was saved. Salvation takes care of the soul; I received a saved soul when I accepted Christ. Salvation takes care of the body. Though death will claim our bodies, at the resurrection we will receive brand-new bodies.

Salvation is great in its power. Consider a person whose life is nothing but a curse on the earth. Everything he touches is harmed. Every place he steps, he brings sorrow and heartache. Yet Jesus can come into that life and save him and make him a blessing.

II. SERIOUSNESS OF OUR SALVATION (2:2-3a)

Now comes a somber note. Don't miss out on the seriousness of your salvation. Hebrews 2:2-3 makes a comparison between God's Old Testament word and His New Testament word. God's first word is the law. God's final word is grace.

A. First Word (2:2)

There is a seriousness attached to God's first word, the law. "For if the word spoken by angels was stedfast"—two verses of Scripture will explain that statement: Acts 7:38 and Galatians 3:19. Those two verses say that when Moses was on Sinai receiving the law from God, the law was brought by angels. If the word spoken by those angels was reliable, "and every transgression and disobedience received a just recompense of reward," we all are in serious trouble. The law of God was so serious that if you transgressed it (if you stepped over the line: sins of commission) or if you disobeyed it (sins of omission), you would receive a just recompense of reward. The Old Testament invariably tells what the punishment will be if a person violates a standard. What God said in the Old Testament is this: If you break My law, it will break you. If you violate My law, you will have to pay the price.

I wouldn't want to live in a universe that was not that way. I wouldn't want to live in a town that was not based on moral law. I wouldn't want to live in a city that did not have a law that said when the light is red you have to stop. The difference between God's law in the universe and man's law in the city is that you may sometimes beat man's law, but you never beat God's law.

B. Final Word (2:3a)

It's true in the natural world just as it's true in the spiritual world: God runs His natural world on the basis of law. Consider God's natural law of gravity. If you stepped off the roof of your house, you would probably break some bones. The law of gravity says that what goes up comes down.

You can disregard God's natural law of gravity if you want to. You can say, "I don't like that law. Who is He to put a law of gravity in His natural world?" Then you climb on top of a building and say, "God I don't like Your natural law. Here I go." You do a swan dive —and you break your back. Are you going to be mad at the law of gravity or the God who designed it? If you break God's natural law, you pay the price. The same thing is true in God's spiritual world. If you break God's moral laws, there is always a punishment.

Let me illustrate with something that's very current—the matter of homosexuality. We are facing a crisis in America because of homosexuality and the whole gender fluidity debate. Romans 1:26-27 says,

> For this cause God gave them up unto vile affections: for even their women did change the natural use into that which is against nature: And likewise also the men, leaving the natural use of the woman, burned in their lust one toward another; men with men working that which is unseemly.

Paul was talking about the sin of homosexuality. The Bible is not obscure or indefinite on that point. I don't care if some liberal preacher tries to tell you that the New Testament or the Old Testament is unclear on that subject. To the contrary, the Bible is crystal clear on the sin of homosexuality.

Throughout the Bible, homosexuality is condemned. Note what Paul said next in the Romans text: "And receiving in themselves that recompense of their error which was meet" (1:27). He was saying that when you violate God's moral laws you must pay the price. Whom do we therefore blame for the current crisis of gender confusion and aberrant sexuality? Do we blame God? No. Do we blame His moral law of sexual purity? I think not. Josh McDowell put it about as well as anybody I've heard. He said that the commandments of God are not primarily negative; instead, they are positive. God is saying to us: Don't hurt yourself. The point of Hebrews 2:2 then is this: in Old Testament law, sin is a serious matter. Consequently, verse 3 says if that was true in the Old Testament, if that is true under the law, then how shall we (believers) escape if we neglect so great salvation?

A Christian may say, "I'm saved. I'm God's child. I'm going to Heaven when I die regardless of what I do, so it doesn't matter how I live." Of course, it is different when a Christian sins. Indeed it is far worse! Suppose your son and the neighborhood boys are playing ball in your front yard, and they get in a fuss. Although you are probably concerned about all of the boys who are involved in the fracas, which boy are you going to deal with? Your boy. You may rebuke them all, but the one you are going to pay special attention to is your boy. When you sin as a child of God He says, "I'm going to deal with you as my child." It is far more serious when a believer sins than when a lost person sins.

How shall we escape? The answer to that is both clear and frightening: *there is no escape*. What would we escape from? Not Hell. Jesus has already paid the price for our sins, and thes when we sin, we do not risk going to Hell. But believers cannot escape the chastisement of God now and the examination of God at the judgment seat if they sin and take lightly the great salvation God has given them.

III. FULLNESS OF OUR SALVATION (2:1)

A. Our Danger

"We ought to give the more earnest heed to the things which we have heard, lest at any time we should let them slip." Without exception, all Bible translations give a picture of the believer here as drifting away from something.

Of course, in the life of a Christian there is the deadly danger of drifting, but here the verb translated "let them slip" has a variety of meanings. A crumb of bread *slips* down into your windpipe. A ring *slips* off your finger. If your husband gave you a ring, and you carelessly let that ring slip off, you would become very concerned. You didn't lose *him*, but you lost something precious that he gave you. The writer may have been saying: Don't lose the preciousness of your salvation.

B. Our Duty

The root of this word *slip* really means "to flow like a river." The verb was used by Jesus in John 7:38 when He said, "Out of his belly shall flow rivers of living water." Yet the verb is passive. So, the picture in Hebrews 2:1 is not of a Christian drifting; it is a picture of a Christian being stationary and a river flowing or passing by. Perhaps we may paraphrase the Hebrews author this way: We must pay the more earnest heed to the things we have heard, lest at any time we should be flowed by.

God's great salvation is like a mighty flowing river. A Christian can just get his feet wet in that river, or he can go beyond the shallow water to the depths of this salvation—to the fullness of it. Thus, the writer was saying to us, "Don't miss out on the abundance of your salvation. Don't let it slip by you. Give more earnest heed. Pay careful attention. Listen to the Word of God. Obey the commandments of Jesus."

Allow me to retell the earlier story of William with a different ending. He continued to cultivate his farm. He drilled and hit oil. He dug and mined gold. When his father and brother came back, they saw that the farm was everything it was intended to be. One of these days our elder brother, the Lord Jesus, is going to come back. We have been given this great salvation. Don't you hope that when He comes back, you and I can say, "Lord, I didn't let it slip me by; I have been everything I possibly could be for You"?

3

Believers' Destination: Glory!
Hebrews 2: 5-13

John Milton, the blind English poet, composed one of the greatest pieces of literature in the English language. In his epic poem *Paradise Lost*, he depicted the creation of man, the fall of man, and the effects of that fall in Heaven, on earth, and in Hell. He described the efforts of God to redeem man from that fall by sending the Lord Jesus into the world. Four years later Milton composed another poem, *Paradise Regained*. In those two poems he captured the essence of the gospel. The Bible is the story of how human beings, by sin, lost paradise and how, by the death of the Lord Jesus Christ, paradise was regained.

Hebrews 2 tells the story of paradise lost and paradise regained. The center of the passage, verse 10, says that God is bringing many sons unto glory. The Bible is about the efforts of God to take fallen sinners, save them, change their lives, and make them fit for glory, fit for the paradise He Himself regained. The gospel is the good news about how God can take sinners and turn them into saints.

The key word of this passage is the word *glory* which occurs in three places. Hebrews 2:7 says that man was crowned with glory and honor. Hebrews 2:9 says our Lord Jesus was crowned with glory and honor. Hebrews 2:10 shows what God does for sinners when He changes them into saints and makes them fit for glory.

I. GLORY REMOVED (2:5-8)

Hebrews 2:5-8 is the story of our human dignity, destiny, and tragedy. The Bible indicates that when God created humankind, He clothed him and her in glory. God gave them the sun to warm their body, the moon to guide them in nightly travels, flowers to freshen their air, and fruit to please their taste. In these verses we see God's intention for the human race.

A. What Humanity Will Be Ultimately (2:5)

God did not put the world-to-come under the subjection of the angels. He has not put the future under their authority. Rather, God has determined that ultimately the world will be under the authority of the redeemed. Several words are translated "world" in our Bible. One of the words is *cosmos,* meaning all of the created universe. Another word for "world" refers to the inhabited earth in the age in which a person lives. In Hebrews 2:5, the writer was talking about the inhabited earth in the millennial reign of Jesus Christ. One of these days there is going to be a millennial reign of Jesus on this earth and every born-again child of God is destined to reign with Him during that period of time. Revelation 20:4 says that believers will reign with Jesus Christ for a thousand years.

B. What Humanity Was Potentially (2:6-8b)

In Hebrews 2:6-8 the writer quoted an Old Testament Psalm (Psalm 8). The quote begins: "What is man, that thou art mindful of him? or the son of man, that thou visitest him?" David the psalmist considered the vastness of the universe God created and became aware of how finite humankind is. We know that in the universe, we are comparatively insignificant physically. The chemical value of a human being, even in these days of inflation, is a little over a dollar.

In addition, we are also mentally insignificant in the universe. While we know a great deal, there is even more that we do not know. We are living in a time of specialization. There are heart specialists, eye specialists, bone specialists. In most fields today knowledge is changing and increasing so rapidly that a specialist has to read a book an hour just to keep up with his specialty. That means you better call your doctor today and make an appointment for no later than tomorrow because he will already be twenty-four books behind on your ailment when you arrive! We have just touched the hem of the garment of the store of knowledge that could be accumulated.

So the psalmist looked at the human race and said: Wonder of wonders —how insignificant in the universe are we, yet God remains interested in us and has even visited us. When we think about the fact that earth is just one of many little specks in the universe, and then consider the fact that out of all those specks, God chose this planet for His Son to visit, we too are filled with wonder. "What is . . . the son of man, that thou visitest him?"

Even more, God gave humankind the potential to rule the universe. "Thou madest him a little lower than the angels" (2:7). Evolution says that man is a little higher than the animals. The Bible says that human beings are a little lower than the angels. God crowned humanity with glory and honor. There are those who believe that when God created humans and put them in the garden of Eden, they were clothed with God's glory-light. Psalm 104:2 speaks of God "who coverest thyself with light as with a garment." So, in Eden Adam and Eve were clothed in the glory of God. They potentially had the power to dominate the universe.

"Thou hast put all things in subjection under his feet" (2:8). That takes us back to Genesis 1 where God said, "Be fruitful, multiply, replenish the earth. I have given you dominion over all created things." That was our potential: to rule God's creation.

C. What Humanity Is Actually (2:8c)

"But now we see not yet all things put under him." I've underlined four words in that verse in my Bible: But now . . . not yet. Those four words tell us what humankind is. Those four words are a summary of Genesis 3 which records our terrible fall into sin and death. Sin robbed mankind's potential of dominion. Human beings don't have control of the universe now.

Ever tried to catch a fish? Unless that fish decides to let you catch him, you don't have much chance of landing him. Ever try to tell a bird where to light? Ever try to control the flight of a bird in the air? Ever try to keep a dog out of your flower bed? Ever try to tame a lion? A lion-tamer may have a lion under his control temporarily, but if he should turn his eyes away for a moment, the lion would rip an arm off his body.

Human beings can't control creation. In fact, we can't even control ourselves. We have fallen from the lofty pedestal where God placed us in the garden. After our willful, sinful catastrophe, we now are totally incapable of recovery. In short, our only hope is a God-sent Savior. You will never understand the human race until you recognize the human condition. We are fallen, sinful creatures. There is no other way to account for the behavior —the inconsistencies—of human beings. One moment a person can be unbelievably kind, the next moment devastatingly cruel. How do you explain such erratic behavior? How do you explain the contradictions in us? The biblical explanation is that people are fallen creatures. They have gone all the way from light to leaves, all the way from glory to nudity. The story of humankind is the story of glory removed.

II. GLORY REVEALED (2:9-10)

In contrast to the sinfulness and failure of humanity, we see Jesus (2:9). When God sent His Son, God revealed His glory once again. As John Henry Newman's 1865 hymn "Praise to the holiest in the height" rings out,

> O, loving wisdom of our God!
> When all was sin and shame,
> a second Adam to the fight

and to the rescue came.

The story of Jesus is a story of the glory of God revealed.

A. Incarnation (2:9a)

Hebrews 2:9-10 tells the whole story of the coming of Jesus into this world. The passage begins, "But we see Jesus, who was made a little lower than the angels." Jesus Christ was on the throne of the universe, yet He entered the narrow confines of the womb of a virgin. Jesus Christ, before whom the angels of God fell in worship, condescended below angelic nature and took upon Himself human nature. Jesus revealed the glory of God in His incarnation. John 1:14 says, "We beheld his glory, the glory as of the only begotten of the Father, full of grace and truth."

When Jesus performed miracles, He was demonstrating the glory of God. Remember the time Jesus went to the wedding in Cana of Galilee? The host ran out of wine so the servants filled up some waterpots with water and in the presence of its Maker, the water became wine. John said, "This beginning of miracles did Jesus in Cana of Galilee, and manifested forth his glory" (Jn 2:11).

Jesus Christ had power over the fish of the sea. Remember the day Jesus was preaching in the boat of Simon Peter? He had been fishing all night and couldn't get a fish to bite. The Lord Jesus said, "Why don't you take your net and throw it on the other side, and I'll let you get a big catch of fish." Word got out in the sea of Galilee that the Lord of the sea wanted some fish. Every fish in the sea of Galilee came running to that net.

Ever try to make a rooster crow? Jesus said to Simon Peter, "Simon, the rooster won't crow until you have denied me three times." Ever tried to keep a rooster from crowing? Daybreak came; Jesus said, "No, not yet." A little later the rooster didn't think he could stand it anymore. Jesus said, "No, not yet." Then when Simon Peter had denied the Lord three times, as Jesus said he would, Jesus pulled the rooster's feathers and said, "Now it's time." Right on schedule. That's Jesus.

When Jesus was tempted, the wild animals in the wilderness did not harm Him. On the day of His triumphal entry, He rode into Jerusalem on a donkey that no one had ridden before. Yet when the Son of God, the Lord of the universe, sat on that donkey, I suspect he didn't flinch a muscle or blink an eye or twitch an ear. God had wanted man to have dominion. But sin came, and man lost that dominion. But the perfect man, the last Adam, the Lord Jesus Christ, came to earth, exercised absolute dominion over the created universe, and revealed the glory of God.

B. Substitution (2:9b)

Jesus also revealed the glory of God in His crucifixion: "We see Jesus, who was made a little lower than the angels for the suffering of death" (2:9). Jesus came into the world to die. See those little feet of the infant Lord? One day they will be grown feet and will walk up a hill called Calvary. See those little hands of the baby Jesus? One day those hands will be driven through with nails. See that little body of the incarnate Son of God? One day that body will be a grown body and will be wrapped in a shroud and put in a tomb. Jesus Christ came into the world for the suffering of death. He was born to die.

Why? Because the wages of our sin is death. The only payment that God will accept for our sin is the payment of death: "That he by the grace of God should taste death for every man" (2:9). Jesus Christ drank dry the cup of death for every one of us. When He was dying on the cross, He was paying the penalty that your sins and my sins deserved.

Death in itself is a terrible reality, but there was never a death like the death Jesus Christ died. The Lord Jesus Christ suffered not only outward torture, but also inward agony. He was on that cross for about six hours and in that finite period of time, Jesus endured an infinite grief. He experienced all of Hell for all the sin of all the people of all the world for all of time. He took your place. He took my place. By the grace of God, Christ became our substitute.

Why did He do it? Not because we are lovable. Not because we deserve it. Jesus paid that kind of price because He loved us. Love sent

Jesus to that cross. Glory removed—that's the tragedy of humanity. Glory revealed—that's what Jesus did.

C. Perfection (2:10)

In His incarnation, in His crucifixion, and also in His exaltation, Jesus revealed the glory of God.

Hebrews 2:10 ends with the following words: "To make the captain of their salvation perfect through sufferings." Those words do not imply moral imperfection on the part of Jesus. The word *perfect* there really means "qualified" or "complete." There was a completeness needed as far as His office was concerned. Jesus could not have been qualified to be our Savior unless He had paid the penalty for our sins by His death. So when Jesus paid the price at Calvary, He became the captain of salvation, being qualified through suffering.

What is more, the word *captain* in verse 10 means the head of the family or someone who founds a city or a pioneer who blazes a trail. Jesus is the One who has blazed the trail. He is the One who leads the way. He is the One who has made it possible for us to go back to glory.

III. GLORY RESTORED (2:11-13)

When God saves us, He restores the glory that Adam lost. Jesus said in John 17:22, "The glory which thou gavest me I have given them." Originally Adam was evidently clothed in the glory of God. When you and I come to the Lord Jesus, that glory is restored. When you receive Jesus as your Savior, you are born again. Now, not only are you God's by means of creation, but you are also God's by means of regeneration. You have been born into the family of God. You are a son or daughter of God, a brother or sister of the Lord Jesus Christ. "For both he that sanctifieth [Jesus] and they who are sanctified [us] are all of one: for which cause he is not ashamed to call them brethren" (2:11).

A. Names Us (2:11-12)

God names us *brethren* when He saves us. Hebrews 2:12 suggests a picture of the church of the Lord assembled in glory, the church of the firstborn in Heaven. The redeemed of the ages are gathered around the throne of God. We are all congregated together with our Savior, who has saved us by His death and washed us in His blood. There you are, and there I am—undeserving, unworthy sinners. And Christ says to the Father, "I will declare thy name unto my *brethren,* in the midst of the church will I sing praise unto thee" (italics added).

B. Claims Us (2:13)

In that scene the Lord Jesus Christ is talking about us. He says, "There is one of Mine I've saved." Verse 13 puts it, "Behold I and the children which God hath given me." That gives each of us some worth today. When Christ saves us and restores glory to us. He displays us to the universe and says, "There they are. Look at the people I died to save."

Christ is not ashamed to claim us as brethren. Are you ashamed of Him? Jesus said, "Whosoever therefore shall confess me before men, him will I confess also before my Father which is in heaven" (Mt 10:32), If Jesus is not ashamed of me up there, then surely I shouldn't be ashamed of Him down here.

4

Why Jesus Became a Man
Hebrews 2:14-18

Hebrews has several purposes, one of which is to encourage us as believers to go on in the Lord and to attain Christian maturity. Another purpose is to explain why, instead of involving ourselves in the Old Testament system of sacrifices, we gather around the Lord Jesus Christ. Hebrews explains to us the reason for the new in contrast to the old. A third purpose is to exalt the Lord Jesus. All through this book the author comes back to the recurring theme that *Jesus is better* in every way.

One of the most astonishing claims in the entire Bible is that when Jesus was born, God became a man. Just think of it. One moment He was dressed in robes of glory; the next He was wrapped in swaddling clothes. One moment He was walking on the streets of gold; the next He was lying on the coarse straw of an animal trough. When Jesus Christ took upon Himself flesh and blood, it was God come down to earth in human form.

Human beings are naturally partakers of flesh and blood. We are born with eyes, ears, mouths, hands, and feet. Hebrews 2:14 says Jesus "took part of the same." He took part of our humanness. Jesus took part of something that was not natural to Him. It was not His nature to be in the form of a man, but He chose to become a man.

When you and I are born, we are tainted with sin (Ps 51:5). You don't have to do anything to be a sinner, but because you are a sinner, you sin. I sin. The Bible tells us that it is the nature of flesh and blood to sin. By birth, we receive a sinful nature (Rm 5:12). Yet when Jesus Christ became human, He was born without human sin.

Moreover, Jesus became a man voluntarily. Taking on human flesh was something He chose to do, He chose to do out of love for us. When you and I are born, we don't have any choice about the matter. But Jesus Christ voluntarily stooped to our level. You and I could not go up to where God is, so God chose to come down to us. That is the mystery, glory, and wonder of the incarnation.

Why did Jesus do become man? Several of the reasons are given in Hebrews 2:14-18.

I. TO RELEASE US (2:14-16)

"He . . . took part of the same; that through death he might destroy him that had the power of death, that is, the devil" (2:14).

A. Disarms the Devil (2:14)

The devil is a real personality. He exists. Yet this verse of Scripture says that through His death, the Lord Jesus destroyed him who had the power of death—the devil. The word *destroy* is a little misleading. It might suggest that the devil is no longer in existence or is no longer at work. Experience tells us the devil is still very much at work. *Destroy* doesn't mean that Jesus Christ put the devil out of existence. A better translation would indicate that Jesus put the devil out of commission. He rendered him at least potentially inoperative in the lives of believers.

A bomb squad can render a bomb inoperative. These experts in detonating and disarming bombs find the trigger and take it out. The bomb is still very powerful; it can still explode and do a great deal of damage. But the squad members have taken the pin out. They have disarmed the bomb. The Bible says that through His death on Calvary, Jesus disarmed the devil. Jesus took away the chief weapon of the devil

—the power of death. When Christ rose from the dead, He showed He had conquered death, Hell, and the grave.

When people who do not know the Lord Jesus as Savior die, the devil rejoices because he knows they are going to Hell forever. They are his forever. He knows that they have lost their opportunities to be saved. The Bible says the wages of sin is death. While the devil can demand the death penalty, the devil has no power over those who have received Christ's resurrection life. Jesus put an end to the devil's dominion over the believer. Christ was able to take away the devil's chief weapon of death because He had a greater weapon—His resurrection life.

A parable in the book of Luke explains what Jesus did to the devil when He died on the cross. Jesus said, "When a strong man armed keepeth his palace, his goods are in peace: But when a stronger than he shall come upon him, and overcome him, he taketh from him all his armour wherein he trusted, and divideth his spoils" (Lu 11:21-22). In that parable the devil is the strong man, but Jesus is the stronger man. When Jesus went to the cross of Calvary, He despoiled the power of the devil.

B. Delivers the Slaves (2:15-16)

"And deliver them who through fear of death were all their lifetime subject to bondage" (Hebrews 2:15). The reference is to the common fear of the reality of death—our normal, natural fear of death. Man born of woman is born to die.

People do unbelievable things because of their fear of death. They go to all kinds of lengths to preserve their lives and to avoid death. But the Bible says that when the Lord Jesus Christ came into the world and died on the cross for our sins, He delivered us —that is, He set us free from the fear of death. He released us. He delivered us from that terrible bondage. True, some believers have more difficulty than others in coping with the problem of death. Some of us have had the experience of waking up in the middle of the night in a cold sweat because of the thought of death. But we have the promises of God. We know that through the Lord Jesus Christ death has been put out of business for us.

Although believers should no longer fear death, sometimes we grapple with that fear. We are like the children of Israel. God had promised to deliver them from the land of Egypt, but when they came up to the Red Sea they were afraid. They didn't know what they were going to do. Just as they stepped into the water, however, God parted the sea and they crossed over on dry ground.

That is what is going to happen to saved people. You may have some fear of death remaining, but one of these days when you step into the chilly waters of death, the Lord Jesus is going to part the waters and you are going to walk over on dry ground. The last enemy that will be destroyed, the Bible says, is death. Jesus became a man to release us from the power of the devil and from the fear of death.

II. TO RECONCILE US (2:17)

Jesus also became a man to reconcile us. "Wherefore in all things it behoved him to be made like unto his brethren, that he might be a merciful and faithful high priest in things pertaining to God" (2:17). This subject is expanded considerably in later portions of the book of Hebrews. The Old Testament system of Jewish religion had many priests whose job was to represent the people to God. The priests would go into the temple and make sacrifices for the people. There was one high priest who would go into the holy of holies. He was the only one allowed to go in there, and he could go only once a year.

The New Testament says that you and I have been made "priests unto God" (Rev 1:6). I do not need an earthly priest today because God has made me a priest. I have the privilege now of going into the presence of God myself.

A. His Priesthood (2:17)

The Lord Jesus is our merciful and faithful high priest. The word *merciful* means He is able to sympathize with us. He has been where we are. He knows what we are going through. He is also a faithful high priest in that He can be depended on to represent us adequately before the heavenly Father. As a man, Jesus is a merciful high priest. He understands us. But as God, He is a faithful high priest. He understands God. Jesus our high priest can do something that no human high priest could do: *He perfectly and completely understands man and God at the same time.*

Christ knew what it was to be tired. He knew what it was to be tried. He knew what it was to be misunderstood. He knew what it was to be maligned. He understands the human situation perfectly and has gone into the holy of holies in Heaven and has adequately represented our needs.

B. His Payment (2:17)

Hebrews 2:17 says Christ became a man "to make reconciliation for the sins of the people." First John 2:2 says that Christ is the "propitiation for our sins: and not for ours only, but also for the sins of the whole world." *Reconciliation. Propitiation.* What do those big words mean? The New International Version puts it this way: "the atoning sacrifice." Reconciliation involves satisfying the demands of the holy law of God. It involves making payment for the broken law of God.

God is a holy God. God's law is a holy law. Sin breaks the holy law of God. Because of sin, man and God are out of fellowship, out of communion with one another. Sin separates man from God. When Jesus came, He was the priest who made the sacrifice for sin, and the sacrifice was none other than His own life. By shedding His blood on Calvary, Jesus paid the price for the broken law of God. He conciliated —that is, He propitiated—He made the atoning sacrifice. Jesus made it possible for sinful man and holy God to be reconciled. Romans 3:25 says that God set Him forth to be a "propitiation... for the remission of sins."

III. TO RESCUE US (2:18)

Jesus also became a man in order to rescue us from temptation. Temptation is something every human being experiences. First Corinthians 10:13 says, "There hath no temptation taken you but such as is common to man." The book of James speaks of *when* you are tempted, not *if.*

A. The Reality of His Temptation (2:18)

When Jesus came and became a man He knew what it was to be tempted: "For in that he himself hath suffered being tempted." His temptations were real. Jesus was tempted all through His life. In the wilderness temptations at the beginning of His ministry, all the temptations of the devil converged at one point in time in His life. For forty days and nights Jesus had not had anything to eat. He was hungry. When people have not had anything to eat for a number of days, they are weak emotionally and mentally. They are not as alert as they could be. The devil moved in on the Lord Jesus Christ, assailing His mind, attacking His soul, stabbing at His heart.

All through His life Jesus had temptations from His friends. Even Simon Peter, one of His closest disciples, tried to tempt Him to avoid the cross. His own family sometimes was a source of temptation. His relatives tried to come and get Him; they thought He had gone crazy; they tried to take Him away from His ministry. It is a severe temptation when your own friends and family want you to do something that you know is not what God wants you to do.

Because He was tempted, He understands the full depths of temptation. The Bible says He suffered being tempted. The fact is, not everybody suffers when temptation occurs. Some people rather enjoy temptation. To them there is something tantalizing about temptation, something enticing. But I really believe that those who know the Lord Jesus suffer when they experience the tempting work of the devil.

Some people of God are suffering being tempted right now. A man reading this book may be tempted to do something illegal in his business. He is wrestling with that temptation, having a terrible battle. A young woman may be tempted to sacrifice her purity and is battling that temptation. I have something to encourage both of you. When Jesus became a man, He knew what it was to suffer being tempted. He understands the battle you are going through. The wonderful truth is that when Jesus suffered being tempted, He did not sin. He was "in all points tempted like as we are, yet without sin" (4:15).

B. The Result of His Temptation (2:18)

Somebody says, "Preacher, if Jesus had sinned, would that have proven that God could sin?" No. If Jesus had sinned, it would have proven He was not God. The temptation of Jesus Christ displayed that He was fully qualified to be our Savior, that He was indeed God become man. The temptation of Jesus put Him to the test to show every one of us that He is adequate to be our Savior and that He can help us when we are tempted.

"For in that he himself hath suffered being tempted, he is able." HE IS ABLE. Those are three of the greatest words in the Bible. Hebrews 7:25 says, "He is able also to save them to the uttermost that come unto God by him." He is able to save. He is able to save you today. If you have never been saved, you are in sin. The devil has his grip on your life. The fear of death has made a slave out of you. He is able to save from the guttermost to the uttermost them that come unto God by Him.

"He is able to succour them that are tempted." What does that word *succor* mean? Literally it means "come to the rescue." It suggests a picture of a little child calling and the parent running to help. This word was used in Mark's account of the boy with a mute spirit. Jesus said to the father, "If thou canst believe, all things are possible to him that believeth," and the father cried, *"Help* thou mine unbelief" (Mk 9:23-24, italics added). The same word was used by the man who appeared to Paul and said, "Come over into Macedonia, and *help* us" (Acts 16:9, italics added). The word succor means "run to the cry of, answer the call of." Jesus is able to run to the call of those who are tempted.

James 4:7 says, "Submit yourselves therefore to God. Resist the devil, and he will flee from you." Here are three steps to help you overcome those temptations of the devil:

Step number one: Look for a lie of Satan in the temptation and confront it. When the devil tempted Adam and Eve, he lied. He said, "Go on and take of this fruit, forbidden because God knows that in the day you eat thereof you will become as God." Somewhere embedded in every temptation is a lie of the devil. The devil says to you, "You ought to have this affair because it will fulfill unmet needs in your life." That is a lie.

Step number two: Claim the truth of the Scriptures. When Jesus was tempted. He answered with the Word of God. Against the lie of the devil, Jesus used the Sword of the Spirit, the truth of the Scriptures. So, when you are tempted, you first must say, "Devil, that's a lie." Then you must use the Scriptures. If you are tempted to have an affair, to be unfaithful to your life companion, claim this truth of the Scriptures: "This is the will of God, even your sanctification, that ye should abstain from fornication" (1 Thes 4:3).

Step number three: Call for the help of the Savior. When temptations come, say, "Jesus, help!" The Lord Jesus will come, and the devil will look up and say, "Oh no, it's you again," and he will flee.

5

Where on Earth Does God Live?
Hebrews 3:1-6

The first Christians who read Hebrews were Jewish people who had received Jesus as their Savior. They had been taught, trained, and brought up in the Old Testament system of sacrifices and priesthood. The center of their worship was the temple. In that temple there were priests who made sacrifices. As we noted earlier, there was a high priest who went to the holy of holies one day a year. He would sprinkle the blood of the lamb on the mercy seat and make atonement for the sins of the people for one year. These Jewish people remembered that Moses was the earthly vessel through whom God had moved to institute that Old Testament system. In John 1:17, the Bible says, "The law was given by Moses." So, they were all wrapped up in Moses and that system of worship.

Then one day on the cross the Lord Jesus Christ cried, "It is finished" (Jn 19:30). In that moment all of the old was swept away, and everything became new. There was now a new high priest. There was now a new sacrifice, the precious blood of the Lord Jesus Christ. When Christ died for sin, all that was partial was replaced by the total. Everything that had been shadow was replaced with substance. When those early believers opened up the Epistle to the Hebrews and read the statements that the old had been superseded by the new, they were aware that in the Lord Jesus Christ they had a brand-new system and a brand-new approach to God.

One of the ways to understand a passage of Scripture is to look for words that reoccur. Seven times in Hebrews 3:1-6 the writer used the word *house*. When you and I use the word house, we think of a physical building. In the Old Testament when God came to dwell among humanity, he did so in a house, a physical place of worship.

While the Jews were wandering through the wilderness, the house was a tabernacle. When God wanted to come down and fellowship with Israel, He descended in the glory cloud; the people and God met together and had fellowship around the tabernacle. Later God replaced the tabernacle with a permanent building— the temple. God's visible dwelling place was that house of worship.

When the Lord Jesus Christ came, a change occurred. For about thirty-three years, God occupied a human body. God dwelt on earth in the person of His Son, the Lord Jesus Christ. Colossians 2:9 says, "In him dwelleth all the fulness of the Godhead bodily." When Jesus was born, "the Word was made flesh, and dwelt among us" (Jn 1:14).

Now look at Hebrews 3:6. Four words there are absolutely mind-boggling: "Whose house are we." The writer was talking about born-again children of God, saved people. He was saying that God now dwells in a spiritual house, a house that consists of God's people—you and me. First Corinthians 3:9 says we are "God's building." First Peter 2:5 says, "Ye also, as lively stones, are built up a spiritual house, an holy priesthood, to offer up spiritual sacrifices, acceptable to God by Jesus Christ."

When you repent of your sins and by faith invite the Lord Jesus into your life to be your personal Savior, you become the dwelling place of God on this earth. Because God today dwells in the lives of believers, certain marks should be evident in our lives.

I. CAREFUL CONSIDERATION (3:1)

Because God lives in us, our lives should be marked by careful consideration. "Holy brethren, partakers of the heavenly calling, consider the Apostle and High Priest of our profession, Christ Jesus."

A, The Believer

First of all, we are "holy brethren." The word *holy* means "set apart." *Brethren* means "brothers and sisters in the same family." We are holy brothers and sisters in the family of God. We belong to God now and partake of the divine nature. We have been set apart. Our lives are not our own.

We are also "partakers of the heavenly calling." To partake means "to have something in common," or in other words "to be partners." This phrase from Hebrews 3:1 explains why a doctor and a laborer, the rich and the poor, gather in the same meeting. They are now partners in a heavenly calling. They have something in common that brings them together.

For many years church-growth experts have been making surveys and writing books. They study what makes churches grow. They give advice to churches concerning growth. These experts say that a church that will grow is one that is made up of the same kind of folks. In other words, if a church in a rich area is to grow, it has to minister to the rich. Or if a church in a poor area is to grow, it has to minister to the poor. These experts say you can't grow a church with all kinds of individuals.

1 say these experts are absolutely wrong. I say that a true genuine church that operates on the basis of the teachings of the Word of God is a church that brings people together around a common allegiance to the Lord Jesus Christ. We don't have fellowship on the basis of the material things we have or do not have. We are not drawn together on the basis of our social standings or intellectual endowments. Rather, we are all partakers of a heavenly calling, an upward calling (Ph 3:14). For the most part the Jews had an earthly calling. Their blessings were tied to a country. For them the place of blessing was the promised land, Canaan. But our blessings don't center around a place; they center around a

person. For us to be in the place of blessing is not to be in Canaan; it is to be in Christ. Our citizenship is in Heaven (Ph 3:20).

B. The Savior

"Consider the Apostle and High Priest of our profession, Christ Jesus." Here are two wonderful statements about the Lord Jesus. First, He is the apostle of our profession. There were other apostles, but only Jesus is the apostle. The original twelve disciples were called apostles. They were the men who did the foundational work in the church. It was through the ministry of those who had the gift of apostle that the Word of God was given to the church. Peter was the apostle to the Jews. Paul was the apostle to the Gentiles.

The word *apostle* means "sent one." It is similar to our word missionary, "someone who is sent with a commission." Hebrews 3:1 says that we ought to put our minds on Jesus because He is the "sent one," the One who was sent from the heavenly Father. John 3:16 says, "For God so loved the world, that he gave his only begotten Son, that whosoever believeth in him should not perish, but have everlasting life."

Second, Jesus is the high priest. An apostle is one who represents the Father to the people. A high priest is one who represents the people to the Father. The Lord Jesus Christ is both. Jesus is the One who represents the Father to us. Jesus comes to us and says, "The heavenly Father loves you. The heavenly Father wants to forgive you of your sins. The heavenly Father wants to take you to Heaven." Jesus is our apostle. And He is our high priest. He is representing us to the Father right now in Heaven.

We have representatives in Washington. Supposedly I have somebody arguing my case in Congress. I can't be too sure of that, but I am absolutely, eternally sure that at the right hand of the Father, I have a faithful high priest who is pleading my case. I am just as sure of Heaven right now as I will be ten thousand years from now, because my high priest has pled my case before the Father in Heaven.

As long as I consider Christ—keep my mind on Jesus, keep my eyes fixed on Him—I do pretty well as a Christian. But sometimes I'm like

Simon Peter. Remember the time he got out of that boat and started walking on the water to the Lord Jesus Christ? When he saw that the winds and waves were boisterous, he began to sink. Simon Peter took his eyes off Jesus. You too will start going down as a believer if you take your eyes off Jesus. Because God indwells us, our lives should be marked by careful consideration of Jesus.

II. GRATEFUL APPRECIATION (3:2-6a)

Because God lives in you, because you are now God's house, your life should be marked by grateful appreciation. You should appreciate the glory, splendor, and superiority of the Lord Jesus. The purpose of the book of Hebrews is to show us that Jesus Christ is better. Hebrews I says that Jesus is better than the prophets. Hebrews 1and 2 say that Jesus is better than the angels. Hebrews 3:2-6a says that Jesus is better than Moses, the great prophet himself.

The Jewish people had heroes such as Abraham and King David, but the greatest hero of all was Moses. Moses was miraculously preserved at birth. His life contained miracle after miracle. He was the human vessel through whom the law of the ten commandments, the tabernacle, and God's beautiful picture of redemption were given. Moses was God's man in every way.

Yet the writer of Hebrews said that in every way Jesus is better than Moses.

A. Fidelity (3:2)

First, we appreciate the great fidelity of the Lord Jesus: "Who was faithful to him that appointed him, as also Moses was faithful in all his house." Moses' life was marked by faithfulness, although at times he was a reluctant servant. God called him to lead the children of Israel out of bondage, and he was reluctant. Read the Exodus passages carefully. The Lord actually got angry with Moses. God called Moses, and Moses kept pointing to somebody else. God wanted Moses to serve Him, and Moses kept saying, "Lord, not me. How about Aaron?" "Here am I,

Lord; send Aaron." But when Moses finally made his commitment to serve the Lord, he was faithful. He wasn't perfect. He made a lot of mistakes. But one thing the Bible says about Moses is that he was "faithful in all his house." Moses did everything God had set him apart to do in the Old Testament economy.

The point of Hebrews 3:2 is that even though Moses was faithful, Jesus Christ was more faithful. Do you know why? Because the faithfulness of the Lord Jesus Christ involved the shedding of His blood. Jesus was faithful to the will of God even when it meant giving His life. Moses was faithful, and you and I ought to be faithful. But Jesus was superior in His fidelity. He is to be appreciated for His great faithfulness to the will of God.

B. Majesty (3:3)

Second, we ought to appreciate Jesus because of His wonderful majesty: "For this man [Jesus] was counted worthy of more glory than Moses." Moses had honor, but Jesus is worthy of more honor—since the one who has built a house has more honor than the house.

Suppose you are in a magnificent building. You look at its lavish furnishings and beautiful craftsmanship. The walls are marvelously built. The floors are gorgeously finished. Probably you ask, "Who built this building?" A magnificent building brings attention to the builder.

Jesus Christ, by His death at Calvary and His shed blood, has brought into existence a household of faith—a family of God, God's born-again people. We who are the building ought to call attention to the Builder. We ought to live so much to the glory of God that when people see our lives they say, "What is causing them to live that way?"

C. Deity (3:4-6a)

Third, we ought to appreciate Jesus because of His deity. According to verse 4, Jesus Christ is God. Many places in Scripture affirm that Jesus is God, but this fourth verse proves it beyond question. "For every house is builded by some man; but he [Jesus] that built all things is God." Jesus is God. That's why, when Christ comes into your life, it means that God is now dwelling in your life.

Moses was a servant in the house, a faithful servant. The word translated "servant" in verse 5 means a servant who has the affection of the master. But even at best, Moses was still pointing toward the future; he was "a testimony of those things which were to be spoken after." Moses was saying, "There is one better than I coming." In John 5:46 Jesus said, "For had ye believed Moses, ye would have believed me: for he [Moses] wrote of me [Jesus]." It's amazing that some people read the Old Testament and say there is no prediction of Jesus there.

In contrast to God's servant Moses, Jesus came into the world as God's son. Yet one time when the Lord Jesus asked His disciples, "Who do people say I am?" they said, "Some people say you are Moses; some say you are Elijah; some say you are Jeremiah; some say you are one of the other prophets." Then Jesus asked, "Who do you say I am?" Simon Peter said to the Lord, "Thou art the Christ, the Son of the living God" (Mt 16:16). Who is Jesus to you?

III. FAITHFUL DETERMINATION (3:6b)

Because God lives in us, our lives should be marked by faithful determination. Hebrews 3:6b is the climax of the passage: "We hold fast the confidence and the rejoicing of the hope firm unto the end." Our continuation in faith is proof of its reality in our lives. This passage is not saying that you have to continue, to hold on, in order to be saved. Rather, the fact that you do continue—you do hold on and are faithful to the Lord—is an evidence, a proof, that you are saved. There is a big difference.

First John 2:19 says, "They went out from us, but they were not of us; for if they had been of us, they would no doubt have continued with us." The word translated "hold fast" is a nautical term meaning "stay on course." With faithful determination we should stay on course showing holy boldness and happy boastfulness.

A. Holy Boldness

The word *confidence* literally means "boldness." It means to speak without fear and restraint. The same word is used in Acts 4:29 when the disciples prayed, "Grant unto thy servants, that with all boldness they may speak thy word." The Bible says that the place where they were praying was shaken. They were all filled with the Holy Spirit and they spoke the Word of God with boldness. One of the ways you know you belong to the Lord is that the Lord gives you a holy boldness. I know some people who couldn't possibly be witnesses for the Lord if the Lord didn't give them boldness.

B. Happy Boastfulness

The word *rejoicing* literally means "boasting." A kind of happy boastfulness ought to be characteristic of a child of God who is staying on course. Does that mean a Christian ought to go around bragging about himself all the time? No, that's not what it means. Here's the boast of the believer: "Not because of anything that I have done, but by the grace of the Lord Jesus I am saved, and I am on my way to Heaven." If God lives in us, that's the kind of boasting we ought to do.

6

The Deadly Danger of Disbelief
Hebrews 3:7-4:11

One purpose of Hebrews is to encourage believers to go on in the Lord to maturity. The danger is not that we will lose our salvation. Rather, we who are born again, who are children of God, who are saved and on our way to Heaven, need to "take heed . . . lest any of you be hardened through the deceitfulness of sin" (Hebrews 3:12-13).

There are Canaan Christians and wilderness Christians. Which kind are you? Are you a victorious Christian or a defeated Christian? In Hebrews 3:7-4:11 we see two kinds of believers: those who are growing in the Lord, and those who are failing to believe and grow. The latter are going through a wilderness experience of defeat and shame; theirs is a miserable existence.

When we invite Jesus into our hearts and lives we become children of God. According to John 1:12, "As many as received him, to them gave he power to become the sons of God, even to them that believe on his name." We are born into God's family through faith in the Lord Jesus Christ. "For God so loved the world, that he gave his only begotten Son, that whosoever believeth in him should not perish, but have everlasting life" (Jn 3:16). But it is possible for a person to be a child of God and yet not become the mature, growing Christian that God intends him to be.

The theme of Hebrews 3:7-4:11 (the second in a series of five warning passages) is the deadly danger of disbelief. To illustrate the danger, the writer began this passage with a quotation from Psalm 95:7-11. There the psalmist recounted the experience of the children of Israel on their way from the land of Egypt to the land of Canaan.

I. AN ILLUSTRATION: THE TRAGEDY OF DISBELIEF (3:7-11,15-19)

The Old Testament is a book of illustrations. I'm not suggesting, of course, that these illustrations are fictitious. The events that are recorded in the Old Testament did occur. But very often they serve as illustrations of New Testament realities. Romans 15:4 says, "Whatsoever things were written aforetime were written for our learning." Here we can learn from the experience of the children of Israel.

Three locations are important in understanding the history of Israel: Egypt, the wilderness, and Canaan. God delivered Israel from the land of Egypt. When they applied the blood of the Passover lamb to their houses, all of the people who were "under the blood" were spared. When they came to the Red Sea, God miraculously opened up that sea so that they could pass over on dry ground. That's a picture of salvation. You and I are "under the blood" of the Lord Jesus Christ. We who have been born again, have been led out of Egypt, so to speak.

But God not only wanted to take Israel out of something; He also wanted to put them into something. They were to be led out of Egypt and they were to be led into the land of Canaan. Between Egypt and Canaan is a wilderness. In the wilderness the Israelites talked about going back to Egypt, but there was no way they could return. Once under the blood and through the Red Sea, they were done with Egypt forever. But because of disbelief, they failed to enter into everything that God had intended for them in the land of promise.

A. How Israel Rebelled (3:7-9,15-16)

What happened to the children of Israel is familiar to most of us. Instead of believing in God's ability to lead them into the land of Canaan, the children of Israel rebelled against the Lord. Instead of going on into Canaan, they went back into the wilderness and wandered around for forty years. Israel disbelieved the promises of God, yet their history was one of miracle after miracle. They had been spared the death of their firstborn when the Passover angel came through the land of Egypt. God opened up the waters of the Red Sea.

Wouldn't you think that those two events alone would be enough to cause them to believe God? But it didn't. Isn't that amazing? Then in the wilderness God gave them manna right out of Heaven—angel food cake—a miracle every day. When they needed water, God said to Moses, "Moses, strike the rock," and when he struck, water came gushing out. When Israel needed guidance, God put a cloud in the sky during the day and a fiery pillar in the sky at night. Yet because they didn't trust Him, God was grieved with that generation. The word *grieved* really means that God was disgusted. He said, "They do always err . . . they have not known my ways." They went astray in their hearts.

B. How God Responded (3:10-11)

"So I sware in my wrath, They shall not enter into my rest" (*rest* is used as a synonym for Canaan). God was saying, "All right, they won't believe in Me, they won't trust Me, and they won't obey Me, so they are not going to get into the land of rest." Hebrews 3:17 asks, "With whom was he grieved forty years? was it not with them that had sinned, whose carcases fell in the wilderness?" With the exception of two men, all of that generation wandered in the wilderness until they died; their graves were testimonies to the danger of disbelief. "And to whom sware he that they should not enter into his rest, but to them that believed not? So we see that they could not enter in because of unbelief" (3:18-19).

What does that illustration, that tragedy in the history of Israel, have to do with modern Christians? Egypt represents our redemption from the land of sin, and Canaan represents victory in the daily life of a believer. Canaan does not represent Heaven. Sometimes the old hymns we sing mislead us. When we read the Old Testament, we see that Canaan certainly wasn't Heaven. There were a lot of fights in Canaan, and there were giants in the land. But in Heaven all battles are over. Canaan was a land of enemies, a land of opposition.

Canaan reminds us that the child of God needs to live a life of victory on a daily basis. You and I, who trust the Lord Jesus Christ for the salvation of our souls and have the victory of redemption in our lives, need to believe that God can help us and be with us day by day.

The wilderness represents defeat in the daily life of a believer. We will never go back to Egypt, but we can live defeated lives. Some people have just enough salvation to make them miserable. They are going to Heaven when they die, but they can't enjoy living for Jesus in the here and now. They are wilderness Christians. But God does not want Christians to live defeated lives. He wants everyone to enjoy the land of promise.

II. AN APPLICATION: THE TREACHERY IN DISBELIEF (3:12-4:3)

A. Departing (3:12-14)

After that illustration the writer of Hebrews added an exhortation: "Take heed, brethren, lest there be in any of you an evil heart of unbelief, in departing from the living God. But exhort [encourage] one another daily" (3:12-13). We who are believers ought to encourage each other. That's why we have Bible studies. That's why we have fellowships. All of these groups are designed to help us "exhort one another daily, while it is called To day; lest any of you be hardened through the deceitfulness of sin."

The deceitfulness of sin really means "the trickery or treachery of sin," the strategy of sin. Sin is deceitful, and it's possible for Christians to be tricked by sin. There are some Christians with sin in their lives; they've lost their families, and they are wrecking their personal lives. They never intended for that to happen. They intended to live for the

Lord Jesus Christ. But their hearts got hardened by the deceitfulness and treachery of sin.

Be very careful. Don't let sin cause your heart to harden. Sin is like cholesterol. Get cholesterol in your system and you are going to have heart problems. Sin is the cholesterol of the spiritual heart. When you have a hard heart, you have an evil heart of unbelief, and you depart from the living God (3:12). Not that you are going to lose your salvation. This verse is referring to apostasy on the part of believers who are out of fellowship with God. God's exhortation here is: Don't depart from the living God because you have sin in your heart. If you do, you are destined to die in the wilderness of failure as a believer.

B. Doubting (4:1-3)

Hebrews 4 begins with a second exhortation: "Let us therefore fear." That's strange. I thought Christians were not to fear. Well, there is bad fear and good fear. We ought not to fear God in the sense of being frightened of God. We ought to be cautious, "lest, a promise being left us of entering into his rest, any of you should seem to come short of it" (4:1). There ought to be a holy anxiety on the part of God's people lest they fail to experience what God has promised for them as believers.

Backslidden, defeated Christians are scattered all over this land. Some so-called Christians out there have probably never been saved. I'm convinced that many people who profess faith in the Lord Jesus Christ have never possessed faith in the Lord Jesus Christ. Yet there are also those who are indeed genuinely born again, who at one time really trusted Jesus, but because of disbelief are not moving on to experience what God saved them to experience. "For unto us was the gospel preached, as well as unto them: but the word preached did not profit them, not being mixed with faith in them that heard it" (4:2).

Israel had God's promises and look what they did. They got right up to the edge of Canaan, the land of promise, the land of rest. God had already preached to them the word that they were to go in and possess the land. It was theirs for the taking. Instead they selected some spies to go in and inspect the land.

There were twelve spies. When they came back there was a majority report and a minority report: ten to two. Ten said, "It's everything God said it was over there in Canaan. It's a land flowing with milk and honey, but there are giants in the land, and we can't take it." We know that the majority is always right. Right? Wrong. Just because the majority says it, doesn't mean it's right.

There was a minority report from Joshua and Caleb—and what a sermon they preached. Its title was "Have Faith in God." They said, "Yes, there are giants in that land. There will be a lot of battles in that land, but God said it's our land. We can take it." They preached the promises of God.

But the sermon of Joshua and Caleb didn't do a bit of good. It wasn't "mixed with faith in them that heard it." The ingredient that gives a Christian the victorious Canaan life is faith. "We which have believed do enter into rest" (4:3). I'm not only saved through faith; I live the daily Christian life through faith.

III. AN APPLICATION: THE TRIUMPH OVER DISBELIEF (4:4-11)

In Hebrews 4:4-11 we see the triumph over disbelief and learn how we as believers enter into the land of rest. The key word of the passage is the word *rest*. Not only is there physical weariness; there is also spiritual weariness. People need rest.

A. A Past Rest (4:4-8)

Hebrews 4:4-5 refers to God's creation rest: "For he spake in a certain place of the seventh day on this wise, And God did rest the seventh day from all his works. And in this place again, If they shall enter into my rest." God created the universe in a six-day period of time. On the seventh day God rested. That doesn't mean God wasn't doing anything. It was the rest of completion. God had finished His creation work. So, the sabbath day commemorates God's creation work.

But sin entered in and so Jesus said in the Gospel of John, "My Father worketh hitherto, and I work" (Jn 5:17). God started His work of redemption and the Lord Jesus Christ came along and picked up the work of the Father. Then, that day when Jesus was on the cross of Calvary He shouted, "It is finished" (Jn 19:30). God's redemption rest had been provided.

Hebrews 4:6-8 refers to God's Canaan rest. "For if Jesus [that is, the Old Testament Joshua] had given them rest, then would he not afterward have spoken of another day" (4:8). God's creation rest and His Canaan rest in the Old Testament point to New Testament realities.

B. A Promised Rest (4:9-11)

Hebrews 4:9-11 describes the threefold rest of the believer: his future rest, his salvation rest, and his sanctification rest. "There remaineth therefore a rest to the people of God" (4:9). Revelation 14:13 says, "That they may rest from their labours." One of these days we are going to a wonderful place called Heaven and it's going to be rest. That's our future rest. That's glorification.

Hebrews 4:10 speaks of past rest: "For he that is entered into his rest, he also hath ceased from his own works, as God did from his." That's salvation rest. When you came to the Lord Jesus Christ and by faith received His work at the cross of Calvary, you laid aside all your efforts to save yourself. You are not saved by anything you do. Salvation is totally dependent on what Jesus Christ did. The minute I believe in the Lord Jesus Christ I enter into His rest. That's what Jesus meant in Matthew 11:28 when He said, "Come unto me, all ye that labour and are heavy laden, and I will give you rest."

Finally, Hebrews 4:11 refers to our sanctification rest. "Let us labour therefore to enter into that rest, lest any man fall after the same example of unbelief."

JERRY VINES

7

Why is the Bible so Special?
Hebrews 4:12-13

The Bible is like a divine kaleidoscope. Every turn reveals new beauty and wonder. So variegated is the Word of God that no one definition is sufficient to explain it. So multifaceted is the Bible that no one description is adequate.

The Bible contains many figures of speech describing itself. For instance, the Bible is compared to a seed. Explaining the parable of the sower, Jesus said, "The seed is the word of God" (Lu 8:11). Planted in a human heart, that seed can change a jungle of weeds into a garden of blessing.

In Jeremiah the Bible is compared to a fire. The Lord says, "Is not my word like as a fire?" (23:29). God's Word can burn like a fire. In that same verse, the Lord also compares the Bible to a hammer: "Is not my word ... like a hammer that breaketh the rock in pieces?" The Bible crushes sin that ought not to be in our lives. The Bible is compared to a sword in Hebrews 4:12 and also in other Scripture passages. For instance, Ephesians 6:17 refers to "the sword of the Spirit, which is the word of God." The writer of Hebrews used this figure of speech to show the superiority of the Word of God.

What makes our Bible so special, above all other books?

I. A LIVING BOOK (4:12)

The Bible is a special book, first of all, because it is a living book. "For the word of God is quick." The word *quick* means "living"; in Greek, the word is a present active participle, indicating continuous life. So we see one difference between a physical sword and the Sword of the Spirit, the Bible: a physical sword stabs physically living people and makes them physically dead; our Sword, the Bible, stabs spiritually dead people and makes them spiritually alive.

A. Its Continuity

The Bible is living in its continuity. It is continuously alive, always alive. There is something up-to-date and contemporary about the Bible. Long ago its human authors, inspired by the Holy Spirit, wrote the words recorded in our Bible. When those words were first read they had living power in that generation. Now, thousands of years later, we read those same words and they are as relevant as if they had been composed this morning. The Bible is eternally the Word of God. The Bible is contemporarily the Word of God.

B. Its Contents

The Bible is living because of its contents. It breathes and bleeds and weeps and sings. It is alive in every generation. Every one of its sixty-six books has been used in the lives of individuals to quicken them into spiritual, eternal life. Take for an example a monk named Martin Luther. He began to give himself to a study of Romans. As he studied, the living power of God came into his life in a saving way. In Romans he discovered that we are justified by faith in Jesus Christ alone. Reading that book transformed the life of Martin Luther, and he became a great reformer.

Then there was the worldly young man named Augustine who lived in the fourth century AD. His mother had been praying earnestly for his conversion, seemingly to no avail. But one day Augustine read the thirteenth chapter of Romans and came upon these words: "Put ye on the Lord Jesus Christ, and make not provision for the flesh, to fulfil the lusts thereof" (13:14). God broke through in the life of that young man, and he became Augustine the great theologian.

The same quickening power transformed the life of Charles Spurgeon when he was sixteen years old. On his way to church one day he was overtaken by a snowstorm. Because he couldn't get to his own church, he stopped in at a little Methodist chapel. The preacher had not been able to get there because of the storm, so a layman stood to speak just a few impromptu words. He chose as his text a verse from the book of Isaiah: "Look unto me, and be ye saved, all the ends of the earth" (45:22). That fumbling layman, doing the best he could, kept repeating that verse, "Look unto me, and be ye saved." Directing his words to Spurgeon, the layman said, "Young man, God says to 'look unto me, and be ye saved.'" Through that one verse Charles Spurgeon had a conversion experience, and he became the greatest preacher of his day.

The Bible is a living book because its words are alive. Jesus said, "The words that I speak unto you, they are spirit, and they are life" (Jn 6:63). Think about the power of one single word from the Bible—for example, that word *repent*. Jesus said, "Except ye repent, ye shall all likewise perish" (Lu 13:3,5). John the Baptist emphasized one basic word, repent. Heeding that one word could transform the lives of individuals who need to turn to the Lord today.

The Bible is a living book because its central personality is not a fictitious character. When you and I open up this special book we are brought face to face with the living, life-giving Lord Jesus Christ. When we read about Him, He steps off the pages of the Bible into our lives. The written Word of God introduces us to the living Word of God.

II. AN ENERGIZING BOOK (4:12)

The Bible is also special because it is powerful. The Word of God has energizing power. I use the word energizing because it is a derivative of the Greek word translated "powerful" in 4:12. Powerful here means "active, productive." The same Greek word is used in 1 Thessalonians

2:13 where Paul referred to the Word of God "which effectually worketh also in you that believe." Paul was saying that the Word of God works in you, energizes you. The Bible does something on the inside of an individual.

A. Converts the Soul

The Bible has power to convert. Psalm 19:7 says that the law of the Lord converts the soul. If you believe what the Bible says, you can be converted. Countless people can testify to that.

B. Comforts the Heart

The Bible has power to comfort. "This is my comfort in my affliction: for thy word hath quickened me" (Ps 119:50). Let me paraphrase that statement: This is my comfort in my affliction: Your promise has renewed my life. The psalmist was saying, "I have gone through an experience that shattered my life, crushed my heart, but Your Word has quickened me. Your promise has renewed my life." There are times when a person needs a word of comfort. The experience of God's people in the hour of bereavement is that they have found comfort in the Word of God.

C. Cleanses the Life

The Bible has power to cleanse. Jesus said in John 17:17, "Sanctify them through thy truth: thy word is truth." Probably you are familiar with the story of *Pitcairn's Island*, a sequel to *Mutiny on the Bounty*. The story is a true account of how nine mutineers, six native men, and twelve Tahitian women escaped to an uninhabited island. Shortly after landing on the island, one of the sailors began to distill alcohol and soon the little colony was filled with debauchery, vice, and violence. They went lower and lower in their sin, and when they hit bottom there was only one sailor left along with a few Tahitian women and children born out of their sinful relationships. Then while rummaging through an old chest, that sailor found a copy of the Bible. He began to read it and to teach its contents to the other survivors. The teaching of the Bible brought cleansing into their lives. Laziness and laxness disappeared and the colony developed into a thriving community. Years later when a sealing vessel stopped at the island, the crew discovered a peaceful community with no jail, no whiskey, and no crime—all because of the power of the Bible.

I experienced that same energizing power in my own life. As a sixteen-year-old, really in an attempt to run from God, I began to take a Bible to high school. Another boy there had made up his mind he was going to be a preacher. (God had nothing to do with his decision; he had made up his own mind.) So he started bringing a Bible to school. I said, "If he can bring one, I can too." I had a little New Testament and I stuck it down in my blue jeans pocket so nobody would see it. Then I made the mistake of pulling it out from time to time and reading it. Every time I read it, God spoke to me. God dealt with me and it was a very unpleasant and disturbing experience. As a result of my reading the Bible, God spoke to me and I committed myself to live for Jesus all the days of my life. The Word of God had power to cleanse my soul.

III. A PENETRATING BOOK (4:12-13)

The Bible is special because it has penetrating power. "The word of God is ... sharper than any two edged sword." The Bible probes deeply into the human heart.

A. Sinners

We need to use the Scriptures in witnessing to lost people. God blesses His Word. It pierces. What if folks don't believe the Bible? Well, it doesn't matter whether they believe it or not; just go ahead and use it. It'll work.

Simon Peter learned that you have to use the spiritual sword, not a physical sword. In the garden of Gethsemane, he decided he would take things into his own hands, and he used a physical sword. He was aiming for a head but all he got was an ear! He learned his lesson, though, and on the day of Pentecost he picked up another sword. He began to preach the Word of God and the Bible says that when he preached, those listening were pricked—literally they were stabbed, stung, cut—in their hearts. The result? Three thousand sinners were saved that day.

B. Selves

We also need to use the Bible on ourselves. The Bible explores our lives, "piercing even to the dividing asunder of soul and spirit, and of the joints and marrow." It penetrates to the depths of our experiences. The Word of God reaches areas no human being is able to see. It gets under our skins. The Bible divides soul and spirit. That means it examines our lives. It is a "discerner of the thoughts and intents of the heart." Other people see what we do, but God's Word examines why we do what we do. It deals not only with our thoughts, but also with the intents behind the thoughts. The word discerner is like our word critic. There are some who would sit as critics of the Bible, but in reality the Bible sits as critics of them. The Bible is a revelation from God and is without error.

The Bible also exposes our lives. It causes us to look at the Lord, and when we stand face to face with the God of the universe, there is no hiding. You can't run from God. God has your number. "Neither is there any creature that is not manifest in his sight: but all things are naked [laid bare] and opened untothe eyes of him with whom we have to do." The word translated "opened" here, literally means "put a knife to the throat." (The medical term tracheotomy is a derivative.) The story is that daggers would be put to the throats of guilty criminals so that they would look into the gaze of the judge instead of dropping their heads. The Bible is a sword that causes us to stand eye to eye with God. We are fully exposed to Him.

C. Satan

We can also use this Sword of the Spirit on the devil. The Word of God is the offensive weapon God has placed in our hands to win victory over the temptations of Satan. Jesus used that weapon when He was confronted by the devil in the wilderness. After forty days and nights of having no food, at a moment when physically and emotionally He was at a low level, the devil tempted Him. Then it's as if Jesus said, "Devil, I know that at the battle of Armageddon I'm going to slay you with a sharp sword out of my mouth, but I'm going to illustrate to the redeemed of all the ages how they can be victorious over your temptations on a daily basis." So the battle was on.

The devil said, "If you are the Son of God, take these stones and turn them into bread." Jesus reached for the sword and said, "It is written, Man shall not live by bread alone." SWISH! The devil retreated, bruised and bitter. Coming back, the devil made his second attack. He said to the Lord Jesus Christ, "If you are the Son of God, throw yourself off the temple." Jesus lifted high the Word, the Sword of the Spirit, and said, "It is written . . . Thou shalt not tempt the Lord thy God." STAB! The devil retreated again, battered and bewildered.

Then the devil gathered his heavy artillery, his most sinister forces, and said, "I will give you all the kingdoms of the world if you will fall down and worship me." Jesus lifted high the Sword of the Spirit and said, "It is written, Thou shalt worship the Lord thy God and him only shalt thou serve." SLICE! The devil retreated, bloody and beaten. Jesus won the victory over the devil. I can imagine He called after the tempter, "I'll see you again at Armageddon!" (See Mt 4:1-11).

We should follow the example of Jesus and put the Bible—this special, penetrating book—to use. As Psalm 149:6 says, "Let the high praises of God be in their mouth, and a two edged sword in their hand."

JERRY VINES

8

Jesus, Our Great High Priest
Hebrews 4:14-16

If you had been born an Israelite two thousand years ago in the city of Jerusalem, your life would be very different from what it is today. For instance, you would not be going to church on Sunday. You would worship on the sabbath day, which is Saturday. In six days, Genesis says, God created the world, and on the seventh day He rested. The Jewish people were to keep the seventh day as a day of rest commemorating God's creation rest. You also would worship at a temple located in the center of the city and only be allowed to go into certain areas of the temple. No pews or chairs existed to sit on. Insteadof a preacher or pastor, a priest would officiate. He would lay an animal on an altar as an offering and sacrifice it. Once a year the high priest would be allowed to go into the innermost sanctuary known as the holy of holies; there he would take the blood of a lamb, sprinkle it on the mercy seat, and make propitiation for the sins of the people. He would follow that same ritual year after year.

Jesus has changed all of that. Things are different now.

In the early days of my ministry in Georgia, one of the boys in my church went to Rhode Island to serve there in the military. He met a young woman in Rhode Island, fell in love with her, married her, and brought her home at Christmastime. During their Christmas vacation,

I had the opportunity to talk to her about Jesus, and she accepted the Lord.

As they were getting ready to go back to Rhode Island, I was giving her some pointers about living the Christian life. I explained that we have the privilege as God's children to come to God in prayer on a one-to-one basis and talk to Him just as a child might talk to his or her father. Contrarily, she had been taught that you cannot go to God directly for yourself in prayer—you have to go to a priest and get the priest to make intercession for you. I told her that we no longer have to do that.

"We don't need a priest," I said. "The Bible says that we have been made priests in the Lord Jesus."

"Unto him that loved us, and washed us from our sins in his own blood, And hath made us kings and priests" (Rev 1:5-6). I explained that she was a priest in the Lord Jesus Christ. She said, "You mean that when I want to talk to God, I don't have to go to a man to get him to talk to God for me?" I said, "Yes, you can get down on your knees by your bed and talk to God for yourself." A light came on in her face that I will never forget. She was so excited and thrilled to know that in Jesus, we have direct access to God.

Here's another wonderful difference Jesus makes: no longer do we have an Old Testament high priest who was just a man, as the Jews had. We have none other than the Lord Jesus Christ Himself. In Hebrews 4:14 Jesus is called "a great high priest." That title is never ascribed to any other person. Right now, this very day, Jesus is our great high priest! We have him. He is our present possession. What makes Jesus a great high priest?

I. HIS POSITION (4:14)

Jesus is our great high priest because of His position. "We have a great high priest, that is passed into the heavens [literally, through the heavens], Jesus the Son of God."

A. Where He Is (4:14a)

Jesus is our great high priest because of where He is. His position right now at the right hand of the Father in Heaven makes Him our great high priest. The high priest in the Old Testament functioned on earth. He performed his work in the temple. He passed through the veil into an earthly holy of holies. He did the work that he was assigned to do and then he came out. The Lord Jesus, our great high priest, has passed into Heaven. That statement reminds us of His ascension. Forty days after His resurrection on Easter morning, He bodily, literally, physically, before the eyes of His disciples, ascended into the heavens!

Why did Jesus ascend to Heaven? Jesus went back to Heaven as our great high priest. He took His own blood and offered it on the mercy seat in the holy of holies in Heaven. As our Great High Priest, He made the one all-sufficient atoning sacrifice for the sins of the whole world. Furthermore, Jesus came as our prophet speaking the sure Word of God. In the Father's own time, He will one day come as our King. But presently He functions as our priest in Heaven.

B. Who He Is (4:14b)

Jesus is our great high priest because of who He is: "Jesus the Son of God." In those two titles we have the humanity and the deity of Jesus tied together. Jesus—that's His human title. The Son of God—that's His divine title. As the human Jesus, He is able to understand our needs. As the divine Son of God, He is able to meet our needs. Whatever the needs of our lives today are, Jesus Christ fully understands them. He knows the burdens we carry.

We have a priest who "is passed into the heavens." That verb *passed* is a perfect tense verb, which means that something that took place in the past bears present results and is a permanent reality. Because Jesus passed through the heavens and remains now in Heaven as our great high priest, we should "hold fast our profession." Note that the Bible doesn't say to hold fast our salvation.

When I was growing up in Georgia I heard saintly people pray, "Lord, help us to hold on faithful to the end." I got the impression that being saved was like holding onto something for dear life. Thus, if you ever lost your grip, you were a goner for sure. I had the idea I had to hold onto Jesus. The Bible doesn't say that you and I are saved because of our hold on Jesus. It's just the opposite. You and I are saved and kept saved because Jesus is holding onto us! That's a big difference, isn't it?

Think about Noah and the ark. Did he drive some spikes into the outside of the ark and say to his family, "A flood is coming in a little while. The boat is going to toss and turn, but if we each hold on to a spike, we'll make it through"? No, they didn't hold on to spikes on the outside of the ark; they were all inside the ark. They were kept safe inside.

First Peter 1:5 says that we are "kept by the power of God." It is God's power that keeps us safe, not our power. Jesus said, "I give unto them eternal life; and they shall never perish, neither shall any man pluck them out of my hand" (Jn 10:28). Hebrews 4:14 refers to our testimony, not our salvation. The writer was saying, "Don't lose (that is, hold fast) your testimony for Jesus."

I don't want to lose my testimony. I don't want to disgrace my great high priest. I want to be faithful in all my ways to the Lord Jesus Christ.

II. HIS PERFECTION (4:15)

Jesus is our great high priest because of His perfection.

A. His Victory

Hebrews 4:15 is a tremendous statement about the absolute perfection of the human life of the Lord Jesus Christ. We read that He "was in all points tempted like as we are, yet without sin." Jesus Christ was victorious over all the onslaughts and temptations of the devil. He endured the full extent of temptation and He never wavered.

Different people have different levels of tolerance of pain. My wife makes the categorical statement that men can't endure much pain. Well, I personally don't mind pain; I just don't want to be around when it happens. Who feels pain most, the person with a low tolerance or the person with a high tolerance? The answer is obvious. The one who has experienced more pain understands pain to a greater degree. The same thing is true of temptation. People have different levels of resistance to temptation. Some people have a low resistance and when the first temptation comes along, WHAM, they fall and it's all over.

Years ago, Evander Holyfield was the world boxing champion. What happened to some guys who walked into the ring with him is what would have happened to me. He wouldn't even have had to hit me—just have the wind go by me, and I'm out. Some guys have gone into the ring and WHAM—one blow and they were out. Other guys have stayed fifteen rounds with Holyfield and taken everything he had. Who knows the strength of Holyfield better? The man who went out in the first blow of the first round or the man who went fifteen rounds with him?

Hebrews 4:15 says that Jesus Christ "was in all points tempted." That means that one day Jesus stepped into the ring with the devil, and was subjected to everything the devil had. Praise God, when the temptation ended, Jesus was without sin!

B. His Sympathy

Because of Christ's victory, He has sympathy for you and me when we are tempted. "We have not an high priest which cannot be touched with the feeling of our infirmities." The Bible uses the negative for emphasis. Put in the positive, the verse would read: We have a high priest who sympathizes with the feeling of our infirmities. The word translated *be touched* is literally translated *sympathize*, which means "suffer with." Jesus Christ knows how to suffer with us. He knows how to sympathize with us.

When you're having a hard time, Jesus understands. When your heart hurts, Jesus understands. He knows what it is to have a heavy heart Himself. We have a great high priest in Heaven who understands everything we're going through.

III. HIS PROVISION (4:16)

Jesus Christ is our great high priest because of His provision. He provides mercy and grace when we come to Him. "Let us therefore come boldly unto the throne of grace." The word *come* means "draw near." As we have noted, if you were an Israelite living two thousand years ago, you could never have drawn near. You worshiped from afar. Now our great high priest says, "You can draw near. You can come near."

The root of the word *boldly* means "freedom of expression, freedom of speech"—the ability to speak unhesitatingly. If you had been living two thousand years ago, you could not have spoken unhesitatingly in the presence of God. "To come boldly" means to have confidence in the presence of God. I don't mean that you are glib in the presence of God. Glibness borders on blasphemy. I'm not talking about that. Hebrews 4:16 is saying that because we have a great high priest, we can open up our hearts and tell Him everything.

When I was a boy, folks used to sing an old gospel song, "Now, Let Us Have a Little Talk with Jesus." If you've got a family problem, have a little talk with Jesus. If you've got trouble on the job, have a little talk with Jesus. If you've got a burden you can't get lifted, have a little talk with Jesus. Jesus Christ has transformed the throne of judgment into a throne of grace. When we come to His throne, our great high priest provides for the past and the present.

A. Mercy for My Past

What we need for our past is mercy. Mercy is something we do not deserve but desperately need. Remember how David sinned against God? He had a heart after God's own heart. God inspired him to write most of the Psalms in our Bible. He was the great king of Israel. He had everything, but he yielded to temptation. He sinned (see 2 Sam 11-12).

We're living in a day when people laugh at sin, minimize sin. But God has not changed His rules. The consequences of sin are the same in the twenty-first century as they were in the 1940s. The guilt is thesame. People may laugh at sin outwardly, but when they sin, guilt starts gnawing inwardly. That's what happened to David. David sinned, and he was guilty. Finally in repentance and remorse, he came into the presence of God. He said, "Have mercy upon me, O God" (Ps 51:1).

I need mercy too. You and I are standing in the presence of the God of this universe. Our mouths are silenced because of our guilt. We don't have a right even to open our mouths in the presence of God. Yet because we have a great high priest in Heaven, the Bible says we can come boldly to the throne of God and obtain mercy in our time of need. Titus 3:5 says, "Not by works of righteousness which we have done, but according to his mercy he saved us." That's what I need: mercy for my past sins and failures.

B. Grace for My Present

I also need grace for my present life. "Let us therefore come boldly unto the throne of grace, that we may obtain mercy, and find grace to help in time of need." Nobody is saved apart from the grace of God. Ephesians 2:8-9 says, "For by grace are ye saved through faith; and that not of yourselves: it is the gift of God: Not of works, lest any man should boast." G-R-A-C-E: God's Riches At Christ's Expense. Because of His mercy, I don't get what I deserve. Because of His grace, I get what I don't deserve! Grace is unmerited favor, or forgiveness.

We are saved by grace, but we also need daily, fresh supplies of grace. Paul said, "By the grace of God I am what I am" (1 Cor 15:10). One day a great preacher walked by an alcoholic in the gutter, looked at him, and said, "There but for the grace of God go I." I need that daily grace of God. There is sufficient grace for whatever need life presents to you.

The Apostle Paul had a problem that he couldn't overcome. He prayed three times about the problem, and it didn't go away. Then God did something better for Paul than removing his problem. God said, "My grace is sufficient for thee" (2 Cor 12:9). We too can "find grace to help in time of need." The Greek phrase in Hebrews 4:16 can be literally translated, "We can find grace to help in the nick of time." Sometimes His grace to help comes at the last minute. William Poole's hymn, "Just When I Need Him" (1907) says it perfectly:

> Just when I need Him, Jesus is near,
> Just when I falter, just when I fear,
> Ready to help me, ready to cheer,
> Just when I need Him most.

9

Our Heavenly High Priest
Hebrews 5:1-7

The opening verses of Hebrews 5 continue the discussion begun in Hebrews 4:14. Why do we spend time studying such things as the Old Testament high priesthood? The problems in the lives of the Jewish people that God dealt with through the priestly system are the same problems people living today experience: sorrow and suffering, death and sin. The basic problems of human life are the same. But we no longer need an earthly priesthood because we have a superior priesthood in the Lord Jesus Christ.

I. EARTHLY PRIESTHOOD (5:1-5)

In Hebrews 5:1-10, a contrast is drawn between an earthly priesthood and the heavenly priesthood of Jesus. The hinge on which this passage turns is in verses 4-5. The contrast is clear: "As was Aaron [the earthly priesthood]. So also Christ [the heavenly priesthood]."

The earthly priesthood was represented by Aaron, the brother of Moses. Aaron was the one whom God set apart to be the priest of the people as they made their journey through the wilderness wanderings on the way to the promised land.

A. His Appointment (5:1,4)

"For every high priest taken from among men is ordained [appointed] for men... No man taketh this honour unto himself, but he that is called of God, as was Aaron." The priest didn't appoint himself; he was appointed by God. (And although we no longer need earthly priests, a person should not undertake a preaching ministry today if he does not have a divine calling). God had ordained that there had to be a man who would represent others. An angel could not understand their needs. When a man went into the presence of God, he went with understanding of human fallibility.

B. His Assignment (5:1)

The Old Testament priest also had an assignment: "That he may offer both gifts and sacrifices for sins." His assignment was to offer those sacrifices for the sins of the people. The basic problem of all people through all the centuries is the same: *sin*. You say, "No, my problem is my marriage." I don't know all the details of the trouble in your marriage, but1know that the root cause is sin—either in your life or your mate's life, probably in both of your lives.

In the Old Testament the priest laid animal sacrifices on the altar to make payment for human sin. The ritual was a picture of the final payment that Jesus Christ would make. We have a better high priest, the Lord Jesus Christ. What is more, He was not only the priest, He was also the sacrifice. When Jesus died on the cross, He was making the sacrifice of Himself for our sins.

C. His Approach (5:2-3)

The priest, if he was what he ought to have been, had to "have compassion on the ignorant, and on them that are out of the way" (5:2). "The ignorant" means those who do not know any better. "Them that are out of the way" means those who are open rebels against God. The word translated *compassion* here is a combination of the Greek for "suffer" and "measured," thus a *measured suffering*. The priest couldn't condone sin, but he couldn't be too severe on sinners either. He had to be able to deal gently with them.

Most of us tend to go to extremes in dealing with people. A parent can be too lenient with his or her child or too severe. Both extremes are bad mistakes. There has to be balance —measured compassion. Similarly, the high priest had to be able to understand people but not indulge them in their sin.

An Old Testament high priest never made an offering for the sins of the people until first of all he had made an offering for his own sins. "For that he himself also is compassed with infirmity. And by reason hereof he ought, as for the people, so also for himself, to offer for sins" (5:2b-3).

Christians ought to keep their own sins in mind when dealing with other people. It's easy to see sin in the life of another person. It's much easier for me to see sin in your life than in mine. Why? We have blind spots. We tend to justify our own behavior. We say that somebody else is quick to lose his temper, but we call our own anger righteous indignation.

In Jesus we have a better high priest because He didn't have any sins. He didn't have to make a sacrifice to atone for His own sins before He could qualify to be our high priest. "Who [Jesus] needeth not daily, as those high priests, to offer up sacrifice, first for his own sins, and then for the people's" (7:27). Our Savior is the sinless Son of God. When He shed His blood at Calvary, it was not for His sins, but for ours!

IL HEAVENLY PRIESTHOOD (5:6-7)

In contrast to the earthly priests represented by Aaron, Christ is our heavenly high priest. When Jews heard the statement that Jesus Christ is the great high priest, they would ask: Does He meet the qualifications of a high priest? Let's see.

A. His Selection (5:6)

First of all, was He appointed by God? Hebrews 5:5 says, "So also Christ glorified not himself to be made an high priest." In other words, He did not call Himself. He was "called of God an high priest" (5:10).

Two Old Testament quotations show us that Jesus Christ was a high priest by divine selection. Hebrews 5:5 quotes Psalm 2:7. "Thou art my Son; this day have I begotten thee." What does this day refer to? Not the day of His birth. Jesus never functioned as a priest in His earthly ministry; He never went into the earthly holy of holies. Rather, on the day of His ascension and exaltation, He began to function as our high priest in Heaven.

Hebrews 5:6 quotes Psalm 110:4: "Thou art a priest for ever after the order of Melchizedek." A Jew considering the qualifications of a high priest would have asked, "What tribe is He from?" The temple records would have shown that Jesus was from the tribe of Judah, and a high priest had to be from the tribe of Levi. Aaron's descendants were from the tribe of Levi. But by mentioning Melchizedek, the writer of Hebrews was reminding those first-century Jews that there was a priesthood before the priesthood of Aaron and the Levites.

The first mention of a priest in the Bible is in Genesis 14. The first mention of any Bible subject is often a key to its meaning. That's why Genesis is so important. It is the seed plot of the Bible. In Genesis 14, Abraham had fought a war, rescued his nephew Lot, and was returning home. "And Melchizedek king of Salem brought forth bread and wine: and he was the priest of the most high God" (14:18). Melchizedek was a king and also a priest.

Later, God separated kings and priests in Israel. If you were a king you were not a priest. If you were a priest you were not a king. This is God's statement concerning the separation of church and state. There are examples in the Old Testament of kings who tried to exercise the role of a priest, and God judged them. Aaron's priesthood never mixed the offices of priest and king. But the Lord Jesus Christ has been selected by God not only to be a king, but also to be a priest. We have a king-priest sitting on the throne of glory for us. "Thou art a priest for ever." High priests in the Old Testament were not forever. They died and were replaced by their successors. But we have a high priest in Heaven who will never die. The Bible says He died once, rose from the dead, and is alive forevermore.

B. His Suffering (5:7)

Does Jesus qualify as a high priest in being able to understand our suffering? If Jesus Christ is going to deal with our sorrows, heartaches, and burdens, He must understand suffering. You never understand what other people are going through until you experience something similar yourself.

I have had very little pain in my life, but for three years I had terrible pain in my shoulders. Often there was not a moment day or night that I didn't have pain. This experience of pain gave me a new understanding of people who have constant pain. And Jesus, our heavenly high priest, is able to understand us because He himself suffered. He does qualify.

Hebrews 5:7 refers to the sufferings of Christ in Gethsemane: "Who in the days of his flesh, when he had offered up prayers and supplications with strong crying and tears." What unusual words to apply to Jesus. These are strong words for prayer, extreme words. A dark shadow falls across this verse. Mark's Gospel says Jesus was "sore amazed" and "very heavy" (14:33). Mark meant He was experiencing fear, panic, crushing depression, and a cyclone of grief. If you and I had been with Jesus that night, we would have been shocked. We would have seen Him prostrate on the ground, His face covered with sweat. We would have heard the loud cries of the Son of God.

Hebrews 5:7 says that Jesus was praying to the One who was able to save Him out of death, and He was heard: "Unto him that was able to save him from death, and was heard in that he feared." That does not mean that Jesus was praying not to die. Jesus realized He was born to die. He prayed, "Not my will, but thine, be done" (Lu 22:42).

Because Jesus was raised from the dead, we have a Savior in Heaven who can say when we suffer, "I understand. I've been there." When we face death, Jesus Christ can say, "I understand. I've been there."

JERRY VINES

10

Let's Talk About Our Salvation
Hebrews 5:8-10

Hebrews 5:8 moves from Gethsemane to Calvary. "Though he were a Son"—even though Jesus Christ is God's eternal Son— "yet learned he obedience by the things which he suffered."

I. HIS SUFFERING (5:8)

Philippians 2:8 says that Jesus "became obedient unto death, even the death of the cross." Our Lord was willing to die on a cross for our sins. Many of us are so familiar with the cross that if we are not careful, the meaning and depth of it evade us. We sing about the cross. We read about it in our Bibles. That kind of familiarity can cause us to miss the profound meaning of the death of our Lord. Jesus suffered death because of our sin and in spite of His sinlessness.

A. Because of Our Sin

The bottom line of the Bible is this: It tells us how Hell-deserving sinners can go to Heaven when they die. Romans 6:23 says, "For the wages of sin is death; but the gift of God is eternal life through Jesus Christ our Lord." Every one of us deserves the wages of sin. The Bible says in Romans 3:23, "For all have sinned, and come short of the glory of God." That verse includes every person reading this book, butnot everyone has sinned in exactly the same way. Most of us have not robbed a bank, but not one of us has been everything he ought to be at every moment of every day in every way.

"There is none righteous, no, not one" (Ro 3:10). You say, "I'm not such a bad guy. I try to treat my family well. I try to do right by the people I work with. I try to be honest in my business. I'm a pretty good guy." The fact is, you are just good enough to go to Hell! Know this: you are not saved on the basis of how good you are.

We have a tendency to compare our own goodness with somebody else's, and there is always somebody down the street who is worse than we are. But God's standard is the Lord Jesus Christ. When He walked on this earth He manifested the glory of God. Compared to that perfect standard we come short. And because of our shortcomings and in spite of His own perfection, Jesus suffered death.

B. In Spite of His Sinlessness

The proper point of comparison is the Lord Jesus Christ. Is there anybody who would claim to be as good as Jesus Christ? Jesus is the only person who never said a word He ought not to have said. The Bible says, "In many things we offend all" (Ja 3:2), and one of the ways we offend is by our words. Maybe we have used profanity. Maybe in anger we have said something unkind to another person. We have all sinned with our words. Yet Jesus Christ never sinned with His.

Jesus never had a sinful thought. When I look at Jesus and discover His absolute purity, then I understand why I'm just good enough to go to Hell. Jesus said that anyone who has sinned in his thoughts needs a Savior, needs salvation. The salvation I need is available because Jesus suffered death. Jesus is our standard, but it is not Jesus' perfect life that saves us. It is His atoning, sacrificial death at Calvary that makes salvation possible. By dying He accomplished the purpose for which He had come into this world. He completed His task. "Being made perfect [perfect here means "complete"], he became the author of eternal salvation unto all them that obey him" (5:9).

II. HIS SALVATION (5:9-10)

A. It Is Powerful

The apostle Paul wrote, "For I am not ashamed of the gospel of Christ: for it is the power of God unto salvation to every one that believeth" (Ro 1:16). Salvation is powerful on the basis of what Jesus Christ did in order to make it possible for us to be saved. I see three ingredients of this powerful salvation that Christ wrought for us.

First, I see the power of the virtuous life of our Lord. Jesus fulfilled all the requirements for being our Savior. He was sinless. He was the perfect Son of God.

Second, I see the power of the vicarious death of Jesus at Calvary. Jesus was destined from all eternity to be the Lamb who would be slain for us (Rev 13:8). Christ suffered bodily pain on the cross, and I want to have a constantly broken and appreciative heart for what He endured physically at Calvary for me. But if I see only the physical sufferings of Jesus, I do not realize the full depths of His agony. Isaiah 53:6 talks about the spiritual suffering of Christ at Calvary: "All we like sheep have gone astray; we have turned every one to his own way; and the Lord hath laid on him the iniquity of us all." The Bible says that when Jesus died on the cross, He who knew no sin was made sin for us. All our sins were laid on Him. All the sin of all of time was laid on Christ. At Calvary the wrath of God fell in full measure on His perfect, sinless Son.

Third, I see the power of the victorious resurrection of Jesus. The Bible says the lifeless form of Jesus was taken down from the cross and put in a tomb. A stone was rolled in front of the tomb, and Roman soldiers stood guard. But God raised Jesus Christ from the dead. God the Father showed He was pleased with what Jesus did at Calvary. The sacrifice of Jesus, our great high priest, was acceptable in Heaven for the sins of the whole world. He was victor over death. Our salvation is powerful.

B. It Is Eternal

The salvation that Jesus Christ provides for sinners is eternal salvation: "And being made perfect, he became the author [originator] of eternal salvation" (5:9).

A little boy in Sunday school was asked to give the meaning of eternal. The little fellow scratched his head and said, "Something that won't quit." Not a bad definition. It means forever. Everlasting salvation. Nowhere in the Bible does Jesus offer temporary salvation. Jesus never offers probationary salvation. Jesus doesn't say, "I'm going to give you this salvation temporarily, and then I'm going to watch and see how much good you do. If you are good enough, I'm going to let you keep it, but if you aren't, I'll take it back from you."

John 3:16 has a wonderful promise: "For God so loved the world, that he gave his only begotten Son, that whosoever believeth in him should not perish, but have everlasting life." When Jesus Christ saves us, we are saved for all eternity; we have eternal security. Christian people, however, sometimes disagree about eternal security. There are sincere Christians who do not believe salvation is eternal. We need to ask them some questions. Upon what does their salvation depend? What is the basis of their salvation? How are they saved in the first place? Who does the saving?

There are two basic views of salvation. One view is that we are saved by something we do. The other view is that we are saved by something God does. If we are saved by something we do, then something we don't do could cause us to lose that salvation. If we are saved on the basis of something God does, then nothing we do could cause us to lose our salvation.

We are not saved because of our works. We don't become "good enough" for God to save us. One of the main reasons people don't come to Christ for salvation is that they have the idea that they have to become "good enough" to be acceptable to the Lord. In other words, they want to clean up their lives a little first. They are putting the cart before the horse. You don't give up bad habits in order to be saved. Jesus helps you straighten things out after you are saved.

Someone may ask, "What about a person who is saved, lives for the Lord for a little while, then later on falls into deep sin and dies in that sinful condition? Is he going to Heaven?" Remember. You and I really have no way of knowing whether a person is saved or not. You don't know whether I'm saved or not. You say, "I think he's saved. He preaches like he's saved. Most of the time he acts like he's saved." But only the Lord and I know whether I'm saved or not.

Consider the man in the Old Testament named Lot (assume you know nothing written about Lot in the New Testament). In Genesis you read about Lot, the nephew of Abraham. Abraham said, "I'm going to walk by faith." Lot said, "I'll go with you." Then Lot pitched his tent toward Sodom, which was a serious mistake. Soon he and his family moved into Sodom. Lot was a man whose life gave no outward indication that he was saved. But, surprise of surprises', the New Testament says that Lot was a righteous man, a just man. He didn't live like a just man. He lost his family. He lost his testimony because of hiscompromise, and barely got out of Sodom alive. There are people who have truly received Jesus as their Savior, yet they don't live for Him the way they ought. Their lives, like Lot's, are a shame and a reproach to their Lord.

Then in the New Testament there is a man who as far as outward appearances were concerned seemed to be saved. Wouldn't you think that a man who was selected by Jesus to be one of His twelve would be a saved man? Wouldn't you think that a man who was selected to be the treasurer of the disciples of Jesus Christ would be a saved man? But the night before His death, Jesus said to His disciples, "One of you is going to betray me." Those words really shook the disciples. Every one of them started saying, "Lord, is it I?" It never dawned on any of the disciples who the betrayer was. By all outward appearances, Judas Iscariot was one of the Lord's own, yet Jesus said he was the son of perdition (Jn 17:12).

Lot and Judas remind us we do not really know whether people are saved, but God knows, and those that are His have eternal salvation.

Note carefully the promise of the Lord Jesus: "My sheep hear my voice, and I know them, and they follow me: And I give unto them eternal life; and they shall never perish, neither shall any man pluck them out of my hand. My Father, which gave them me, is greater than all; and no man is able to pluck them out of my Father's hand" (Jn 10:27-29).

Our salvation is eternal, not on the basis of our hold on the Father, but because of His hold on us. Someone may say, "If you preach that, you are going to encourage people to sin." No. To believe that I have eternal redemption provided for me by the sacrificial work of Jesus Christ does not cause me to say I can do as I want. Being saved changes my attitude toward sin.

One reason I know I'm saved is that my attitude toward sin has changed. If you have really been saved, you can still sin, but you can't sin and enjoy it. There are people out there in the world reveling in every minute of their sinning. Later on, we'll discover Hebrews talks about delighting in the "pleasures of sin for a season" (11:25). But the saved person understands that his sins are responsible for the death of the Lord Jesus Christ and his heart is broken when he sins.

If he has been born of the Spirit, he can't enjoy sin. The moment you receive Jesus Christ as your Savior, the Bible says you receive the Holy Spirit. God's Holy Spirit comes to dwell in your life and places His seal on you (Eph 4:30). A seal means ownership, and it also means preservation. Do you remember seeing your mother putting away preserves in those Mason jars and sealing them—preserving them? How long am I sealed? Until the day I sin? Until the day I disobey the Lord? No. Until the day of redemption.

Because Jesus our high priest went into the holy of holies and obtained eternal redemption (9:12), we are sealed until the Lord comes. We have an eternal salvation!

11

Let Us Go On Hebrews 5:11-6:3

Hebrews contains a series of encouragements. Although some people call these segments *warning* passages, I prefer to call them *encouragement* passages. Hebrews 5:11-6:3, the third of five warning/encouragement passages, deals with the tragedy of arrested development. On the basis of the superiority of Jesus, the salvation He provides, and the Christian life He offers, we are encouraged to move on to maturity and to become full-grown, mature believers in the Lord. There is nothing wrong with being a baby when you are born, but it is a problem if you remain a baby all your life.

In the physical realm there is nothing sweeter than a newborn baby. There is nothing so thrilling as seeing a baby begin to mature physically. To see that little one begin to use his hands and arms is exciting. It's exciting to see a baby beginning to develop mentally. You notice the way a little child begins to make sounds. He starts off—ba, ba, ba, ba. You think she's saying bye, bye. Probably she's not, but you like to think so. Then comes the first word—da, da. Yes! She's surely talking about daddy!

And what is more exciting than a brand-new Christian? In our church every Sunday we have the joy of seeing people come to know the Lord. Perhaps you have had the joy of going into people's homes, opening up your Bible, and explaining to them how they can know Jesus as their Savior. Every time a sinner repents of his sin and invites Jesus into his heart, a brand-new birth occurs. Jesus said to Nicodemus, "Ye must be born again" (Jn 3:7).

It is essential to be born into God's family in order to go to Heaven. A person who is born only once will die twice. A person who is born twice will die only once. You have to be born into God's family.

But birth is only the beginning point. Birth is not the end of our Christian experience. The Bible says we ought to grow into maturity in the Lord. Second Peter 3:18 instructs us to "grow in grace, and in the knowledge of our Lord and Saviour Jesus Christ." Ephesians 4:13-14 says, "Till we all come in the unity of the faith, and of the knowledge of the Son of God, unto a perfect man [unto a full-grown, mature man], unto the measure of the stature of the fulness of Christ: That we henceforth be no more children." God intends for new-born Christians to mature.

The writer of Hebrews described the condition of spiritual immaturity—arrested development. Then he prescribed the solution and told us how to get beyond spiritual babyhood in our lives.

I. HE DESCRIBED THE CONDITION (5:11-14)

A. Restrained Development (5:11-12a)

Spiritual immaturity is not necessarily proportionate to the number of years one has been a Christian. It is possible for a new Christian to grow rapidly, to advance in his Christian life and achieve amazing spiritual maturity in one or two years. On the other hand, it is possible for a person to be a Christian for years and years and still be in kindergarten in his spiritual life. I have seen seventy-year-old baby believers, still in their diapers spiritually. They have never learned to crawl. They have never learned to grow and mature in their Christian lives.

Hebrews 5:11 begins to describe this condition of spiritual immaturity: "We have many things to say, and hard to be uttered, seeing ye are dull of hearing." The writer was saying, "I would like to say more to you. I would like to go a step further, but the problem is, you are dull of hearing." The word *dull* means "slow" or "sluggish." Sluggish or dull hearing is something we don't normally think about. More often we talk about dull preaching or dull teaching. I've heard some dull preaching, and to be honest I've done some myself!

I heard about two laymen who met one Monday morning uptown. One said to the other, "How was the preaching over at your place?" His friend said, "It was the same old ding dong, ding dong." The first guy smiled and said, "Well, you ought to be thankful. At our place it was the same old ding, ding, ding, ding."

But dull preaching is not the problem dealt with in Hebrews 5:11; this verse is talking about dullness of hearing. The first indication of spiritual underdevelopment is that believer-babies are dull of hearing. Spiritual things are not interesting and exciting to them. They go to small group Bible study and the teaching seems dull. They attend a church worship service, and the music sounds dull. They hear the gospel, and the preaching is dull to their ears; they don't get anything out of the sermon. The problem might not be dull teaching and preaching and singing. The problem might be that there is spiritual dullness in their lives because they're not growing and maturing in the things of the Lord. Dullness of hearing is a symptom of restrained spiritual development.

There is another indication that certain people are not growing beyond spiritual babyhood: when they ought to be sharing the gospel with others, they need instead for somebody to go back over the basics of the faith with them, "the first principles of the oracles of God." The phrase "the first principles" is a translation of a word that means "the rudiments of any subject ,the beginning lessons, the basic elements."You don't walk into a group of first graders and hand them copies of a novel. Rather, you teach them a-b-c, d-e-f. The writer of Hebrews was talking about the first truths of the gospel.

Of course, there is nothing wrong with the first truths of the gospel. But when you are a spiritually immature person, you have to be taught those first principles over and over again. You never get beyond them.

Instead of teaching, you have to be taught yourself. This does not mean that every Christian is intended to be a teacher. I personally believe that a person needs to be called by God to teach Scripture in small group Bible studies just as I need to be called by God to preach. Not everybody has been called to teach. What the writer of Hebrews was saying is that as you mature in your life as a Christian, you ought to begin to have the ability to share the basics of the gospel with other people.

I don't agree with those who say that soulwinning is a spiritual gift, and that some people have it, and some people don't. I do believe that some people seem to have more ability than others to lead people to Jesus Christ. I believe that some people have the spiritual gift of evangelism. But as I understand the New Testament, every child of God is given the commission from Jesus Christ to be a witness for Him and to strive to lead other people to faith in Him.

You may not be the greatest soul-winner in the world, but you can tell somebody else about Jesus. Don't worry about how timid you are. There is somebody out there who can be won to Jesus Christ by a timid soul like you. You may not be able to present the gospel as skillfully as somebody else. You may be frightened. But I have seen God use that kind of fright to lead somebody else to the Lord Jesus Christ. There are some folks I can lead to the Lord, and there are also some folks you can lead to the Lord. However, if you're underdeveloped spiritually, you will not be able to teach or get into the solid food of the Bible.

B. Restricted Diet (5:12b-14)

The last part of Hebrews 5:12 says that you "are become such as have need of milk, and not of strong meat." Notice the contrast. Milk and meat. Milk and solid food. Milk is baby food; we all understand that. The Bible teaches that we should desire milk: "As newborn babes [literally, just now born], desire [earnestly desire] the sincere milk of the word, that ye may grow thereby" (1 Pe 2:2). God has built into a baby the natural desire for milk. You don't have to teach a baby to want milk. That's one of the ways you can know you are a born-again child of God. If you are truly saved, there will be a natural desire for the milk of the

Word of God. You will want to know the Bible. Baby Christians need the simpler truths of the Bible.

I never get tired of the simpler truths. I like milk. I still drink milk. We don't discard milk when we are grown. But the Bible not only points us to the simpler truths of the gospel, it also talks about its teachings as meat, solid food. "For everyone that useth milk [those who feed on milk] is unskillful [inexperienced] in the word of righteousness: for he is a babe" (5:13). How do we know when we are getting into the solid food, the meat of the Word?

> Strong meat belongeth to them that are of full age [those who are mature, those who are grown], even those who by reason of use have their senses exercised to discern both good and evil (5:14).

We are maturing in our Christian lives and developing in our understanding of the Bible when we get to the point where we are able to apply the principles of Scripture to our daily lives. Then we are able to use those principles to help us judge—to discern between—what is right and what is wrong.

The Bible is not merely to be believed; it is also to be obeyed. The Bible says, "Be ye doers of the word, and not hearers only" (Ja 1:22). It's wonderful to hear the truths of the Bible, the basic gospel, the milk of the Word. But we are to be doers of the Word.

Suppose you are in the business world. You go to work and sit down at your desk at seven in the morning. You face a decision that needs to be made that day. If you are a mature Christian, you will ask yourself, "What does the Word of God say about this issue? What have I found in my Bible study lately that has a practical bearing on this decision?"

Young people in high school are faced with all kinds of decisions—some involving pressures from their peer group. If one of these students is a growing Christian, he will say, "How does what I've been reading in my quiet time apply to these decisions?" God did not give us the Bible just to read and receive as information. God gave us the Bible to help us make correct spiritual decisions in our daily lives.

Nowhere in the Bible does it say, "Thou shalt not drink a beer." It's been a long time since I've read Leviticus, but I don't think such a statement is there. Rather, we find principles in the Bible. The Bible says, "Wine is a mocker, strong drink is raging: and whosoever is deceived thereby is not wise" (Prv 20:1). The Bible says that my body is the temple of the Holy Spirit, and that I'm to glorify God in my body (1 Cor 6:19-20).The Bible says, "Whatsoever ye do, do all to the glory of God" (1 Cor 10:31). If you apply those principles to the question of whether or not you're going to drink, you'll come out with the right decision.

Again, no where in the Bible does it say, "Thou shalt not play the lottery." But there are principles in Scripture about not doing anything that causes your brother to be offended or hinders your brother. The Bible teaches that I am not to let anything have dominion over me and rule my life, and I am to work for what 1get. People who don't apply the principles of the Bible to their daily lives are spiritually immature. The writer of Hebrews described them as babies needing milk, but showed how they could become spiritual adults on solid food.

II. HE PRESCRIBED THE SOLUTION (6:1-3)

A. Forsake Immaturity

"Therefore leaving the principles of the doctrine of Christ, let us go on unto perfection; not laying again the foundation of repentance from dead works, and of faith toward God." The phrase the principles means "the first truths, the elementary truths"—like the foundation of a building. The word *leave* here means "move beyond." A baby bird moves beyond the shell. A builder moves beyond his foundation. Some foundational truths have their base in the Old Testament. There is a mingling of New Testament truth and Old Testament truth in verses 1-3. (The first readers of Hebrews would have especially understood references to the Old Testament system better than we do).

In these verses are six truths—in three groups of two. The first couplet is "repentance from dead works" and "faith toward God," the initial truths of the gospel. The writer used Old Testament terminology talking about the works of Old Testament believers in keeping the law. He used New Testament terminology talking about faith in the Lord Jesus Christ.

Repentance and faith are two sides of a coin. No one who hasn't repented can put faith in Jesus Christ. No one who repents fails to put faith in the Lord Jesus Christ. The word repentance means "an about-face, a turning around." You turn from and you turn toward. You repent from dead works. Dead works are considered sin. You repent from sin and turn toward the Lord Jesus Christ.

The next two truths are symbolic: "the doctrine of baptisms" and "laying on of hands." The doctrine of baptisms is the doctrine of washings. In the Old Testament there were washing ceremonies that we don't perform today. But there is a New Testament application. Titus 3:5 says, "Not by works of righteousness which we have done, but according to his mercy he saved us, by the washing of regeneration, and renewing of the Holy Ghost." We don't have to go through all those washing ceremonies in the Old Testament. If we've been born of the Spirit of God, we have had the washing of regeneration. The other symbolic truth is the "laying on of hands." In Old Testament times the Jews would bring a sacrificial animal to the priest and lay their hands on it. The priest would then take the animal, kill it, and offer it on the altar. You and I by faith have laid our hands on the Lamb of God, the Lord Jesus Christ, who was slain for our sins.

The final couplet is "resurrection of the dead" and "eternal judgment," eternal truths. The resurrection of the dead is a truth that is only partially unveiled in the Old Testament. The Old Testament teaches that there is going to be a resurrection. The New Testament reveals more, teaching that there will be a resurrection of both believers and the unsaved. The eternal judgment of God is an Old Testament concept. Malachi, the last book of the Old Testament, ends with the word curse

(Mal 4:6). But this Old Testament truth is fully expanded in the New Testament where we discover that there is no judgment for those who are in Christ Jesus. He bore our judgment at Calvary.

These six foundational truths are wonderful, but we must move beyond them.

B. Follow Maturity

Leaving the first principles, "let us go on unto perfection." Let us go on to maturity. In the original the verb is passive as in, "let us be carried on to maturity." God carries us on to maturity—"This will we do, if God permit."

The Lord will help us grow beyond the baby stage in our Christian lives. He will bring us to maturity in the Lord if we allow Him to. I want to be a mature Christian, don't you?

12

Tragedy of a Backslidden Life
Hebrews 6:4-9

The verses in Hebrews 6:4-9 are not easy to understand; not surprisingly, this passage has evoked a great deal of disagreement. Three questions we should ask when studying any portion of Scripture. First ask, What do these verses say? The only way you can find that out is to read the verses for yourself. A second question is, What do the verses mean? What do these verses teach? What is the interpretation? A third question is, What do these verses tell me to do? There is no purpose in reading and studying the Bible for the sake of gathering a store of information. The purpose of Bible study is always practical. You want to find out what the Bible says and means in order to help you do what the Bible says to do.

If you have read Hebrews 6:4-9, you know what those verses say. But what do they mean? There is a great deal of difference of opinion among fine Bible scholars about the interpretation of this passage.

Some commentators say these verses refer to a person who had been saved but subsequently apostatized from the faith. That is, he or she departed from the faith—repudiated the faith—and in so doing lost their salvation. According to this interpretation, it is possible for a person who has been saved to depart from the faith; that is, to forfeit salvation. If you take this view, you also have to take the view that such an individual cannot be saved again. "It is impossible ... If they shall fall away, to renew them again unto repentance" (vss. 4, 6).

Other commentators believe these verses do not refer to a saved person but to a lost person who had been at the very edge of salvation. While he had tasted of the heavenly gift, experienced it through a little taste, but then turned away. He went back into his previous life. Those who offer this interpretation would also have to say that such a person could never again come to the point of being saved. These verses specifically say that if he falls away, it's *impossible* to renew him again unto repentance.

Those are two main views taken by earnest, sincere believers concerning the meaning of these verses of Scripture.

I'm going to suggest a third alternative, which I believe gets to the heart of what Hebrews 6:4-9 has to say to believers today. There are several considerations to keep in mind as we study these verses of Scripture.

First, we must never allow an obscure passage of Scripture to override clear passages. There is virtually no difference of opinion about some verses in the Bible. They are completely clear in their teaching. We must not let difficult verses cause us to lose the blessing of verses we do understand. Mark Twain said, "It is not the verses in the Bible I don't understand that bother me; it's the verses in the Bible I do understand that bother me."

A second consideration to keep in mind is that we must always understand a passage of Scripture in the context in which it is found. We don't read verses in isolation. We look at what is said before and what is said after. A text out of context is a pretext. Virtually all of the false cults today are built on Scripture passages lifted out of context. Hence, we must remember that Hebrews 6:4-9 is part of a passage encouraging believers to go on to full maturity in their Christian lives. Believers must not allow anything to keep them from moving on to maturity in the Lord, to be everything God saved them to be. That is the context.

A third consideration is that we must ask the question, Is this a salvation passage or a fellowship passage? Some passages in the Bible have to do with salvation; they deal with our relationship to the Lord, how we are saved, how we become members of God's family forever. Other passages are fellowship passages; they deal with our relationship to God not as children to our Father but as servants to our Lord.

Once we are saved, it is not possible for us to lose our salvation, but it is possible for us to lose our fellowship with Jesus. Fellowship has to do with bearing fruit, living close to the Lord, and abiding in Him. John 15, for example, is a fellowship passage. If you look at that passage as a salvation passage, you will wind up losing your salvation in that chapter. If you keep in mind that the subject is fellowship, abiding in Jesus on a daily basis, you will see that He is talking about bearing fruit as an obedient Christian who lives close to Him.

Hebrews 6:9 says, "But, beloved, we are persuaded better things of you, and things that accompany salvation." The pasage is not about salvation, but about things that *accompany* salvation.

What things are being talked about? Hebrews 6:7 helps us understand what the answer to that question is: "For the earth which drinketh in the rain that cometh oft upon it, and bringeth forth herbs meet for them by whom it is dressed, receiveth blessing from God." When the writer of Hebrews referred to the things that accompany salvation, he was talking about bearing fruit in our fellowship relationship with the Lord Jesus Christ.

Based on the above considerations, I believe Hebrews 6:4- 9 is a picture of a tragedy, the tragedy of a backslidden Christian life.

The Bible teaches that it is possible for a Christian who is saved to get out of the will of God. We call such a person a backslidden Christian. We all know someone in that condition. David was a saved man, a man after God's own heart. Yet David was so backslidden that he was even willing to commit murder. David came back to God, but he never fully recovered from the consequences of his sins. He clearly had a backslidden phase. Multitudes of people are backslidden today.

They are truly saved (though God alone really knows) but not bearing any fruit for the Lord Jesus Christ.

Three alarming characteristics of a backslidden Christian are revealed in Hebrews 6:4-9. A backslidden Christian is a tragedy because he or she is pitiful, disgraceful, and finally unfruitful.

I. A PITIFUL CHRISTIAN (6:4-6a)

A. A Contradiction (6:4-5)

A backslidden Christian is pitiful because his life is a contradiction. He is saved, but he allows sin in his life. He was "once enlightened" (6:4). The word *enlighten* means "turn the light on." The word *convict* means "turn the light on" too. A lost person is in spiritual darkness, but when the Spirit of God convicts him of his lost condition, he is made aware of his sins. He receives the light of the knowledge of the Lord Jesus Christ, and he is saved.

Second Corinthians 4:6 says, "God, who commanded the light to shine out of darkness, hath shined in our hearts, to give the light of the knowledge of the glory of God in the face of Jesus Christ." Hebrews 10:32 says, "But call to remembrance the former days, in which, after ye were illuminated, ye endured a great fight of afflictions." A person who has been illuminated— enlightened—is a saved person.

A backslidden Christian has "tasted of the heavenly gift" (6:4). Some say that the word *taste* does not mean "eat," but only "nibble" or "sample." However, the meaning here is "experience."

Psalm 34:8 says, "O taste and see that the Lord is good" (cp. 1 Pe 2:3). Hebrews 2:9 says, "But we see Jesus, who was made a little lower than the angels for the suffering of death, crowned with glory and honour; that he by the grace of God should *taste* death for every man" (italics added). Jesus didn't sample death. He experienced death for everyone. And a backslidden Christian has experienced the heavenly gift. "The wages of sin is death; but the gift of God is eternal life through Jesus Christ our Lord" (Rm 6:23).

A backslidden Christian has been made a partaker of the Holy Spirit (6:4). The word *partaker* literally means "lay hold of with someone." It is a picture of partnership or working with someone in a common endeavor. When we are saved, we and the Holy Spirit are working together in a common endeavor. We are to endeavor to become like the Lord Jesus Christ and serve Him. The Holy Spirit wants to sanctify us—that is, make us more and more like Jesus. He also wants to work through us—that is, make our service fruitful. Our role is to cooperate with the Holy Spirit, to "lay hold of with the Holy Spirit," to engage in this common activity with the Holy Spirit.

The Lord has a hard time with us sometimes, getting us to be what we ought to be. We are all going to be what we ought to be when we get to Heaven, but it would be nice if the Lord wouldn't have such a cleanup job to do at the judgment seat. Wouldn't it be better if we could make a little progress down here?

A backslidden Christian has "tasted [same word] the good word of God, and the powers of the world to come" (6:5). He knows what it is to be blessed by the teaching and preaching and personal study of God's Word. He has had a foretaste of what is awaiting him over in the glory land. One of the joys of being saved is that sometimes God gives us a little down payment of what Heaven is going to be like.

A backslidden Christian has been enlightened, has experienced the heavenly gift, has partaken of the Holy Ghost, has been blessed by the Word of God, and has had a foretaste of Heaven, but he has fallen away. *Fall away* is not the same as *apostatize*, which means "stand off from." The word translated *fall away* in 6:6 means "fall alongside." (It is not used anywhere else in the entire New Testament).

If you are walking down a road, you might fall alongside the road. A saved person, put on the road of salvation, intended to grow and mature in the Christian life, can fall alongside. He can deviate from the purpose. He can allow sin to get into his life. His life can become a contradiction of everything salvation means.

If you are truly a child of God, and you are living a backslidden Christian life, your life is a total contradiction of everything the Bible stands for, of everything Jesus Christ ought to mean to you, of everything your church stands for. You are a pitiful Christian.

B. A Complication (6:6a)

A backslidden Christian is a complicated problem to anyone who wants to help him. If a Christian falls away—if he gets into a life of sin and is not growing and maturing in the Lord and is not serving the Lord the way he ought to—it is impossible to renew him again unto repentance. I have repented far more since I've been saved than I did when I got saved. One could almost say that a Christian life is a life of repentance. First John 1:9 says, "If we confess our sins, he is faithful and just to forgive us our sins, and to cleanse us from all unrighteousness." There's hardly a day in my life when I don't have to claim that verse and repent.

But a backslidden Christian is not repentant. Nobody can turn him around from the course of destruction down which he is headed. Hebrews 6:6b uses present tense verbs when describing the time of backsliding. A clear translation would be "While they are crucifying to themselves the Son of God afresh, and while they are putting him to an open shame." When a Christian is in a backslidden condition —while he is in that condition of crucifying Jesus all over again, while he is in that condition of putting Him to an open shame—nothing can be done with him. As long as he is in that condition it is impossible to renew him again unto repentance.

So you had better be careful about what you are doing. You had better be cautious about what you play with. Even if you are a child of God, you can get yourself in such a condition, so blinded by the devil, so deeply in sin, so shackled by lust, that there is nothing anybody can do about you until you finally hit bottom. You could become a pitiful Christian. A backslidden Christian is a tragedy because he is pitiful and disgraceful.

II. A DISGRACEFUL CHRISTIAN (6:6b)

A. Slays the Son of God

A backslidden Christian is disgraceful because he repeats Calvary. It's the cross all over again. A Christian who is letting sin remain in his life is saying, "Give me the hammer; I'll drive another nail in His hand." He's saying, "Give me a sword; I'll plunge another sword in His side." He is saying, "Let me strip off every bit of His clothes; I'll expose Him to open shame."

B. Shames the Son of God

The people who know a backslidden Christian look at his life and jeer and leer and mock and ridicule the name of Jesus. A person who claims to be saved but whose life contradicts everything Jesus stands for can do a lot of damage. The souls of people damned to Hell because of his inconsistent, disgraceful life hang heavy, heavy over his head. A backslidden Christian is a tragedy because he is pitiful, disgraceful, and unfruitful.

III. AN UNFRUITFUL CHRISTIAN (6:7-9)

The purpose of a piece of land is to bear fruit. The worth of the land is determined by the fruit it is able to bear. The purpose of a Christian life is to bear fruit.

A. A Useful Life Brings God's Blessing (6:7)

A Christian who is walking with the Lord is bearing fruit and is a blessing. "For the earth which drinketh in the rain that cometh oft upon it, and bringeth forth herbs meet for them by whom it is dressed, receiveth blessing from God."

B. An Unfruitful Life Brings God's Curse (6:8)

If a Christian is in a backslidden condition and is not walking with Jesus, his life is unfruitful, and he brings a curse. "But that which beareth thorns and briers is rejected." Paul said in 1 Corinthians 9:27, "Lest . . . when I have preached to others, I myself should be a castaway."

A backslidden Christian is going to become a castaway, a reject. He will not lose his salvation. The land is still the same land. It's not the land that is burned, but the thorns and briers that the land produced. The land "is nigh [right near, next] unto cursing; whose end is to be burned."

God is saying, "I'll deal with the backslidden Christian at the judgment seat of Christ." It's going to be a sad day for him when he stands there. He is saved and is going to go to Heaven, but he is saved "so as by fire" (1 Cor 3:15). When he could have had a fruitful, righteous, beautiful garden of a life to offer the Lord Jesus at the judgment seat, instead all he will have is a piece of land that has been burned over.

That's tragic, but let me conclude this chapter on an encouraging note. Hebrews 6:9 begins, "But, beloved [that's one of the sweetest terms of endearment for God's people], we are persuaded better things of you, and things that accompany salvation." Let me encourage you to go on to produce the things that accompany salvation, fruit that will bring honor and glory to our Lord Jesus Christ.

13

Dancing on the Promises
Hebrews 6:10-15

One of the most encouraging aspects of the Christian life is that God has given us wonderful promises. Literally thousands of them are recorded for us in the Bible. Someone said, "Christians do not live by explanations; they live by promises."

Experiences that defy explanation come to all of us. Mysteries, perplexities, and enigmas come to God's people, just as to everyone else. But when there are no explanations, there are always the promises of God. In His good time He will help us understand what is taking place.

When you are facing a situation you do not understand, which would you rather have: an answer to that specific problem or the One who has the answer to every problem? When answers aren't enough, there is Jesus.

You and I need to learn to appropriate the promises of God in our lives. We need to find and claim those promises. God never, ever fails to do what He says in the Bible He will do. Russell Carter's hymn "Standing on the Promises" (1886) says it perfectly:

> Standing on the promises that cannot fail,
> When the howling storms of doubt and fear assail,
> By the living Word of God I shall prevail,

JERRY VINES

Standing on the promises of God.

I. APPRECIATION (6:10)

Before referring to the promises, the writer of Hebrews offered words of appreciation. God does not fail to see what you do. God appreciates everything His children do for His honor and glory. Hebrews 6:10 says, "For God is not unrighteous [not unfair] to forget your work and labour of love." God never has a memory lapse.

Malachi 3:16 says, "Then they that feared the Lord spake often one to another: and the Lord hearkened, and heard it, and a book of remembrance was written." God in Heaven is keeping record. Everything you do for Him is written down in His book of remembrance. That's not hard to believe when you think of today's computers that can file unbelievable amounts of material.

God notices when we help the other members of His family. As members of the same family, we ought to pray for one another. We ought to bear one another's burdens. We ought to love one another. We ought to forgive one another. We ought to help weaker brothers and sisters. We ought to give to those who are needy. God expects us to minister to one another. The word *minister* means "serve." *Deacon* comes from the same root word.

A. Motivation for Service

In Hebrews 6:10 God expresses His appreciation for the motivation behind our Christian service. Love for Christ is our motivation. We serve others for Jesus' sake. Our service is done as unto the Lord. God will not forget our "labour of love."

A missionary on furlough was describing his work and the difficulties of dealing with the people he served. Somebody said, "It really must take a whole lot of love for you to love those people enough to go over there and be a missionary to them." The missionary said, "I didn't go over there because I love them. I went over there because I love Jesus, and Jesus told me to go over there. When I got over there, Jesus taught me to love those people."

B. Continuation of Service

God notices when we continue to serve the Lord. "Ye have ministered to the saints and do minister." You just keep on.

A friend of mine said, "Retirement means that you were tired yesterday, and you are tired again today." I don't know if that's true or not, but I know that we should never retire from serving Jesus.

Sometimes people say, "Oh yes, I used to teach Sunday school." That's wonderful, but what are you doing for Jesus today? Some of the most effective Christian witnesses are retired people. God has let them loose from secular jobs so they can work for Jesus fulltime.

II. ADMONITION (6:11-12)

A. Diligence (6:11)

Here is a word of admonition. "We desire that every one of you do shew the same diligence to the full assurance of hope unto the end: That ye be not slothful, but followers of them who through faith and patience inherit the promises" (vv. 11-12). We are to be *followers*. From the Greek for this word we get our English word *mimic*. A mimic imitates. We are to be imitators. We are to imitate those who have gone on before.

Old Testament believers and Christian saints who have gone on before us have set a tremendous example for us to follow. They showed diligence and every successive generation has to show the same diligence in order for God's work to go on effectively. A successful church doesn't just happen. Dedicated, diligent people make it happen. We are admonished to imitate the diligence of those who inherit the promises.

B. Patience (6:12)

The promises of God are inherited "through faith and patience." The promises have a trust element and a time element. Faith is the trust element. If we don't make the promises our own by faith—if we don't trust them—they won't do us any good. Patience is the time element. The word *patience* here means "longsuffering." Hebrews 10:36 says, "For ye have need of patience, that, after ye have done the will of God, ye might receive the promise." We need to follow the example of patience. We need to wait for the promises of God to be fulfilled. We must keep on believing. Fulfillment of the promises may not come when we expect it, but we are to be patient in our trust that God is going to do what He said He would do.

III. APPLICATION (6:13-15)

The author of Hebrews provided an illustration from the life of Abraham. Abraham is the foremost Old Testament believer who by faith claimed the promises of God and then was willing to wait for the fulfillment of those promises. Romans 4:11 says that Abraham is the "father of all them that believe."

A, Extended (6:13-14)

God extended a promise to Abraham. Abraham once was a pagan, a moon-god worshiper in Ur of the Chaldees. One day God came to Abraham and said, "Get out of this country to a country I will show you" (Gen 12:1-3). God didn't even tell him where he was going. But He told him He would bless his seed and make his seed a blessing to the world.

The Bible says that Abraham believed God. Can you imagine what happened next? One day Abraham came strolling into the First National Bank of Ur. The clerk said, "Hello there, Brother Abraham. It's good to see you. What can we do for you today?"

"I want to take all my money out of the bank." (He was very rich.)

"Excuse me, Brother Abraham?"

"Yes, I want my money."

"Oh, Brother Abraham, is there a problem somewhere?"

"No. No problem."

The teller ran into a back office to see the president. He said, "Listen, Brother Abraham is out there, and I don't know what's wrong, but he wants to take out all his money." They ushered Brother Abraham to the president's office.

"Sit down, Brother Abraham. Would you like a cup of coffee? Sugar? Cream? Anything I can do to help you? Are you happy with our services?"

"Yes, everything's fine."

"Has a teller been rude? I'll fire him on the spot."

"Oh no, they've all been just as kind as they can be."

"Brother Abraham, we have connections all over the country. Could we transfer your account to a sister bank?"

"No, I don't know where I'm going."

"You don't know where you're going?"

"No, I'm just leaving this part of the world."

Abraham went home and said to Sarah, "Load up. Pack up. Get everything ready."

"What for?"

"We're moving."

"Moving? We just got this house remodeled. Where in the world are we moving?"

"I don't know where we are going."

"Abraham, have you been to the doctor for a checkup lately?"

Hebrews 6:14 says, "Surely blessing I will bless thee, and multiplying I will multiply thee." God gave Abraham that promise and on top of the promise He made a pledge. When a person puts his hand on the Bible and swears to tell the truth, he is pledging on the basis of something greater than himself. Because God could swear by none greater than Himself, He said, "I'll put My personal character on the line. I will swear by Myself that My promises are true."

B. Experienced (6:15)

Abraham first experienced the trust element, then the time element of inheriting the promise. Though God said, "You are going to have descendants like the stars and sand," years and years passed, and no child was born. But the time came when God kept His promise and gave Isaac to Abraham and Sarah. I can almost see old Abraham looking up into the face of God and hear him saying, "God, I didn't know how, but I knew You would keep Your word." He was experiencing the thrill element of the promises of God. Abraham wasn't only standing on the promises; he was *dancing* on the promises. Have you ever gotten to the point where you were dancing on the promises of God?

Perhaps you are not experiencing delight like Abraham's today. Perhaps you are concerned about a serious problem. Some of God's people have problems with child abuse. Others have problems with parent abuse. Maybe you have problems with your spouse. Maybe there is a problem on the job.

Let me tell you what to do. Get your Bible. Search that Bible and dig and bury your mind and heart in that Bible. Stay at it until you come upon a promise from God for the problem you are experiencing. Find it. It's there. When you find a promise from God for that problem, by faith lay hold of it. Exercise the trust element. Claim it. Say, "That's my promise, God." Then be prepared for the time element and just keep on holding on, enduring, believing, trusting. One of these days you will look up into the face of God and say, "I didn't know how, but I knew You would keep Your word." Then you can dance on the promises!

14

My Anchor Will Forever Hold
Hebrews 6:16-20

It is interesting that in the same chapter used by some people to teach that Christians can lose their salvation, we find one of the strongest affirmations of the eternal security of the believer to be found anywhere in the Bible. The verses in Hebrews 6:16-20 turn our attention to the future dimension of our faith as God's children. The word that summarizes the Bible teaching about what God has in store for us is *hope*. Hebrews 6:18 tells us "to lay hold upon the hope set before us."

The theme of hope was introduced earlier. In Hebrews 6:11 we found: "We desire that every one of you do shew the same diligence to the full assurance of hope unto the end." In 6:19 the word was picked up again: "Which hope we have as an anchor of the soul." Christians have a hope. Colossians 1:5 describes it as "the hope which is laid up for you in heaven." First Peter 1:3 says that God "hath begotten us again unto a lively hope by the resurrection of Jesus Christ from the dead." First Timothy 1:1 says that Christ is our hope.

The Christian life is lived in three dimensions: past, present, and future. Each dimension is cared for by our personal relationship with the Lord Jesus Christ. Our past is cared for by faith in the Lord Jesus. By that faith our past sins are under the shed blood of our Savior.

We obviously have to live in the present dimension. How can I live the way I ought to live? The word that describes our victory in Jesus in the present is *love*. The love of God is poured into our hearts by the Holy Spirit. The love of the Lord Jesus Christ comes into our lives when we are saved. He teaches us how to love Him more and how to love each other. Thus, our present life is cared for in Jesus because of the love that He puts in our hearts.

We look to the future and are aware that death awaits us. Beyond death there is judgment. Beyond judgment there is eternity. But we don't have to be afraid. We have a blessed hope for the future in the Lord Jesus Christ.

Sometimes today, the word *hope* includes an element of fear. If a mother learns that her son has been in a car wreck she may say, "Oh, I hope he's all right." But in the Bible the word *hope* does not have that element of fear. There *hope* has an element of faith.

Sometimes we use the word *hope* with an element of uncertainty. A mother who has a son who is away in the war may say, "I hope and pray he's going to get back." She's not sure. But that's not the way the Bible uses the word *hope*. The Bible uses the word to indicate certainty.

The wonderful door of hope we have in the Lord Jesus hinges on three assurances.

I. A SURE PROMISE (6:16-18a)

We are going to Heaven because we have a sure promise from the Lord. When a promise is made, that's the end of strife, the end of the argument.

A. God's Promises (6:16-18a)

God has given us certain promises. We are heirs of hope, heirs of the promises, and God cannot lie.

I have had opportunities in my ministry to help folks who have had problems with assurance. I have taught them that the way to know you are saved is to claim the promises of God. Every time I go over the plan of salvation with lost people, I share with them a promise. For instance, Romans 10:13 says, "Whosoever shall call upon the name of the Lord shall be saved." That is a promise of God. If you have called on the name of the Lord and have asked Him to save you, then you're saved. His promises are sure.

The word *immutable* is used twice in Hebrews 6:17-18. The word means "unchangeable." God does not change. God can't change. If God could change for the worse, then He would cease to be God. If God could change for the better, He wouldn't have been God in the first place.

Since God is immutable, His promises are dependable. God is not going to walk out on His promises to us. God is not a turncoat. He does not take back what He has given. Romans 6:23 says, "The gift of God is eternal life through Jesus Christ our Lord." If God gave us eternal life and then took it away, it wouldn't have been eternal in the first place. Eternal means forever and ever.

Eternal life doesn't end when you sin. That wouldn't be eternal life; that would be conditional, probational life. God promises eternal life and His promise is sure.

B. God's Pledge (6:17)

But God went a step farther. He not only made us a promise, He gave us a pledge on top of that promise. Hebrews 6:17 says, "Wherein God, willing more abundantly to show unto the heirs of promise the immutability of his counsel, confirmed it by an oath." He put His character on the line. God guaranteed His promise of eternal life on the basis of His own integrity. If you lose your salvation, God loses more than you do. He loses His holy, sacred character.

God wants us to know that our salvation is guaranteed. We have a blessed door of hope set before us and it hinges on a sure personal promise from God Himself and the assurance of a safe refuge.

II. A SAFE REFUGE (6:18b)

Hebrews 6:18b says, "We might have a strong consolation, who have fled for refuge." That brief statement about fleeing to Jesus for refuge has its background in the Old Testament.

A. Old Testament Teaching

The Levites, who were the priests, were given forty-eight cities, six of which were known as cities of refuge. Three were scattered on one side of the Jordan, and three were scattered on the other side.

In the case of an accidental killing, the killer was known as a manslayer. The next of kin of the victim was known as the avenger of blood. In his anger the avenger would pursue the manslayer. If the manslayer were caught, the avenger would kill him immediately. That's the way justice was meted out in the Old Testament. But if a manslayer could get inside the gate of a city of refuge, the avenger of blood couldn't touch him. The manslayer could stay there until the death of the high priest. When the high priest died, the manslayer was free to go back to his home and possessions, and the avenger of blood was not allowed to touch him at all.

B. New Testament Teaching

The writer of Hebrews had in mind that Old Testament picture of the cities of refuge when he said that in Jesus we have a safe refuge. Sin makes fugitives of everyone. If you are a sinner, the devil is after you. Sin haunts and hounds you. In addition to that, you have an avenger of blood; the holy wrath of God is on your trail. John 3:36 says, "The wrath of God abideth on [those who are lost]."

You are in a dangerous situation today if you have never been saved; you are a person on the run. Unsaved people run from place to place and from experience to experience and from pleasure to pleasure. They have restlessness in their hearts. They are fugitives from God.

If you are a fugitive, you need to head for the city of refuge. When you enter, you can stay there forever. That's what our hope is all about.

The door of hope hinges on a sure promise, a safe refuge, and the assurance of a safe anchor.

III. A SECURE ANCHOR (6:19-20)

Hebrews 6:19 says, "Which hope we have as an anchor of the soul, both sure and stedfast." An anchor keeps a ship from drifting with the tide, drifting with the flow of the ocean. To keep our souls from drifting we need to be anchored to the Lord Jesus Christ.

A. The World Around Us

We are living in a world where people are being tossed to and fro by every wind that comes along. Our society has lost the heritage that many of us were brought up with.

When I was growing up there was no question about the authority of the Bible. Anybody who dared to question the authority of the Bible was immediately labeled an infidel. Almost every small town had one infidel. He would make fun of the Bible, make fun of the church, make fun of the preacher, make fun of the Christians. Now we are living in a time when the town infidel may be standing in the pulpit of a church.

Now, the majority of folks don't go to church. Everybody didn't go to church even when I was young. But back in those days a lost person who never darkened the door of the church would say, "I know I need to go." He wouldn't say that now. He would say, "Why should I go? I have enough problems in life without all that church business."

The moral values on which this country was built, which made this country great, have largely been washed away. We have a generation of young people who are at sea, adrift in the world around us. They have nothing to hold on to. As a result, we are facing a crisis of suicide among youth. We are facing a crisis of drug use. We are facing alcoholism: in our country there are three million teenage alcoholics.

We need to anchor young people to the Lord Jesus Christ. He is an anchor for the soul. A ship's anchor reaches down through the dark murky waters of the ocean to the unseen ocean bed and grounds that ship. But our anchor for the soul doesn't reach down. Our anchor for the soul reaches up through the unseen world to the realms of glory.

B. The World Ahead of Us

When a person receives the Lord Jesus Christ, his or her soul is anchored to the rock of ages that is in the holy of holies in Heaven. The Lord Jesus Christ is the forerunner who has entered for us "within the veil." There is no cloud of incense to separate our great high priest from God because He and the Father are one. On the basis of His shed blood, our salvation is secured.

Being saved, however, doesn't prevent you from having problems. Storms may beat against your vessel even if you are saved. Some problems will still shake you severely. But if youare anchored to the Lord Jesus Christ, your anchor is already up there in Heaven. When death comes, you will go to God because your anchor will hold.

If the devil gets after me, my anchor holds. If I have temptations and trials, my anchor holds. If I fail the Lord along the way, my anchor holds. If I disappoint the Lord and my friends, my anchor holds. The Lord forgives and cleanses. When the tide of death comes for me, I'll head into the shore. I'm anchored in the Lord Jesus Christ.

A little boy was flying a kite. It went up and up out of sight. He was standing there holding the cord to that kite when a fellow came by and said, "Son, what are you doing?"

He said, "I'm flying my kite."

The man looked up and said, "I don't see a kite up there. Do you see a kite up there?"

"No sir, I don't see it either."

"If I can't see the kite and you can't see the kite, how do you know you have a kite up there?"

The little boy thought for a second and said, "I can't see that kite, but I can feel it pull."

Every now and then I can feel the pull of my anchor in Heaven. I can feel that upward pull of the Lord Jesus Christ.

15

The Mystery of Melchizedek
Hebrews 7:1-28

It is difficult for a person whose faith has been deeply ingrained in one religious system to move from that into a different one. For centuries the Jewish people had been accustomed to having a priest represent them before God. That is what God had taught in the Old Testament. That is the way God had set it up.

Now, because of the Lord Jesus and His death at Calvary, the writer of Hebrews was saying, "It's all over for that system. God has opened up a new and living way. The old priesthood has passed away. You don't have to go to a man anymore to get into the presence of God."

Those ideas were hard for Jews to understand and accept, and they began to raise a series of objections, or at least bring up questions. For example, the Jews would say that Jesus couldn't be a priest because He was not born in the tribe of Levi to the family of Aaron. The writer of Hebrews dropped a bombshell on the Jews: "Called of God an high priest after the order of Melchisedec" (5:10).

After a long and involved exhortation to go on to the fullness of the Lord Jesus Christ, the writer returned to the subject of Melchizedek in chapter 7. Who in the world was Melchizedek? Why was this allusion so revolutionary to the thinking of people steeped in Judaism's priestly religion? This mysterious personality is mentioned only three times in the Bible.

Melchizedek appeared suddenly on the pages of Scripture in the book of Genesis. We are told that he was a priest of the most high God who came out to meet Abraham as he returned from the battle of the kings. Genesis 14:18-20 says that he brought bread and wine to Abraham, that Abraham gave tithes to Melchizedek, and in turn this priest blessed Abraham. That is the only *historical* mention of Melchizedek. Several centuries later, in Psalm 110:4, David mentioned him and said that the Messiah, the coming Savior of the world, would be "a priest for ever after the order of Melchizedek." That was a *prophetical* mention of Melchizedek. He was not referred to again until the book of Hebrews was written. Its author gave a *doctrinal* explanation of what Melchizedek is all about.

Looking at this mysterious personality typically, legally, and practically can help us understand several aspects of the priesthood of the Lord Jesus.

I. TYPICALLY (7:1-10)

Melchizedek in the Old Testament is a type of the Lord Jesus Christ. A type is an Old Testament picture of a New Testament truth. For instance, the serpent lifted by Moses on a pole in the wilderness is a picture of the death of Jesus Christ on the cross of Calvary. And the blood of a lamb on an Old Testament altar is a picture of the blood the Lord Jesus Christ shed for our sins.

So Melchizedek is an Old Testament picture of a New Testament truth. That doesn't mean Melchizedek never existed, because he did. But in Hebrews, he is an illustration of New Testament truth about the Lord Jesus Christ.

A. Titles (7:1-3)

Notice Melchizedek's titles in Hebrews 7:1: king of Salem and priest of the most high God. That combination must have startled the Jewish people, because in the Old Testament, God made it clear that there was to be a separation of the offices of priest and king. If a man were a priest, he couldn't be a king. If a man were a king, he couldn't be a priest. In fact, when King Uzziah went into the temple to offer sacrifices for himself, God smote him with leprosy. But Melchizedek was a priest and a king at the same time. He was a picture of the Lord Jesus who is our priest and king. He combines what was intended to be separate among men.

The only time we are ever going to find a correct joining of spiritual things and governmental things is in the coming kingdom of the Lord Jesus Christ. One of these days Jesus is going to reign as king on this earth. I'll be glad when we get into a world that's run by Him. I'll be glad when we have someone sitting on the throne who is qualified. The only hope for our world is the Lord Jesus Christ.

In Hebrews 7:2 Melchizedek is given two other titles: king of righteousness and king of peace. The role of every Old Testament priest was to show people both how to be righteous (right with God) and how to have peace in their hearts. The only way to have peace is to get right with God. Romans 5:1 says, "Therefore being justified by faith [made right with God by faith in Jesus], we have peace with God through our Lord Jesus Christ." The reason many people don't have personal peace is that they have never had a salvation experience with the Lord Jesus Christ. Jesus is King of righteousness. He is King of peace. He's the One who brings the two together; He gets us right with God, and He brings the peace of God into our hearts.

Psalm 85:10 says, "Righteousness and peace have kissed each other." That took place when the Lord Jesus Christ, who knew no sin, was made sin for us that we might be made the righteousness of God in Him. On the basis of His sacrifice, we can now be right with God; we can know our sins are forgiven. That knowledge would bring tremendous peace into anyone's heart and life.

As King of righteousness the Lord Jesus makes us right with God. As King of peace, He brings the peace of God into our hearts. So Melchizedek is a picture of our Savior in his titles.

Melchizedek appeared suddenly on the scene; he just stepped out of nowhere and then suddenly disappeared. "Without father, without mother, without descent" (7:3). That doesn't mean Melchizedek didn't have a father and mother; he did. It means that as far as the record is concerned, no mention is made of them. Melchizedek had "neither beginning of days nor end of life" (7:3). That's a picture of the Lord Jesus, our priest. Jesus Christ existed before His birth, and He exists after His resurrection. He is the eternal Christ. When He was born, He made His entrance into time. Yet Christ is the Christ of all eternity. He is going to live forever, and that is the kind of priest we need.

B. Tithes (7:4-10)

When Abraham came back from the battle of the kings, Melchizedek brought him bread and wine. They observed the Lord's supper ahead of time, looking forward to the coming of Jesus. Then Abraham gave tithes to Melchizedek, thus acknowledging the superiority of this priest.

Hebrews 7:4-10 explains that the Levitical priests existed embryonically in their father Abraham. So when Abraham gave tithes to Melchizedek, they were also giving tithes to Melchizedek. In the days of the Lord Jesus it was the Levitical priests who received tithes from the people. In Abraham they were giving tithes to a superior priest. The writer of Hebrews was saying that Melchizedek is a picture of Christ because Jesus is a superior priest who ultimately receives our tithes.

"Abraham gave the tenth of the spoils" (7:4). He gave a tenth right off the top of the heap. That's the way we ought to give to the Lord. We shouldn't give to Jesus after we have done everything else we wanted to do for ourselves. (The first check I write is always my tithe. The Lord gets the first.)

Do we tithe in order to earn merit and favor before God? No. We give because we love Jesus. The Jewish people had no choice about tithing; it was the law. Now we give tithes because of love.

II. LEGALLY (7:11-22)

Jesus does not qualify to be a priest because He meets the legal requirements for the priesthood, but because He, like Melchizedek, has "the power of an endless life" (7:16).

A. Tribes (7:11-17)

The former priesthood was built on the Old Testament law. The first five books of the Old Testament are packed full of requirements and legal statements concerning the priesthood: how they were to dress, how they were to perform their ceremonies. A human priest never could do his job fully and completely (7:11). But another priest, the Lord Jesus Christ, can bring us into the presence of the God of this universe.

The Levitical priest became a priest strictly on the basis of a physical law. He had to be born into the tribe of Levi. It didn't matter how good he was or how qualified he was. If he wasn't born into the physical family of Levi, he couldn't be a priest. That was the only requirement.

Christ was not born into the tribe of Levi. He came from the tribe of Judah. But He qualifies to be our priest because He lives forevermore.

For the Lord Jesus Christ to be a priest, there had to be a change of law: "Who [the Lord Jesus] is made, not after the law of a carnal commandment" (7:16). When Christ became our high priest, the Old Testament system of priesthood was over, and no one ever again had to be represented before God by another man. That was hard for first-century Jews to take. It is also hard for some folks to understand today; there are still groups who want to put believers back under the Old Testament law.

B. Testimony (7:18-22)

Hebrews 7:18 says, "For there is verily a disannulling of the commandment going before for the weakness and unprofitableness thereof." The Old Testament law has been set aside —not the moral law, but the ceremonial law. The word *disannul* means to "set aside and replace with something else."

Was the Old Testament law not any good? No. Ought we to disregard what the Old Testament law says to do? No. Look at Romans 8:3: "For what the law could not do, in that it was weak through the flesh." The problem is not with the law of God, but with human weakness. The law says, "Do this and you will live." The problem is we can't do it. The law shows us how totally helpless we are to save ourselves. The law is weak because my flesh is not able to live up to its standards.

God sent His Son to do for me what I could not do for myself. My salvation is not based on my outward keeping of the law; it is based on my inward relationship with the only law keeper, the Lord Jesus Christ. That's good news. You can't earn salvation by trying to reform your life. You can't say, "I'm going to get good enough and God will be so thrilled with the way I'm living He'll save me."

The law has been disannulled; it's been set aside. "For the law made nothing perfect, but the bringing in of a better hope did; by the which we draw nigh unto God" (7:19). The Old Testament way was never a completed way because of the weakness of man (7:11). So God brought in a better way, a better hope.

In the Old Testament the high priest entered the holy of holies once a year. Because we have a better way in the Lord Jesus, we ourselves can draw nigh unto God as often as we want to. We can come boldly to the throne of God because we have a priest after the order of Melchizedek.

III. PRACTICALLY (7:23-28)

Melchizedek is a type of Christ because he "abideth a priest continually" (7:3). Such permanence has practical implications.

To help yourself understand the disadvantage of impermanence, suppose for the moment that your doctor moves away or dies. You have to get all your records, find a new doctor, and go through your wholecase history all over again. It's not easy. For Jews under the old order there were many priests, but they all died.

A. A Permanent Salvation (7:23-25)

"And they truly were many priests, because they were not suffered to continue by reason of death" (7:23). Because priests died, they had to be replaced. "But this man [Jesus], because he continueth ever, hath an unchangeable priesthood" (7:24). Jesus never dies. He is always there to represent us. "Wherefore he is able also to save them to the uttermost that come unto God by him, seeing he ever liveth to make intercession for them" (7:25). Jesus is praying for us right now. At the cross He acquired our salvation, and His prayer in Heaven today maintains it. Somebody would have to stop the prayers of Jesus before we could lose our salvation. Our salvation is permanent in the Lord Jesus.

B. A Permanent Sacrifice (7:26-28)

Some of the Old Testament priests were ungodly sinful men. And even the best had to offer daily sacrifices for his own sins and the people's. But Jesus was absolutely pure. There was no defilement in Him, not one moral stain on His life. He was "separate from sinners" (7:26). Though He was a friend of sinners, He was altogether different from them. The Lord Jesus Christ will never let us down. When Jesus made the sacrifice of Himself at the cross, He did it once and for all.

The author of Hebrews concludes, "[Jesus, our great high priest] Who needeth not daily, as those high priests, to offer up sacrifice, first for his own sins, and then for the people's: for this he did once, when he offered up himself..." Our salvation rests on a perfect sacrifice made by a perfect Savior.

JERRY VINES

16

The New and Better Covenant
Hebrews 8:1-13

Everything we have in Jesus is better. Nonetheless, there is a tendency among those who come out of a cult or some other religious system to cling to some of their former practices. So all through the book of Hebrews we find this emphasis: Why do you want to go back to what is inferior?

The first four chapters of Hebrews show that in Jesus we have a better person. Chapters 5-7 show that in Jesus we have a better priest. Chapters 8-10 show that in the Lord Jesus we have a better provision. The sacrifice that the Lord Jesus made for us at Calvary is a provision totally superior to any made before.

More specifically, Hebrews 8 speaks of our high priest, the Lord Jesus, as the One who gives us a better covenant. The first five verses say that Jesus Christ is the minister in a better tabernacle. Verses 6-13 say that Jesus is the mediator of better promises and a better testament.

I. MINISTER IN A BETTER TABERNACLE (8:1-5)

"Now of the things which we have spoken this is the sum: We have such an high priest, who is set on the right hand of the throne of the

Majesty in the heavens; A minister of the sanctuary, and of the true tabernacle, which the Lord pitched, and not man" (Hebrews 8:1-2).

A. Where He Sits (8:1)

Jesus sits on the right hand of the throne of the Father. In the Old Testament system, the priests went in and out. No chair was provided for them since their work was never finished.

In New Testament days, the supreme court in religious matters was known as the Sanhedrin. The high priest presided over the Sanhedrin and at his left and right hands scribes were ready to record the verdicts. If someone was guilty of a crime or some act of disobedience, the terms of his prosecution were written out by the scribe on the left side of the high priest. If someone was innocent and was no longer condemned, the terms of his acquittal were written out by the scribe on the right side of the high priest.

We have a God-man in Heaven who is on the right hand, the place of authority and power, who has written out the terms of acquittal for our sins. Our sins have been forgiven; they are held against us no more. Our wonderful Savior is seated on God's right hand.

In the Old Testament system, the high priest could not sit on the mercy seat. That was God's earthly throne, so to speak, and for an earthly high priest to sit down there would have been an act of blasphemy. But the Lord Jesus Christ is entitled to sit down at the right hand of the Father. Our high priest is better and is seated in a better tabernacle.

B. Where He Serves (8:2-5)

The Lord Jesus serves in the realities which are in Heaven. The earthly tabernacle was just an example, a copy, or a pattern of heavenly realities. In the Old Testament God gave His people object lessons. He gave them pictures to help them understand spiritual things.

> "Who serve unto the example and shadow of heavenly things, as Moses was admonished of God when he was about to make the tabernacle: for, See, saith he, that thou make all things according to the pattern shewed to thee in the mount (8:5)."

Every item of furniture, every detail of that tabernacle was a picture of the reality that was going to come in the Lord Jesus. Jesus Christ is operating in the heavenlies. As our high priest, He ministers in the true tabernacle that the Lord pitched. He works *for* us, *on* us, and *in* us.

Old Testament people saw the shadow; they didn't see the substance. Have you ever been afraid of a shadow? To a child, a shadow can be ominous. But a shadow has no power at all. There is no substance to a shadow. It is simply a representation of a reality somewhere. In Jesus we have the spiritual realities. We aren't walking in the shadows anymore. That's why it's futile for people to try to put themselves under the Old Testament law. We don't live the Christian life on the basis of the Old Testament law. That's only a shadow. Why walk in the shadows when the sunshine, the Lord Jesus Christ, has come?

II. MEDIATOR OF A BETTER TESTAMENT (8:6-13)

"But now hath he [Jesus] obtained a more excellent ministry, by how much also he is the mediator of a better covenant" (8:6). A mediator is a go-between, someone who represents two parties. Job cried out for a mediator. He had a grievance with God and realized he needed somebody to represent him, so he longed for a daysman, a mediator (Job 9:33). First Timothy 2:5 says that there is "one mediator between God and men, the man Christ Jesus." Jesus Christ, the God-man, is now the mediator. He's the go-between. A mediator needs to understand both parties in the dispute. That's why Jesus became human. Now, having been a man, He understands what we go through. Jesus is able to lay hold of man, having become a man; He is able to lay hold of God, being God.

A covenant, or testament, is an agreement between two parties. We have in our Bible an Old Testament and a New Testament. That means we have an old covenant and a new covenant. The new covenant is better and Jesus is its mediator. Why is the new covenant better? What was wrong with the old one?

A. Failure of the Old Covenant (8:6-9)

"For if that first covenant had been faultless, then should no place have been sought for the second" (8:7). What was the first covenant? We have to go back to Exodus to see how God set up this first agreement with man. The law was the first covenant. When God was getting ready to give the ten commandments, the ceremonial law, and all the other judgments He said, "Now, therefore, if ye will obey my voice indeed, and keep my covenant, then ye shall be a peculiar treasure unto me above all people: for all the earth is mine" (Ex 19:5).

Here's what the people said: "And all the people answered together, and said, All that the Lord hath spoken we will do" (Ex 19:8). That was their part of the agreement. After the law had been given, Moses "took the book of the covenant, and read in the audience of the people: and they said, All that the Lord hath said will we do" (Ex 24:7). They were saying, "Okay God; we'll do what You tell us to do."

There was a problem, however. The law can show you that you are a sinner, but it can't put away your sins. The law can show you what's wrong with you, but it can't give you power to change. A yardstick can tell you how tall you are, but it can't make you one inch taller. The law of God can show you what you ought to be and what you ought to do, but it has no enabling power.

The problem was not in the law that God gave in the first covenant, nor was the problem in God's ability to keep His part of the agreement. The problem was not in God, not in the law, but in the people (8:8). The people said they would obey, but they couldn't. Neither can we.

The law, the first covenant, shows us that we are sinners and that we desperately need a Savior.

B. Nature of the New Covenant (8:10-13)

The new covenant is better because Jesus does the saving. The Old Testament was based on the statement, "We will." In the New Testament God says, "I will" (six times in Hebrews 8:8-12). He is saying, "I know you can't handle this. I'll do it."

Look at the difference between the covenants. "For this is the covenant that I will make with the house of Israel after those days, saith the Lord; I will put my laws into their mind, and write them in their hearts: and I will be to them a God, and they shall be to me a people" (8:10). The old covenant was external, written on tablets of stone. The new covenant is internal, written on the human heart. That's a big improvement. External law can control people, but it can't change people. Consider a thief. Stealing is illegal, but he steals just the same.

The law can control him by putting him in prison. While there he can't steal. But if he gets out of prison, he will steal again. The prison system is not designed to make thieves honest. It's designed to punish those who are thieves. The prison system can't change anybody; it just controls people. But if while the thief is in prison he has a personal experience with the Lord Jesus Christ, God will write His law on his heart and give him a desire to do what God says. Jesus will change that man. When he walks out of prison, he won't need to be controlled anymore. He won't want to steal.

When you get saved, God puts a desire in your heart to do what is right. You may not always do what's right, but you *want* to do what's right. One reason I know I'm saved is that when I do wrong it breaks my heart. I want to do right. Under the new agreement, God works on the inside. Salvation is an inside job. God puts His law in our minds and in our hearts.

Another difference between the covenants is in Hebrews 8:11: "They shall not teach every man his neighbour, and every man his brother, saying, Know the Lord: for all shall know me, from the least to the greatest." In the Old Testament there were special teachers who taught people the law of God. But in the new covenant, the new agreement, we have a teacher living in our hearts. When we are saved God comes into our lives in the person of the Holy Spirit and He, Jesus says, will teach us all things. That doesn't mean we don't need human teachers and we can't learn from them; rather it means we are not dependent on them. The blessed Holy Spirit, the resident teacher, is on the job all the time.

This new covenant is based on forgiveness. "For I will be merciful to their unrighteousness, and their sins and their iniquities will I remember no more" (8:12). When we come to the Lord Jesus Christ, He forgives our sins. The Bible says He covers them with a thick cloud. He removes them as far as the East is from the West. He casts them behind His back. He casts them into the depths of the sea and remembers them no more. They are gone forever.

At the time this letter to the Hebrews was written, the temple was still standing. The Levitical priests were still going through outdated, obsolete sacrifices. The writer of Hebrews was saying to that generation, "Why are you still living in the shadows when you can have the reality in Jesus?" That question is addressed to us also.

17

Our Great Tabernacle Revealed
Hebrews 9:1-14

Everybody in the world has problems similar to yours and mine. One of those problems is this: What must I do to bring myself into fellowship with a holy God? I know down deep in my heart that I have sinned against this holy God and my sins have separated me from Him. I have a second problem also. My sin has done something on the inside of my being. Sin has stained my conscience and soul.

The ancient Israelites had the same problems. God gave them an object lesson to show them how to deal with these problems—how to deal with the problem of a guilty conscience.

Let us imagine that we are floating on a magic carpet, back in time and over continents and oceans toward that Middle Eastern wilderness called Sinai. Once there we meet a group of people known as the Jews —not just a handful of people, but more than a million. They are living in tents arranged according to tribe. In the middle of those tents is an unusual building made of unattractive badger skin. The building is oblong and not very large.

I ask one of the Jews, "What's the building in the center of your encampment?"

"Oh, that's the tabernacle."

"Why are all of your tents gathered around it?"

"Oh, that's where God comes down and meets with us."

"You mean the God of this universe comes down in that little building there?"

"Right."

I say, "You know I am very interested in that building. Tell me about it."

Hebrews 9 describes the meaning of this building, why it was so important to the Jewish people, and why it is also important to you and me. Verse 1 says, "Then verily the first covenant had also ordinances of divine service, and a worldly sanctuary." The word *worldly* here means the sanctuary was built on the earth. The writer was referring to that tabernacle we see in the camp of Israel.

In Hebrews 9:11 we are given a contrast: "But Christ being come an high priest of good things to come, by a greater and more perfect tabernacle, not made with hands, that is to say, not of this building." The tabernacle we see in the Jewish encampment was not the final tabernacle. It was only a representation of a greater, more perfect tabernacle: "Which was a figure for the time then present" (9:9). The word *figure* means parable. So in Hebrews 9, we are going to discover a parable, an object lesson. We are going to see what was to be fulfilled when Jesus Christ would come into this world to be our Savior.

I. THE SANCTUARY EXAMINED (9:1-5)

That wilderness tabernacle had three parts: an outer court and then two rooms in the tabernacle itself. The first room was called the holy place, or sanctuary. A veil separated it from the second room, known as the holy of holies, the holiest place. If you and I were Jewish priests, we would be allowed to go into that first room, but since we are not, we are excluded.

A. Outer Room (9:1-2)

Our Jewish guide explains what's on the inside. On the south side of the room is a candlestick or lampstand made of pure gold. The top of each one of its branches is cup-like, holding a wick and oil. The light in the holy place is provided by this lampstand. The lampstand is a picture that points to the coming of Jesus. He is the light of the world. Only the presence of the Lord Jesus Christ can illuminate the darkened heart of a sinner. When Jesus comes in, the light turns on. We have enlightenment in the Lord Jesus Christ.

On the opposite side of the room is a table made of acacia wood overlaid with solid gold. Placed on the table are twelve pieces of bread—showbread, it is called. (Not corn bread, not white bread, but showbread.) New showbread is put there every sabbath day. The priest then eats the bread that has been removed. The showbread, too, points to the Lord Jesus Christ. The Bible tells us that Jesus is the bread of life. It is Jesus who feeds the hungry soul. Jesus says, "I am the bread of life; he that cometh to me shall never hunger" (Jn 6:35).

B. Inner Room (9:3-5)

"And after the second veil, the tabernacle which is called the Holiest of all" (9:3). Our guide continues his explanation. That inner room is a perfect cube, as wide as it is long and as high as it is wide and long. Inside is the golden censer, a utensil like a pan or a shovel made of pure gold. On the pan are coals of fire. Once a year the high priest goes into the holy of holies and throws incense in the fire. A sweet smell wafts upward and billows of smoke. Incense in the Bible is always a picture of prayer. Here incense pictures the prayers of our Lord Jesus on our behalf.

In the inner room there is also the ark of the covenant, a chest made of acacia wood and overlaid with gold. Inside the ark are three articles, one a golden pot containing manna. When the Israelites were wandering in the wilderness, God had a supernatural way to provide for them. Every morning they would discover that God had covered the ground with angel food cake, heavenly bread.

Also inside the ark of the covenant is Aaron's rod that budded. When Aaron was the priest, some rebelled against him and said, "Who do you think you are to be a priest?" So God said, "We'll put everybody's rod in this ark and the one whose rod blossoms with little flowers will be proven to be my choice." Aaron's rod budded. The rod is a picture of the death, burial, and resurrection of the Lord Jesus Christ.

Third, the ark contains the tables of the ten commandments, which God with His own finger wrote on tablets of stone — the law of God.

So, the contents of the ark of the covenant teach that God is interested in the basic needs of people. The manna reminds us that God meets our physical needs. The rod of Aaron reminds us that God meets our spiritual needs in the Lord Jesus. The tablets of stone remind us that Christ fulfills our moral needs and gives us power to live the way God wants us to live. If a person has a personal relationship with the Lord Jesus Christ, every need of his life can be marvelously, supernaturally met.

II. THE SERVICE EXPLAINED (9:6-10)

A, What the Priests Wrought (9:6-7)

Looking into the outer room we notice a group of men known as the priests. They go in there every day (9:6). They trim the lamp and put in new wicks. Priest after priest, generation after generation, they perform this daily service for God.

Our guide explains that once a year the high priest enters the inner room. "Into the second [room] went the high priest alone once every year, not without blood" (9:7). That means he goes in with blood. (This short statement explains the Jewish day of atonement, Yom Kippur.) Clothed in magnificent robes, the high priest enters the inner room. The smell of incense and smoke fills the holy of holies. He sprinkles the blood of a sacrificial animal on a piece of furniture, the mercy seat (9:5), which is a slab of solid gold. Part of the slab, on the ends, are two figures of cherubim, angelic heavenly beings, facing one another and looking at the mercy seat. The mercy seat is a place of covering. It covers the ark of God, containing the law.

What does all that have to do with us? God sent Jesus Christ forth to be a mercy seat, a place of covering. The Greek word translated "mercy seat" in Hebrews 9:5 is found in the New Testament two other significant times, and in those verses it is translated "propitiation." Romans 3:24-25 says, "Being justified freely by his grace through the redemption that is in Christ Jesus: Whom God hath set forth to be a propitiation through faith in his blood." And 1 John 2:2 says, "And he [Jesus] is the propitiation for our sins: and not for our's only, but also for the sins of the whole world."

The Old Testament mercy seat points us to the Lord Jesus Christ. When He died on the cross, He shed His blood for our sins. Because our sins are covered by the blood of Jesus, a holy God and a sinful man can have fellowship.

B. What the Holy Spirit Taught (9:8-10)

"The Holy Ghost this signifying, that the way into the holiest of all was not yet made manifest, while as the first tabernacle was yet standing" (9:8). The Old Testament ritual was limited. The way was not yet open for God and man to have fellowship. There was still a barrier between sinful man and a holy God. The Old Testament tabernacle was just a picture of something yet to come. "Which was a figure for the time then present, in which were offered both gifts and sacrifices, that could not make him that did theservice perfect, as pertaining to the conscience" (9:9). All of that outward worship and ceremony couldn't deal with the inside where our problems really are.

III. THE SAVIOR EXALTED (9:11-14)

"But Christ ..." I like that. What a difference those two words make. In our high priest, the Lord Jesus, we have the remedy that solves both of the problems we human beings have. First, he solved the problem of alienation between us and a holy God.

A. A Superior Payment (9:11-12)

"Neither by the blood of goats and calyes, but by his own blood he entered in once into the holy place, having obtained eternal redemption for us" (9:12). The word *redemption* means "a setting free by the payment of a price." The Lord Jesus Christ made the eternal payment for our sins. All the blood on Jewish altars couldn't end the alienation. It just rolled our sins one more year toward Calvary. But when the Lord Jesus Christ shed His precious blood, He paid the price that remedies the alienation of the sinful heart from a holy God. If you are a believer, the payment for your sin has been made and you have direct access to the God of this universe.

B. A Superior Purging (9:13-14)

What about the second problem, my guilt on the inside? The Old Testament offerings in the tabernacle were only ceremonial. They never got to the root of the problem. The blood of Jesus Christ does what the blood of animals could never do. It goes down deep into the human personality, down deep in the soul where the stain is, down deep in the conscience where the guilt is. The blood of Jesus washes us clean and our guilt is removed. There is no other way to approach a holy God or to deal with the sin problem in our hearts. "For if the blood of bulls and of goats, and the ashes of an heifer sprinkling the unclean, sanctifieth to the purifying of the flesh: How much more shall the blood of Christ, who through the eternal Spirit offered himself without spot to God, purge your conscience from dead works to serve the living God? (9:13-14)

A young man attending a revival crusade was prompted by the Holy Spirit to go forward and give himself to Christ, but he didn't go. The service was dismissed, and the boy walked away to his car. Under deep conviction, he decided to go back to the church, where the evangelist was busy packing up. The young man said, "Sir, I have come back because I want to know what I have to do to be saved."

The evangelist hardly lifted his eyes from what he was doing. "I'm sorry, son; you are too late."

The boy said, "Too late, sir? You're still here. I know the service is over, but surely I'm not too late. Surely there's time for me to find out what I have to do to be saved."

Then the evangelist looked at him with a twinkle in his eye. "You are two thousand years too late. Jesus did it all. Jesus paid it all. Jesus Christ at Calvary's cross did everything necessary for you to be forgiven of your sins."

What a wonderful day it is when each of us understands and accepts that fact for himself.

JERRY VINES

18

Christ's Last Will and Testament
Hebrews 9:15-28

The night before the Lord Jesus was crucified He gathered His disciples together in an upper room to observe the Passover supper. At that supper, which God had commanded the Jews to observe, Jesus said, "This cup is the new testament in my blood, which is shed for you" (Lu 22:20). There at the observance of the Passover supper, the Lord Jesus Christ inaugurated what He called the "new testament." That's why our Christian Bible is divided into an Old Testament and a New Testament. Jesus Christ made the change from the old to the new.

Hebrews 8:8 says, "Behold, the days come, saith the Lord, when I will make a new *covenant* with the house of Israel" (italics added). Hebrews 9:15 says, "And for this cause he is the mediator of the new *testament*" (italics added). *Covenant* and *testament* are two different translations of the same word in the original language. In Hebrews 8 the word is used to describe the new agreement (covenant) that God has with His people grounded in the cross. In Hebrews 9 the word is used to describe a will (testament). So the phrase *the new testament* means "the new agreement" that Jesus Christ has made with those who receive Him by personal faith, but it also means "the new will" that Jesus Christ has made for believers.

A will is a legal statement of how a person intends his earthly possessions to be disposed of after death. At least three individuals are involved in a will. First, there is the person who makes the will, the testator. "Where a testament is, there must also of necessity be the death of the testator" (9:16). Then there is the heir, the person who is the beneficiary of the will, the one who is to receive the property of the person who makes the will. The third person is the executor, the one appointed by the testator to carry out the terms of the will after the testator is dead.

Hebrews 9:15-28 is a statement that the Lord Jesus Christ has made out a Last Will and Testament. This will is mediated, validated, and activated.

I. MEDIATED (9:15-17)

In the opening verses of the passage, we see how the will is mediated. Jesus Christ is the mediator of the new will (v. 15). "There is...one mediator between God and men, the man Christ Jesus" (1 Tim 2:5). Jesus is "the mediator of a better covenant," a better agreement (8:6). We have come "to Jesus the mediator of the new covenant [the new agreement, the new will], and to the blood of sprinkling, that speaketh better things than that of Abel" (12:24). In other words, Jesus is the go between, the mediator of God's will.

A. Its Benefits (9:15)

There are several benefits of our new agreement with the Lord Jesus. First, by means of His death there is the "redemption of the transgressions that were under the first testament" (9:15). By the death of Jesus and His shed blood, all the sins of believers in all ages have been fully paid for. When Jesus died, His death took care of all future sin and all past sin. Jesus is the Lamb who was slain before the foundation of the world. The power of the blood of Jesus Christ is retroactive; all of those Old Testament saints were saved on credit, so to speak, looking forward to the death of Jesus. You and I living in this age are saved because we look back to the death of Jesus. We all have been set free by the payment of a price.

The Bible pictures a sinner as a person who is under a tremendous load of debt. Let's suppose that you have a crushing debt —all kinds of mortgages and liens against you. You are facing financial ruin and don't know where to turn. Then one morning you wake up to discover that a billionaire died, and his will names you as heir to his wealth. On the basis of the death of another, all your debts are paid and you are fabulously rich. That is quite a change.

Each child of God once had a load of sin weighing down on his heart. The burden was unbearably heavy. But when he received the Lord Jesus Christ as his Savior, he became a beneficiary of His will. The load was lifted off his shoulders. That is the good news of the new will of the Lord Jesus Christ.

Hebrews 9:15 gives a second benefit of the new agreement: "They which are called . . . receive the promise of eternal inheritance." In other words, we are now heirs of God and joint¬ heirs with the Lord Jesus Christ.

We used to be like two homeless people who were lying around one morning. One started crying and the other said, "What are you crying for?"

"Well, I just heard that Rockefeller died."

"Well, what are you crying for? You're not related to Rockefeller."

"That's why I'm crying!"

But by the new birth, we are heirs of God!

B. Its Benefactor (9:16-17)

Because the one who wrote out the will and made us the beneficiaries of everything He owns has died, everything Jesus Christ owns is yours and mine today. The testator had to die before the will could take effect. "For a testament is of force after men are dead: otherwise it is of no strength [it is not in force] at all while the testator liveth" (9:17). Our benefactor died at Calvary; that's how the new will is mediated.

II. VALIDATED (9:18-23)

The old testament and the new testament were validated by the shedding of blood. "Whereupon neither the first testament was dedicated without blood .. . And almost all things are by the law purged with blood; and without shedding of blood is no remission" (9:18,22). In Old Testament times people were required to bring a lamb to the priest to be offered for their sins. (Some were too poor to have a lamb, so they were allowed to bring flour, but that was the only exception.) There is never any basis of salvation apart from the principle of the shedding of blood.

A. Pictured (9:18-21)

Scripture gives an Old Testament picture of what is required for validation of the new will. In Hebrews 9:18-21 is a reference to Exodus 24. Just after the giving of the law, Moses "took the blood of calves and of goats, with water, and scarlet wool, and hyssop, and sprinkled both the book, and all the people" (9:19). Hyssop was a bush that was used as an applicator. The bush would betied toa piece of cedar wood with a string of scarlet wool. (They used hyssop the way we use *a* brush to apply barbecue sauce to a chicken.) Moses dipped the hyssop in the blood and water and applied it to the book and the people. The Old Testament agreement was validated by the shedding of blood.

B. Provided (9:22-23)

What was pictured in the Old Testament is fulfilled in the New Testament. "It was therefore necessary that the patterns of things in the heavens should be purified with these; but the heavenly things themselves with better sacrifices than these" (9:23). In the Old Testament picture, animals provided the blood. But Jesus shed His own blood.

How can you tell whether or not you are in a gospel preaching church, a true Bible-believing church? Such a church will make much of the shed blood of the Lord Jesus Christ. If a sinner comes to your church and you do not preach the blood of Jesus, you don't give that sinner any hope. Don't just tell a sinner he must try to do better; there is no way he can ever do any better. The only way any of us can ever do any better is by being made better. The only way to be made better is to be purged of our sins by the blood of the Lord Jesus Christ.

Some may object, "I don't like all that preaching about blood. It's offensive." Maybe they even call ours a slaughter-house religion. But a radical disease requires a radical cure. The offensive element is not the blood of Jesus; it's our rotten, filthy sin. The Lord Jesus Christ had to shed His blood because our sin is like cancer, and it has to be cut out with a surgical procedure.

Sinful people don't need to go to unbelieving psychiatrists who will help them submerge the guilt of their sins down into their subconscious. Genuine guilt is a symptom of sin. The lost will never eliminate the symptom until they deal with the cause. What they need is to be forgiven of their sins. Only the gospel of Christ deals with this need; apart from the blood of Jesus there is no forgiveness of sin.

III. ACTIVATED (9:24-28)

Even when a will is made out, problems can develop after a person dies. Wills are contested all the time. A will can be tied up in litigation so long that the heir never receives any benefits. Or the executor might turn out to be a crook. So when the implementation of a will gets complicated, someone might say, "I wish the person who made out this will could be here and just tell us what he really wants. If only the one who made the will could be the executor!"

The new will described in Hebrews was made out by the Lord Jesus Christ; He died to put the will into effect; and He also rose again to be the executor of His will! That is good news. He's going to carry out all its details to the letter until His promised appearing.

A. His Present Appearing (9:24)

There are three appearances of Jesus in Hebrews 9:24-28. First is His present appearing in Heaven right now (9:24). He is in the presence of God for us. The word *presence* means that He is face to face with God.

The Old Testament high priest had to have a cloud of incense smoke in the holy of holies so that he couldn't see the face of God.

B. His Past Appearing (9:25-26)

Mentioned second is Christ's appearance on earth when He came to die for us. The Old Testament priest had to enter the holy of holies *often* (). "But now *once* in the end of the world hath he [Jesus] appeared to put away sin by the sacrifice of himself" (9:26, italics added). Jesus Christ made one sacrifice for sin. It is never repeated. Any religious system that teaches that the death of Christ has to be continually repeated is based on a blasphemous doctrine. In the Lord's supper the sacrifice of Jesus is not repeated. We do not believe that Jesus has to be sacrificed over and over again. He did it one time forever when He died at the cross of Calvary.

C. His Promised Appearing (9:27-28)

Mentioned third is the appearance we are waiting for. "Unto them that look for him shall he appear the second time without sin unto salvation" (9:28). He will not come back to deal with the sin question a second time. He has already dealt with that. Just as we die once (verse 27 eliminates any idea of reincarnation), Jesus Christ died once to bear the sins of many.

Jesus is going to come back to finish the job as executor of His will. When Jesus returns, the full salvation experience will be completed. When the high priest came out of the holy of holies, the people knew the sacrifice had been accepted. Jesus will appear the second time, and we will see Him.

The Lord himself shall descend from heaven with a shout, with the voice of the archangel, and with the trump of God: and the dead in Christ shall rise first: Then we which are alive and remain shall be caught up together with them in the clouds, to meet the Lord in the air: and so shall we ever be with the Lord (1 Thes 4:16-17).

When Jesus died at Calvary, He was making a sacrifice for sin. That single sacrifice was for all people, for all sin, forever. That is what is meant by Jesus' "finished work." There can never be another sacrifice for sin. "But this man [the Lord Jesus], after he had offered one sacrifice for sins for ever" (10:12). That concept is at the heart of the gospel. It is the focal point of everything the Bible has to say about our salvation. You and I cannot do anything to pay our sin debt. Jesus paid it all. Jesus did it all. That is what this tenth chapter of Hebrews is about.

That one sacrifice was expected in the Old Testament, established by Jesus when He came into the world, and explained in the book of Hebrews.

JERRY VINES

19

One Sacrifice Offered Forever
Hebrews 10:1-18

Old Testament sacrifices were preparatory, preliminary, anticipatory. Hebrews 10:1 says that those sacrifices were "a shadow of good things to come, and not the very image of the things." Those sacrifices were shadows of the real thing.

A shadow is merely an outline of an object, not the object itself. Your shadow is an outline of you, but it is not you. It is only a representation of you. It is an indication there is a "you" somewhere that has cast a shadow.

The shadow of a key cannot unlock a door. The shadow of a meal cannot feed a hungry person. The shadow of a Calvary could not do the work for sin that needed to be done.

I. EXPECTED (10:1-4)

A. Repetitive (10:1-2)

Why were those sacrifices merely representations of the real thing? One reason is that the Old Testament sacrifices were repetitive in nature. Those sacrifices were "offered year by year continually" (10:1). They had to be repeated time after time. Every year the repetition of those sacrifices let the worshiper know that he still was not dealing adequately with his sin problem.

The sin problem is deep-rooted. That's why it doesn't do any good just to try to get rid of habits in our lives. Our problem is not just outward habits. Our problem is the root of those habits—what causes us to do what we do. Romans 3:23 says, "For all have sinned, and come short of the glory of God," but it can also be translated, "All have sinned, and have a sin nature."

The Old Testament sacrifices were primarily outward in form. They didn't get to the root of the matter. "It is not possible that the blood of bulls and of goats should take away sins" (10:4). A material remedy was not able to deal with a moral problem down on the inside.

Suppose you are in debt. You go to the bank and borrow a certain amount of money to pay your debt. They ask, "Do you have anybody who will sign the note with you?" It happens you have a wealthy friend who is concerned for you and he says, "I'll sign the note with you. I'll guarantee the repayment of the debt." It's to come due in twelve months. At the end of twelve months, not only are you unable to pay the first debt, but you have also accumulated additional debt. You need another note tacked onto the original note. The wealthy friend says, "I'll stand good for that too." Now you owe more. The next year the same thing happens.

Somewhere down the line you finally realize that there is nothing you can do to pay off your former debt and you are accumulating new debt all the time. Then comes good news. Your wealthy friend says, "1see you are not able to pay your debt. You've been accumulating more debt year after year. I'm just going to pay it off in full, so you will be totally out of debt." That's what Jesus Christ did.

All through the Old Testament, there was only the repetition of the signing of promissory notes. When Jesus paid the debt in full, provision was made to get us out of debt. If those Old Testament sacrifices had taken care of the sin problem, they would have "ceased to be offered" (10:2). If sins had been cleansed by those sacrifices, the Jewish people wouldn't have had any more consciousness of sin. The yearly day of atonement merely tormented their consciences; it reminded them that they had a deep-seated sin problem.

B. Reflective (10:3-4)

The Old Testament sacrifices were only shadows of the real thing because they were reflective. They would bring to mind everything wrong the Jews had done. But when we accept Christ, God remembers our sins no more; they are put away forever.

Sins already committed were covered by the yearly sacrifice, but sins committed after the sacrifice had to be remembered until the next day of atonement. In contrast, when Jesus died for our sin, He not only covered our sin; He also cleansed our sin. He got down into the depths of our hearts. He made provision for the root problem of our sin nature.

II. ESTABLISHED (10:5-10)

The one sacrifice was established when Jesus came into the world. It is clear, of course, that Christ lived before He was born in Bethlehem. The Bible teaches the pre-existence of Christ: "In the beginning was the Word [that's Jesus], and the Word was with God, and the Word was God. The same was in the beginning with God. . . . The Word was made flesh, and dwelt among us" (Jn 1:1-2,14).

In Hebrews 10:5b-7 we read an Old Testament statement of the thoughts of Jesus before He was incarnated, the mind-set of the Son of God as He came into the world: "Sacrifice and offering thou wouldest not, but a body hast thou prepared me: In burnt offerings and sacrifices for sin thou hast had no pleasure. Then said I, Lo, I come (in the volume of the book it is written of me,) to do thy will, O God."

A. Revealed in a Body (10:5-6,10)

Jesus Christ was going to be born in a body that was prepared by the heavenly Father. When you and I were born, we were each born of the union of a man and a woman. When Jesus was born and received a physical body, it was a supernatural birth: He was conceived in the womb of the virgin Mary by the Holy Spirit.

Some people ask, "Does it make any difference whether Jesus was born of a virgin?" It certainly does. Those who deny the virgin birth of the Lord Jesus Christ undermine God's plan of salvation. If Jesus Christ had not been born of a virgin, if He had been conceived by natural means, as we were, He would have had original sin. He would have been born with a body tainted by sin.

You and I are born sinners. It doesn't take parents long to find out that their children are sinners. That little bundle of innocence, however cute and cuddly, has inherited a sinful nature. But that was not true of Jesus Christ.

Jesus Christ chose to be born. He is the only one who ever chose to be born. Jesus chose to come into this world to do the will of God. All through His life Jesus Christ was engaged in doing the will of God.

Remember the day He was sitting by Jacob's well, weary from His journey? A woman came to draw water. Jesus said, "I can give you water to drink and you will never get thirsty again." Before that discussion was over, she had drunk the water of life. Another soul was saved. About that time the disciples came to the well. "Lord, here's some food. Eat." Jesus said, "I have meat to eat that ye know not of. . . . My meat is to do the will of him that sent me, and to finish his work" (Jn 4:32,34).

There came a night when the Lord Jesus Christ went to a grove at the foot of the mount of Olives. In the midst of that experience in the garden of Gethsemane Jesus said, "Not my will, but thine, be done" (Lu 22:42).

B. Written in a Book (10:7-9)

"In the volume of the book it is written." God has put it all in a book. I've been studying the Bible since I was a sixteen-year-old boy, and I know that the bottom line of the Bible is this: God loves us so much that He sent His Son to die on a cross for our sins. If you can understand and accept that, you understand the message of the Bible.

Our job is to go into a lost world to those who don't know what's in this Bible. There are people all around us who have no idea that God loves them. They have no conception at all of what Jesus did at the cross for them. If we could just explain to them what the Bible has to say, they would be knocking at the doors of our churches.

III. EXPLAINED (10:11-18)

The writer of Hebrews explained the implications of the one sacrifice.
A. The Finished Work of the Savior (10:11-14)
"Every priest standeth daily ministering and offering oftentimes the same sacrifices, which can never take away sins" (10:11), but Christ finished His work. The one sacrifice He made paid not only for all past sins and all present sins; it also paid for all future sins. The sacrifice of Jesus at Calvary paid for every sin you will ever commit.

Does that mean people are free to sin? That's not the way the realization of the finished work of the Savior affects me. What put me out of the sin-enjoying business was understanding that every sin I have ever committed or ever will commit is responsible for Jesus' dying on the cross.

That work of Jesus Christ is eternal in its ramifications. When Jesus died, He conquered His enemies (10:13). He conquered demons (Col 2:15). He conquered the devil (Heb 2:14).

By the payment Jesus made for our sins, we who have been sanctified (set apart, and also in the process of being set apart) are brought ultimately to completion, to everything God saved us to be. "By one offering he hath perfected for ever them that are sanctified" (10:14). We are not all we ought to be right now. But praise God, we aren't what we used to be. And, wonderful truth, we are not all we are going to be one day.

B. The Faithful Witness of the Spirit (10:15-18)
"Whereof the Holy Ghost also is a witness to us" (10:15). The Holy Spirit takes the fact of the death of Jesus for our sins —the fact of the

one sacrifice—and makes it real to our hearts. Hebrews 10:16 says, "This is the covenant that l will make with them ... I will put my laws into their hearts, and in their minds will I write them." The Lord is saying, "I'll put them in your heart to help you want to do My will. I'll put them in your mind to help you know My will." Then Hebrews 10:17-18 adds, "Their sins and iniquities will I remember no more . . . where remission of these is, there is no more offering for sin." When there is forgiveness, it's all over. God is saying, "I'll forgive, and I'll forget."

20

Come On In! Hebrews 10:19-25

The Jewish people were tied into a system that kept them away from the presence of God. In the wilderness they worshiped God in a tabernacle. In the land of Israel, they worshiped God in a temple. In those places of worship there were barriers that kept them from approaching God. So, when these Hebrew believers read for the first time that because of the death of Jesus on the cross, they could come into the presence of God themselves and for themselves, they were confronted with a revolutionary thought.

Hebrews 10:19-25 brings to a climax one major division in the book of Hebrews. The theme of Hebrews thus far has been that everything we have in Jesus is far better than anything we ever have had before. On that basis, the writer could give us three admonitions to encourage our hearts. He wrote: "Let us draw near" (10:22); "Let us hold fast the profession of our faith" (10:23); and "Let us consider one another to provoke unto love and to good works" (10:24). He was admonishing us to enter, endure, and encourage.

I. ENTER (10:19-22)

A. Provided (10:19-21)

Provision has been made by Jesus for us to enter into the presence of God. "Having therefore, brethren, boldness to enter into the holiest by the blood of Jesus, By a new and living way, which he hath consecrated for us, through the veil, that is tosay, his flesh" (10:19-20). The word *having* is a present-tense participle. Therefore boldness is something we have right now as our present possession—that is, freedom or liberty to enter into the presence of God. The word *new* means "freshly slaughtered." The word *veil* is a figure of speech comparing the incarnate body of the Lord to the veil of the temple that was torn when Jesus died. These words indicate that we have access to God through the shed blood and the torn body of Jesus Christ.

Hebrews 10:21 means that Jesus has led the way for us into the holy of holies. Jesus is our forerunner—somebody who goes on in advance, someone who prepares the way for us to come into the presence of God.

Hebrews 10:22 is an open invitation for us to come: "Let us draw near." God in Heaven says, "Come on in, friend; it's good to see you. How's your family doing? How are things on the job? How is it with your children? Where are you going? Stay a little longer. Are you going to come back tomorrow?" The Old Testament kept us out. The New Testament brings us in. What a wonderful provision has been made for us.

B. Pursued (10:22)

This entrance into the presence of God must be pursued. "Let us draw near with a true heart in full assurance of faith, having our hearts sprinkled from an evil conscience, and our bodies washed with pure water" (10:22). This verse reminds us of what a priest had to do before he went into the presence of God (Lev 16). The blood of the sacrificial animal had to be sprinkled on him, and he had to stop by a laver that was filled with water and wash himself. Those rituals represented the fact that in order to come into the presence of God, you have to be clean on the inside as well as the outside. Your heart has to be sprinkled with blood and your body has to be washed with pure water.

When you go into the presence of God, you have to deal with any sin that's in your life. We can't come to God unless we come on the basis of the shed blood of the Lord Jesus Christ. We do not have access to God based on our own good deeds and merit. We come into God's presence saying, "Lord, I don't deserve this, but the precious blood of your Son has cleansed me from my sin. I'm coming in based on Your Son's blood."

We believers have the privilege of washing our lives with the precious water of the Word of God. We need to have a time every day when we get into the Word and let it wash our outward lives, rearrange things, and make us what we ought to be—practical sanctification.

When we come to God having confessed our sins, having washed in the water of the Word, we have an entrance into God's presence, and we can have fellowship with Him in prayer. That means that you are a priest. I'm a priest. Every born-again Christian is a priest. We can enter into the presence of God for ourselves. If you have a need you don't have to find a preacher. You can speak to God for yourself. Of course, we also ask other Christians to pray for us. When somebody comes to me after a service and asks me to pray for him, I pray for him right on the spot. I don't want to forget. I take requests for prayer seriously. We now have access into the presence of God. Let us enter.

IL ENDURE (10:23)

The second admonition is "Let us hold fast the profession of our faith" (10:23). The better texts translate that last word as *hope*. Let us hold fast the profession of our hope. Here is the admonition to endure. The words *hold fast* convey the idea of perseverance on the part of believers. The writer is not talking about holding fast our salvation.

A. No Wavering (10:23)

The Greek word translated *without wavering* in Hebrews 10:23 means "not leaning." We are not to lean back to the old life, but rather to move forward, to go on. Even though there is that constant pull of the old life, the child of God ought to endure without wavering, leaning toward Jesus all the time.

B. No Doubting (10:23)

We are to endure without doubting. Look at that statement in parentheses in Hebrews 10:23: "For he is faithful that promised." The basic truth about perseverance is not that we hold onto the Lord, but that He holds onto us. He is faithful.

Sometimes I'm unfaithful. Sometimes you are unfaithful. Sometimes we don't hold on. But the wonderful truth is that He who has promised is faithful and He has laid hold on us. We are not kept saved by our hold on the Lord—though we are called on to endure. We are kept by the power of God. We can count on the Lord.

III. ENCOURAGE (10:24-25)

The third admonition is "Let us consider one another to provoke unto love and to good works" (10:24). The word *consider* means to "fix your eyes on, focus your attention on." Believers are admonished to pay attention to, to fix their minds on other believers. One of the most psychologically healthy things you can do is to focus your attention on the needs of others.

In our church the singles ministry is not built around the problems of being single. Our singles reach out to other singles who need the Lord. We don't dwell on the fact that our young people are young people. We teach our young people to consider others, to get interested in others. Our senior adults have a soulwinning ministry. They say, "Why should we sit around bemoaning the fact that we are getting old or our bodies are not what they used to be? Instead, we consider each new day as a chance to tell someone about the Lord Jesus Christ."

A. Personal Stimulation (10:24)

The word *provoke* in Hebrews 10:24 means to "stir up or stimulate." We ought to stimulate other people to be loving and to do good works. Are you an encourager to your fellow believers? Is your life a stimulation to others? You and I ought to be so loving that other people are challenged to be loving by our example. We ought to work so faithfully for the Lord Jesus Christ that by our example other Christians are challenged to work for the Lord.

B. Public Celebration (10:25)

We are to encourage others by public celebration: "Not forsaking the assembling of ourselves together" (10:25). The word translated *assembling* here is used in 2 Thessalonians 2:1 to describe the second coming of Jesus, when believers are gathered in the air. Here in Hebrews, it refers to the gathering of believers on the earth in local churches. The same word is used to describe both the rapture and our assembling on earth, I think that our gathering in God's house should be exciting. I don't understand dead services. What a contradiction they are for people who claim that they have new life in the Lord, that they serve a living Savior, and that they look forward to the blessed hope of the glorious coming of our great God. Our coming together ought to be a celebration.

The word *forsake* means "abandon." It is the custom of some to abandon gathering together with God's people. Such believers are spiritual deserters. Such Christians are AWOL. They belong to a church and yet have forsaken their church. It's a sad thing.

If there ever was a time when Christians ought to be gathering together in their churches, it is today. How does anybody get along without a church? I heard about two boys hoeing. A big jet plane flew over and one of them said, "I sure would hate to be up there in that plane." The other one said, "I sure would hate to be up there without it." I would hate to be in the world without a church.

You don't like your church? Well, go join another one. I never understand people who criticize their church. I love my church. If I didn't, I'd join one I did enjoy. The Bible does not teach lone-ranger Christianity.

If live coals are stirred and banked up together, those coals will be red hot. If one of those coals falls off to the side, it will be fiery and hot for a little while. But then it will begin to cool off and the next thing you know there is just a little wisp of smoke. Soon you can reach over and pick the coal up with your bare hand. That's what happens to some of God's children. When they separate from God's house, they get cold.

Every time God's house is open, you ought to assemble yourselves together, "exhorting one another: and so much the more, as ye see the day approaching" (10:25). Church ought to be an encouraging experience, not a discouraging experience. Jesus is coming, and when He comes I don't want Him to find me slacking off; I want Him to find me stirring up.

21

Can Christians Get by with Sin?
Hebrews 10:26-31

Some people have the idea that when you come to know the Lord you are saved eternally and it really is not a serious matter when you sin. The Bible does teach the eternal security of the soul; the person who has received Jesus as Lord and Savior is kept by the power of God. But the Bible also teaches that sin is a very serious matter in the life of a believer. A Christian cannot sin and get by with it. In some ways sin in the life of a believer is even more serious, more dangerous, than in the life of a nonbeliever.

Hebrews 10:26-31 has elicited great differences of opinion. Devout Bible teachers hold diametrically opposite views about the meaning of these verses. The question is, Do these verses have to do with a lost person or with a saved person?

Opinion seems fairly evenly divided on this matter. Some Bible-believing teachers think that these verses are addressed to those who have never been saved but are on the verge of being saved; they are being encouraged not only to come to the door but also to enter through the door, to know Jesus as Savior. Other teachers believe that these verses have to do with those who are already genuinely saved. I believe these verses concern deliberate sin in the life of a Christian.

This portion of Scripture is the fourth of five encouragement passages in the book of Hebrews. Here is encouragement and also warning that believers can get themselves in such a position that they actually despise the Word of God. They can allow sin to get a firm grip on their lives. Basically, the author of Hebrews was saying that Christians cannot sin and get by with it. I see four reasons in these verses for assuming he was talking about Christians.

First, I see the use of the word *we* twice in Hebrews 10:26: "For if we sin wilfully after that we have received the knowledge of the truth." The context makes clear that the reference is to believers: 10:22, "Let us draw near"; 10:23, "Let us hold fast the profession of our faith"; 10:25, "Not forsaking the assembling of ourselves together." This focus on truly saved people continues in 10:26. Clearly it is Christians who are being addressed.

Second, I see the clause, "after that we have received the knowledge of the truth" (10:26). The word *received* refers to a definite act. We have received in a definite manner the knowledge of the truth. The Greek word for *knowledge* here means "full knowledge," not just an acquaintance with the way of salvation. Using similar language the apostle Paul wrote, "God our Saviour . . . will have all men to be saved, and to come unto the knowledge of the truth" (1 Tim 2:3-4). And Paul alluded to those who are "ever learning, and never able to come to the knowledge of the truth" (2 Tim 3:7). I believe people who have definitely received full knowledge of salvation are truly saved people.

Third, I see the clause, "wherewith he was sanctified" (10:29). The word *sanctified* means "set apart." When you are saved, you are sanctified; you are set apart for the Lord. Of course, the process of sanctification is gradual. But as far as our position in the Lord Jesus is concerned, at the moment of our salvation, He set us apart. A person who has been sanctified is a saved person. Note again 10:14: "For by one offering he hath perfected for ever them that are sanctified." A sanctified person is a person who has been perfected; he has been made complete by the one sacrifice of the Lord Jesus Christ.

Fourth, I see the sentence, "The Lord shall judge his people" (10:30). The Lord is going to judge His own—saved people. Thus, I believe that this passage deals with deliberate sin in the life of a believer. I am not talking about an occasional failure, a slip, a trap a person falls into inadvertently. The use of the word *willfully* in Hebrews 10:26 means the writer was thinking of intentional sin, defiant sin.

Do you ever sin on purpose? Do you ever know you ought not to do something, but you go ahead and do it anyway? Do you ever know you ought not to say what you're about to say to your wife, yet you go ahead and say it? Do you know you ought not to drive the way you do in traffic, yet you do it anyway?

The verb *sin* in Hebrews 10:26 is a present-tense word, and it therefore means not one act of sin but a lifestyle of sin. In other words, you don't do it just one time; you do it over and over again. The reference is not to irregular, occasional sin, but to a Christian who chooses to revert to his old lifestyle and gets into a habit pattern of intentional sin.

Why is it such a serious matter when a person who is a believer deliberately sins? Deliberate sin in the life of a Christian is disturbing, damaging, and distressing.

I. DISTURBING (10:26-27)

A. Excludes Christ's Sacrifice (10:26)

Sin in the life of Christians is disturbing because it excludes the daily power of the sacrifice of Christ. If you sin deliberately after you've received the knowledge of the truth "there remaineth no more sacrifice for sins" (10:26). What does that mean? Reference to the Old Testament sacrifices will help to explain this statement. On the day of atonement, the high priest would make a sacrifice for all the sins of the people for all of the year. But on a daily basis, no provision was made for what is called in the Old Testament presumptuous sin. But when Jesus Christ made His sacrifice at Calvary's cross, it was for *sin* and also for *sins*.

Hebrews 9:26 says, "But now once in the end of the world hath he appeared to put away *sin* by the sacrifice of himself" (italics added). Hebrews 10:12 says, "This man, after he had offered one sacrifice for *sins* for ever" (italics added). What is the distinction between *sin* and *sins?* The Bible teaches that we are sinners in two ways; we are sinners not only because we commit acts of sin, but also because we are born with sinful natures. You and I commit acts of sin because we are born with sinful natures.

When Jesus died, He had to pay the price not only for our individual sins, but He also had to deal with our sin natures. The moment you receive Christ as your personal Savior that "one sacrifice" is made effective in your life. That old sin nature has been changed, and you have a brand-new nature down inside you.

But now you have to deal with the problem of sins, s-i-n-s. You have to claim the power of the cross for the sins you commit on a daily basis. Please don't misunderstand me. It is not necessary for a Christian to sin. A Christian can sin, but it is not necessary for a Christian to sin. (I am not saying that you are never going to sin again.)

By His sacrifice, the Lord Jesus Christ has paid the price for "daily" sins. He has also made available to Christians the power to deal with sin, so that when we are tempted to sin we have a choice. Before we were saved, we didn't have a choice. We sinned because it was our nature to sin; we didn't have power to keep from sinning. When temptation came, we were like sitting ducks for the devil because we did not have the power of the cross in our lives. But when we came to Christ, we received power to overcome sin.

It is disturbing when a Christian deliberately sins because he is in some sense repudiating the sacrifice of Jesus. Such a Christian is basically saying, "It doesn't matter to me if the power of the cross is available in my life or not." If you reject the power of the cross in your daily life, there is nothing else God can do to help you overcome sin: "There remaineth no more sacrifice for sins." Jesus is not going to die on the cross again when you sin. He has made one sacrifice for sin (singular) and for sins (plural) forever.

B. Expects Christ's Judgment (10:27)

Sin in the life of a Christian is also disturbing because it can expect the judgment of God. "But a certain fearful looking for of judgment and fiery indignation, which shall devour the adversaries" (10:27). If you allow deliberate sin in your life, God will judge you concerning that matter. Of course, our sins were judged two thousand years ago at Calvary. But the Bible teaches that there is going to be a judgment seat of Christ where believers are going to be examined for their deeds, whether good or bad. If a believer has unconfessed, deliberate sins in his life, he is going to face the fiery indignation of God at the judgment seat of Christ.

In 1 Corinthians 3:11 the apostle Paul said, "For other foundation can no man lay than that is laid, which is Jesus Christ." In other words, the only way you are saved is to have the foundational experience of faith in the Lord Jesus. Next Paul described how a believer builds on that foundation. He can use permanent materials like gold, silver, and precious stones. Or he can use materials that are not pleasing to God, like wood, hay, and stubble —including deliberate sin.

> Every man's work shall be made manifest: for the day shall declare it, because it shall be revealed by fire; and the fire shall try every man's work of what sort it is. . . . If any man's work shall be burned, he shall suffer loss: but he himself shall be saved; yet so as by fire (1Cor 3:13,15).

It will be a sad day when people who have truly been born again but who haven't lived for Jesus stand at the judgment seat of Christ and see a lifetime of wasted opportunities go up in smoke.

II. DAMAGING (10:28-29)

Deliberate sin in the life of a Christian is damaging to the cause of Christ.

A. The Older System (10:28)

Under the law of Moses, when a person rejected God's Word, when he lived in open rebellion, he died without mercy at the word of two or three witnesses. This older system had some severe requirements. For example, a rebellious son was to be stoned to death.

The Old Testament is severe for two reasons. First, God wants us to know that He is a holy God. Second, He wants us to know He hates sin. That doesn't mean He hates the sinner. God loves you, but He hates anysin that is wrecking and ruining your life. God hates sin as parents would hate a rattlesnake coiled up in their baby's crib.

B. The Newer System (10:29)

If that's the way it was in the Old Testament, what do you think it's going to be like in the New Testament? Hebrews 10:29 answers, "Of how much sorer punishment...shall he bethought worthy," and then paints one of the saddest pictures in the whole Bible of a backslidden Christian who is living in open sin. That kind of Christian does three things that we recognize by the word *hath*. "Who *hath* trodden under foot the Son of God, and *hath* counted the blood of the covenant, wherewith he was sanctified, an unholy thing, and *hath* done despite unto the Spirit of grace" (italics added).

First, if you are in a backslidden condition today, you are rejecting God's Son, repudiating God's Son. You are treading on (stomping under) the Son of God. In the sermon on the mount when Jesus was talking about the salt that had lost its savor, He said that that salt was worth nothing except to be trodden underfoot. It was useless. When a Christian deliberately sins, he or she is saying to a lost world, "Jesus is no more than the dirt under my feet; that's what I think of the Lord Jesus Christ."

Second, if you are deliberately sinning, you are also rejecting God's sacrifice. If I allow deliberate sin in my life, I am repudiating the blood of the Lord Jesus Christ. In other words, I am saying to Jesus, "I don't care that you died and shed your blood for me."

Third, if you are deliberately sinning, you are insulting the Spirit of grace. When you are saved, the Holy Spirit comes to live in you, and He never leaves you. Your body is the temple of God; God's Holy Spirit is that divine presence in you that causes you to live a holy, clean, dedicated life. When you sin as a Christian, the Holy Spirit inside you is grieved. If you start living in intentional sin, you are treating that precious indwelling Holy Spirit of grace with contempt. You are like a husband who brings a disease-infested prostitute into his home and says to his sweet, loving wife, "You'll just have to endure it. I'm keeping this prostitute right here with us."

A Christian with open sin in his life is useless to the cause of Christ. His life openly ridicules everything that the Lord Jesus Christ stands for. It gives the lost world another opportunity to laugh and mock and jeer at the Christian faith.

III. DISTRESSING (10:30-31)

Deliberate sin in the life of a Christian will cause him distress. God says, "Vengeance is mine; I will repay" (Rm 12:19). "The Lord shall judge his people. It is a fearful thing to fall into the hands of the living God" (10:30-31). God will deal with the backslidden Christian through discipline or through death.

A. Discipline (10:30-31)

David in the Old Testament was God's man, but he allowed open defiant sin in his life. So God disciplined him, and the rest of his life he bore the scars of that sin. God may judge the backslidden Christian through discipline.

B. Death (10:30-31)

God may even judge the backslidden Christian by taking him home. First John 5:16 says, "There is a sin unto death." It is a terrible thing to fall into the hands of the living God for chastisement. The wonderful good news is that we don't have to. Instead, we can fall into the hands of the living God for cleansing. David said, "Let us fall now into the hand of the Lord; for his mercies are great" (2 Sam 24:14).

22

When There's No Turning Back
Hebrews 10:32-39

The theme for the entire book of Hebrews could be "No turning back." If you are a child of God and have set your course on following the Lord, being what Jesus wants you to be, the writer of Hebrews is saying to you, "Don't turn back."

Hebrews 10:32-39 gives compelling reasons why those of us who know Jesus ought to keep going forward for Him.

I. PAST VICTORIES (10:32-34)

We ought not to turn back because of past victories. One source of encouragement for the days ahead is the memory of victories we have experienced in the past. We can remember when the light came into our spiritual darkness—when Christ first came into our lives. Hebrews 10:32 says, "Call to remembrance the former days, in which, after ye were illuminated, ye endured a great fight of afflictions."

For the Hebrews, coming to Christ was a dramatic experience—and it brought them reproach and suffering. We may not experience persecution to the same degree, but those of us who have had a genuine, life-changing experience with Christ will encounter difficulties like the Hebrew Christians faced.

A. They Struggled (10:32-33)

The Hebrews began their Christian lives with a great struggle. The writer was saying, "Remember the battle you were in. You didn't turn back then." What struggles did they experience? Hebrews 10:33 gives an example: "Ye were made a gazingstock both by reproaches and afflictions." We get our word *theater* from the word translated *gazingstock*. It is as if they were on a stage to be made a public spectacle. In fact, some first century believers were taken to the Roman coliseum and martyred for their faith; they were thrown to the lions.

In those days the general public was bloodthirsty; people were always looking for some new thrill. One of their sports was burning Christians. Thousands of people would watch as believers were placed on public display. The more the Christians suffered, the more the crowd enjoyed it. They cried for more. Many times the life of a believer was left to the capricious whim of a Roman emperor who would give him either a thumbs-up or a thumbs-down.

In our day you could suffer reproach at school. Have you ever been publicly embarrassed at school because of your faith in the Lord, or because you wouldn't go along with something you knew to be wrong? It's not easy for a Christian teenager to say no, especially when others are saying, "I'm a Christian and I'm free to go where I want to go. What's the matter with you? You're just a legalist, aren't you?"

It's not easy on the job to take your stand for the Lord when everybody else is betting on the ballgame, telling dirty jokes, and flirting around the office. If you dare to be different—maybe you have a Bible on your desk—you may become an object of public scorn.

When you come to know the Lord as your Savior, you are involved with everybody else who knows the Savior. Every other Christian is your brother or sister in Jesus—not just the members of your church, but also saved people who belong to other churches. Because you identify with them, you sometimes have to bear the reproach that comes on them. "Partly, whilst ye became companions of them that were so used" (10:33).

Sometimes it's embarrassing to be identified with other Christians. There are some kooky Christians in this world. There are times when it's tough to be identified with believers, because believers can do some absolutely nutty things. But that's my crowd. It's like being in the ark. The only reason Noah could stand the stench on the inside was the judgment on the outside. He'd rather be in than out. It's not easy to endure the stench of inconsistent Christian living. But I'd rather be with the Lord's crowd on the way to Heaven than to be with the other crowd.

Occasionally, there is reproach attached to the church you belong to. When I was a teenage boy, not everyone loved my home church. Occasionally people made snide remarks about it. They would say things that hurt me. That can happen. If you belong to a cocktail-sipping crowd in a worldly church, you will be respected in some circles. But if you belong to a church that takes a stand for Jesus and is unashamed of the Bible, you may suffer reproach.

I want the whole world to know that I identify with the born-again crowd. I belong to the crowd who believes in the whole Bible instead of a Bible full of holes. I belong to that crowd on the way to glory. I'm homeward bound. No turning back.

Some football teams adopt the motto, "No pain, no gain." If a player is not willing to go through the pain of giving all he can during the game, he may not experience the gain of winning the game. Christians too need to be willing to struggle for victory.

B. They Survived (10:34)

One way to survive struggles is to focus your mind on others. The Hebrew Christians were good to the writer of the Epistle in the midst of their afflictions. "Ye had compassion of me in my bonds" (10:34). He went on to say, you "took joyfully the spoiling of your goods" (10:34). Evidently, they had lost personal property because they had come to Christ. How would you feel if your personal possessions were seized because you were a believer? For example, take that new car you bought. You come out to the garage one day, and it's gone because the government heard you had become a Christian. How would you respond? Would you stand out there in your driveway praising God?

Why could they be so happy when they were losing personal possessions, when things were being taken away from them? The answer is found in the rest of Hebrews 10:34: "Knowing in yourselves that ye have in heaven a better and an enduring substance." These people had come to realize the true value of things. They understood that what we have over yonder is far more precious and lasting than what we have down here. I don't care what you have in the way of possessions; they are temporary in nature and eventually they will mean nothing to you. But what you have in Heaven will have everlasting value. The Bible says that we have an "inheritance incorruptible, and undefiled . . . reserved in heaven" (1 Pe 1:4). No one can take that inheritance away. Jesus says, "Lay up for yourselves treasures in heaven, where neither moth nor rust doth corrupt, and where thieves do not break through nor steal" (Mt 6:20). The Hebrew Christians could remember how their sense of values helped them survive their struggles.

My Father is rich in houses and lands, He holdeth the wealth of the world in His hands! In 1877, Harriet Buell wrote "A Child of the King." The last stanza captures this perfectly:

> A tent or a cottage, why should I care?
> They're building a palace for me over there;
> Though exiled from home, yet still may I sing:
> All glory to God, I'm a child of the King!

II. PRESENT NECESSITIES (10:35-36)

We ought not to turn back because of present necessities for confidence and endurance. We can claim the promises of God as we keep going forward.

A. Confidence (10:35)

"Cast not away therefore your confidence, which hath great recompense of reward" (10:35). The word *confidence* means "assurance." The writer of Hebrews was not saying, "Don't cast away your salvation." Rather, he was saying, "Don't toss out your assurance." Christians can't lose their salvation, but they can lose their confidence. If we waver and begin to look back, we begin to lose our assurance in the Lord. What we need is a present-tense confidence in the Lord: staying with it, continuing to press forward for Jesus. There is a reward for that kind of life.

B. Endurance (10:36)

"Ye have need of patience" (10:36). The writer was referring to endurance, the ability of a faithful soldier to hold up. When the Bible says that you need patience, it doesn't mean you should grin and bear it. It means that you should hold up under whatever the enemy hurls against you and press on through to victory.

One thing about God's people is that they have a tendency to keep on keepin' on. I've come a long way in my journey for Jesus. I've been living for the Lord a long, long time. Has there ever been a time when I was tempted to turn back? Of course. There have been times when the struggle was great, and the devil would whisper sweet cajoling in my ear. Does the devil ever talk to you? He talks to me every now and then. He says, "You've done enough. Cool it, ease up, back off a little."

The devil says that to people close to retirement too. "You've taught Sunday school. You've been there every time the church is open. You've already done your share." Admittedly, some people can't do all they used to do; I'm not talking about that. But isn't it a shame that some people who have lived for the things of Heaven all their lives get to retirement age and then suddenly switch their attention back to the things of this earth? Of course, others use their new-found freedom to be more active for Christ than ever before.

How exciting it is to do the will of God and claim God's promises in your life by faith. Don't quit doing the will of God. Just keep on doing what's right. Keep moving forward so that "after ye have done the will of God, ye might receive the promise" (v. 36).

III. PROSPECTIVE REALITIES (10:37-39)

Hebrews 10:37-39 whets our appetites for what's out there in the future. Bright prospects give us added incentive not to back up but to keep on going for Jesus.

A. The Sure Return (10:37)

The first prospective reality is the sure return of Jesus Christ. "For yet a little while"—in just a little while, or literally, for yet how little how little—"and he that shall come will come, and will not tarry" (10:37). How long has it been since that statement was written? Around two thousand years.

When you are looking forward to something, the wait can seem to last forever. Do you remember when you were looking forward to being sixteen so you could get your driver's license? It seemed like you had to wait forever. But suddenly the day arrived. Or, do you remember waiting for your high school or college graduation? I remember how anxious I was about getting out of college. I had the date circled on my calendar, and I crossed off the days as they passed. I thought that date would never come. But you know, it was just a little while.

The coming of Jesus Christ is imminent. Isn't it going to be great to meet the Lord in the air and say, "Lord, I never turned back."

B. The Solemn Review (10:38-39)

The second prospective reality is the solemn review. "Now the just shall live by faith: but if any man draw back, my soul shall have no pleasure in him. But we are not of them who draw back unto perdition; but of them that believe to the saving of the soul." Are you among those who draw back? If you are on the verge of being saved, but cringe back in fear, the Lord will not be pleased. You have to come to Him by faith or He will not save you. Those of us who are saved do not turn back; we live by faith and move forward to be what God wants us to be.

23

Christians Live Only by Faith
Hebrews 11:1-7

The Christian life begins with personal faith in the Lord Jesus Christ. Ephesians 2:8-9 says, "For by grace are ye saved through faith; and that not of yourselves: it is the gift of God: Not of works, lest any man should boast." We are saved when we put our faith in the finished work of Jesus at Calvary's cross.

The Christian life is also lived by faith. Galatians 2:20 says, "I am crucified with Christ: nevertheless I live; yet not I, but Christ liveth in me: and the life which I now live in the flesh I live by the faith of the Son of God, who loved me, and gave himself for me."

Actually, you cannot live a day of your life apart from faith. By faith you eat your breakfast, trusting that no one has sprinkled arsenic on your cereal. By faith you believe what you read in the morning newspaper. (Sometimes your faith is misplaced if you believe what you read!) By faith you drive your car to work, trusting in automobile designers you have never seen. By faith you take medicine, trusting the diagnosis of the doctor and the prescription supplied by the pharmacist. And so on. You put your faith in people you see and in people you do not see.

The object of our faith for salvation is the Lord Jesus Christ. The Bible says, "Neither is there salvation in any other: for there is none other name under heaven given among men, whereby we must be saved"

(Ac 4:12). So, we put our faith in the finished work of the Lord Jesus, and having done that, we put our faith daily in the promises of God.

Living by faith is what the remaining chapters of Hebrews are about. We have seen that in Jesus Christ we have a better person, a better high priest, and a better provision. Beginning in Hebrews 11 we discover that in the Christian faith we have a better principle: We live based on faith in the Lord Jesus and in the promises of His Word.

I. FAITH DECLARED (11:1-2)

A. Definitions (11:1)

Hebrews 11:1 gives a twofold definition: Faith is substance and faith is evidence. "Faith is the substance of things hoped for." The word translated *substance* literally means "that which is placed under." It means a foundation or a support. The author was saying that faith is to the Christian's life what a foundation is to a house. Faith is what gives foundation and confidence and assurance for our lives.

In New Testament times, the word translated *substance* was used to describe a business document that served as proof of ownership, a title deed. Our faith is the title deed of things that are still in the future. When Jesus comes again, or when I die, I will have a wonderful home in Heaven. I've never seen that home, but I know that I have it because of my title deed. My title deed for things that I hope for is faith. By faith I trust what God says and I bring the future into the present because I believe what God has to say.

Faith is also "the evidence of things not seen." The word translated *evidence* in Hebrews 11:1 could be translated "proof." Faith is the proof of things that we cannot see. Faith is evidence we could take into court to prove our case.

When you are saved, the Bible says that in an instant you are born again. You can't see *born-again* because that is a spiritual term. The Bible also says that when you come to Christ, you are justified. You can't see *justified*; it is a spiritual term. When you are saved, you are washed in the blood of the Lamb. Has anybody ever seen that take place? Then, how do we know that those invisible things are real? We know by faith. Faith is trusting what God has said.

A. Illustrations (11:2)

"For by it [that is, by this spiritual commodity, faith] the elders obtained a good report" (11:2). The word *elders* there refers to Old Testament believers, people who functioned based on faith; who did what they did because they were obeying what God had revealed in His Word to them. The elders are practical examples of faith in action. Sometimes the doctrines of the Bible are better understood and make more sense when they are illustrated in people's lives.

The elders "obtained a good report." God took notice of them and bore witness to the reality of their faith. It's as if God is saying in Hebrews 11:2, "Look at them; they are my men. Look at them; they are my women. Look at them; they are my people." I wonder what kind of record Heaven is writing about us today.

II. FAITH DESCRIBED (11:3-7)

A. Present Belief (11:3)

It is on the basis of faith that we understand the universe. "Through faith we understand that the worlds were framed by the word of God, so that things which are seen were not made of things which do appear." Isn't that an amazing statement written almost two thousand years ago? You and I know that visible things are made up of invisible things. We know that material things are composed of atoms that the naked eye cannot see. But people didn't know that when Hebrews was written. Yet the writer said the visible world came into existence on the basis of invisible realities.

The writer was saying that only by an act of faith can we understand the origin of the universe. This is the doctrine of creationism. We creationists do not believe that the world came into existence accidentally. We believe that the world originated by an intelligent Creator.

Creationism has been laughed out of the academic, intellectual community in America. It has been called pseudoscience. We are told that we cannot teach creationism in our schools because it is not scientific. Well, evolution is not scientific either, because when you start talking about the origin of the universe, you are getting outside the realm of science. All science can do is deal with processes that are going on now.

Science has nothing to say about the ultimate origins of anything. So when a person talks about origins, he is not talking as a scientist, but as a philosopher. When a person discusses how the world came into existence, if he is honest, he does not say, "We have proved this." He says, "We think this." The fact is, if he is honest, he will say that what he thinks today is not what he thought ten years ago.

A college student was racing across campus with a book under his arm. Someone stopped him and asked, "Where are you going?" The student replied, "I just bought the latest physics book, and I'm trying to get to class before it goes out of date."

I taught eighth-grade science for a while when I finished college. Even then, I wouldn't have thought of letting my students use a five-year-old textbook. Science is constantly in a process of change. Many theories thought to be true yesterday are not believed today.

Whatever you believe about the origin of the universe, your beliefs are not based on scientific observation. Your beliefs are based on faith in something because no one was present when this world came into existence. There are only two alternatives: you can believe in the theory of evolution, or you can believe in creation. You can put your belief in human speculation, or you can put your belief in divine revelation.

To repeat Hebrews 11:3, "Through faith we understand that the worlds were framed by the word of God." If you live your life based on faith in the Creator, that is present belief.

B. Previous Belief (11:4-7)

To illustrate past belief the writer of Hebrews referred to individuals in Old Testament times who lived their lives based on faith in God. The three examples in Hebrews 11:4-7 are taken from Genesis 4, 5, and 6.

The first illustration is from the life of Abel, the second son of Adam and Eve.

Abel's life demonstrates *worshiping faith*. Evidently at the end of a period of instruction during which Adam taught his sons how to approach God, Cain and Abel each brought a sacrifice to God. Cain's sacrifice was fruit. He was a farmer and he brought some of his produce. Abel's offering was from the firstlings of his flock. Abel brought what the Lord had instructed him to bring.

Now where did Abel get his instruction? I believe he got it from Adam. Where did Adam get his instruction? I believe he got it from God. When Adam and Eve disobeyed, God took the skins of animals and clothed them. They were clothed based on the slaying of an animal. I believe that right there in the garden of Eden, God was teaching them that they could not approach Him apart from the shedding of blood.

I believe that right there in the garden of Eden God gave a preview of Calvary where Jesus the Lamb of God would be slain. He thus established for all time that the only way to come into the presence of a holy God is based on the blood of the Lamb. The Bible says that without the shedding of blood there is no remission of sin.

Abel came God's way; Cain came his own way. That's why "Abel offered unto God a more excellent sacrifice than Cain" (11:4). The only way to come to God is to come God's way. God decides how we are to come into His presence. You say, "I'll come my way." That's the way of Cain (Jude 11). God's way is the only way we can be saved. Jessie Pounds wrote "The Way of the Cross Leads Home" (1906). It rightly declares:

> I must needs go home by the way of the cross,
> There's no other way but this;
> I shall ne'er get sight of the gates of light,
> If the way of the cross I miss.

Enoch is the second illustration. His life demonstrates *walking faith*. Enoch's career is revealed to us in Genesis 5, which I think of as the death chapter. We read about one after the other: "And he died," "And he died," "And he died." Then right in the middle of that chapter we read, "And Enoch walked with God" (Ge 5:24). Enoch didn't die, "for God took him." God just translated him, transposed him.

Musicians know what it is to transpose a piece of music; they take a piece out of one key and put it into another key. That's what happened to Enoch; he was transposed. He was carried from one sphere of life into another sphere. His body "was not found, because God had translated him" (Heb 11:5). Enoch's body was not found. That means people looked for him. He was missed.

Often God's children are not appreciated by their own generation. They are considered extreme, rigid, narrow-minded, or too old-fashioned. But when they are gone, people may begin to realize that a saint has walked in their midst.

The Bible says that Enoch "had this testimony, that he pleased God" (11:5). It wasn't easy for Enoch to walk with God in his day, but he did. It isn't easy to walk with God in our day either. But we can walk by faith, just doing what God says to do.

Noah is the third illustration. His life demonstrates *witnessing faith*. Noah was "warned of God" (11:7). In other words, God revealed to Noah that there was going to be a flood. It seems that it had never rained on the earth, but God told Noah that a flood would destroy the whole world. The next morning Noah was obeying the word of God, building the ark just like God said.

Eyewitness News sent a reporter who said, "What are you doing, Noah?"

"I'm building an ark; there's going to be a flood."

They took off to the local university and checked with the meteorology department: "Has there ever been a flood?"

"No, there's never been a flood in the history of the world."

You can imagine the ridicule on the evening news.

But Noah took God at His word and started building a boat. He also began to preach, warning others that there was only one way to be saved. He built an ark "to the saving of his house" (11:7), for the flood came. That is what faith is all about. Faith is confidently obeying what God says regardless of the circumstances and the consequences.

24

Abraham: Looking for a City
Hebrews 11:8-10

Hebrews 11, the great chapter of faith, is a series of studies of Old Testament characters whose lives illustrate what it means to live by faith. Because definitions of faith can be hard to understand, the Bible provides flesh and blood illustrations.

We've got to keep in mind that these Old Testament characters were real people. They were like you and me and had heartaches, sorrows, and other difficulties. Sometimes they soared to the heights as they trusted God in faith. Other times they plunged to the depths of despair as they faltered in their faith. We can identify with these people, so it is an encouragement to us to read about their lives.

As we consider their lives, we should ask ourselves, "How are we going to live our lives?" We have only two possible choices. One, we can live by sight. In other words, we can live based on things we can see; we can live for the present instead of the future; we can live for the temporal instead of the eternal. Two, we can live by faith. In other words, we can live based on things we cannot see; we can live for the future instead of the present.

We are called to live by faith when we come to know Christ as our Savior. We are called to put our trust in a person we have never seen. The Bible says about Jesus, "Whom having not seen, ye love . . . [and]

rejoice with joy unspeakable and full of glory" (1 Pe 1:8). We are called to live our lives going toward a city that we have not seen.

The predominant illustration in the Old Testament of what it means to live by faith is the life of Abraham. The New Testament calls Abraham the father of the faithful. God came to Abraham and made a promise to him; Abraham believed that promise and began to live a life of faith.

I. LISTENING TO GOD'S PROMISE (11:8)

"By faith Abraham, when he was called to go out into a place which he should after receive for an inheritance, obeyed." To understand this statement fully, we must remember Abraham's background. Abraham was living in an ancient city known as Ur, near the Persian Gulf and not far from the city of Babylon. Ur of the Chaldeans had a sophisticated civilization. They had highly developed art, a well-organized system of government, and a complex religious system. The patron god of Ur was the moon god. Abraham was born and reared in a pagan culture and was heading for a lost eternity. In the midst of this godless yet advanced civilization, Abraham was a successful, well-to-do businessman. He had a beautiful wife. He had everything that a man could want in terms of the visible and the temporal.

There came into the life of this Abraham an amazing call from God. Abraham probably had no plans to go anywhere. I imagine that Abraham thought he would live and die in the surroundings of Ur. Yet we learn in Genesis 12 that the Lord called him right out of that pagan darkness. God had different plans for his life.

It is God who takes the initiative and approaches the human soul. God always takes the first step. We don't know how God broke through to Abraham—whether it was an audible voice or not. Sometimes in the Old Testament God did speak to men in an audible voice. However God called, the call was so clear that Abraham listened.

I believe God gives everyone a chance to know Him. God may speak in a church service; He may use the preaching of the Bible or the singing of a gospel hymn. In a pagan land, He may speak to a person through the world of nature and let him know that there is a God who is a creator. However God speaks, we need to listen to the promises and respond. The Lord calls us to His Son, and when we respond, we move from being pagans on our way to a godless eternity to being children of God on our way to a city that He has promised to give us. We turn our backs on an old way of life and in faith turn our faces toward a new way of life. That is what salvation is all about. We are called and we obey.

A. Sudden Obedience (11:8)

The tense of the verbs in Hebrews 11:8 makes it clear that when Abraham heard the call of God, he instantly obeyed. The moment he heard God call, he started packing.

B. Stunning Obedience (11:8)

"He went out, not knowing whither he went." *The Living Bible* puts it this way: "Away he went, not even knowing where he was going." Think about that uncertainty. When God called Abraham, He didn't say, "Here's a map. You're going to be here today, and there tomorrow." There was no map, no itinerary. He took off not knowing where he was going. That was stunning obedience.

If you give the Lord stunning obedience, you will have the greatest life you could possibly have. I believe that the worst day I live serving Jesus is better than the best day I could ever have living for the devil.

On the way of faith God doesn't show you everything ahead of time. If you take one step of faith, the Lord will show you the next step. You don't have to know it all. To live by faith is to obey God when He says, "Just follow Me and I promise you that it's going to come out all right. Trust Me and I'll show you the rest of the steps down the road." Abraham could live by faith because he listened to the promise.

II. LIVING BY GOD'S PROMISE (11:9)

Abraham also lived by God's promise. "By faith he sojourned in the land of promise, as in a strange country, dwelling in [tents]."

A. Separation

Abraham left a city and plunged into a desert. Having been used to urban dwelling, the rest of his life he lived in tents. Everywhere Abraham went in his walk of faith, he always constructed an altar and erected a tent. The altar was the place where Abraham met God in prayer. The altar represents Abraham's faith and reminds us of his dedication to God.

The tent represents separation from the world. God said, "Go out to a land, Abraham, that I will afterward give you." When Abraham got there, however, he found that it was already populated and controlled by a godless and wicked people. There were Canaanites in the land. So, Abraham remained separate from the rest of the population and spent the rest of his life living in a tent in a land that God had said was going to be his. All he really possessed of that land in his lifetime was a burial place for himself and his family.

Likewise, God has promised to give this world to His children. "The meek…shall inherit the earth" (Mt 5:5). Every morning we wake up and see the sun; that's our sun shining on us. God has said the sky and sea and stars are ours. But it doesn't look like the world is ours. We are in possession of very little of it. But we live here by faith.

When we come to Christ we are like Abraham, who turned his back on his old life, separated himself from the godless culture around him, and began to live a new lifestyle. We have new, God-oriented thought patterns. We have new behavior patterns. Some activities that used to be perfectly all right are not acceptable anymore. We have a brand-new set of desires. We now want to do the things we ought to do. We derive a new set of standards and values from what God says in the Bible. We are no longer victims of the temporary fads and fashions of this world.

The tent reminded Abraham of the temporary nature of this world. We also remember that "the things which are seen are temporal; but the things which are not seen are eternal" (2 Cor 4:18). Our eyes are on Heaven.

B, Participation (11:9)

Living by the promise is a life of separation and participation. Abraham was "dwelling in tabernacles with Isaac [his son] and Jacob [his grandson], the heirs with him of the same promise." Abraham not only lived a life of faith himself, but he also passed on that faith to his family. Acts 16:31 says, "Believe on the Lord Jesus Christ, and thou shalt be saved, and thy house." You can claim your family for Jesus. Wouldn't it be a shame for you to live for Jesus and your children to live for the devil?

You may say, "I have lived for Jesus and I have tried to teach my family to live for the Lord and they're still living for the devil." Just hold on and keep trusting in God; keep living for Jesus and keep sharing the promises of God with your family. Somewhere down the road they'll come to the same faith in Jesus you've come to. We can trust God for the salvation of our families.

III. LOOKING FOR GOD'S PROMISE (11:10)

Abraham was looking for God's promise. "For he looked for a city which hath foundations, whose builder and maker is God."

A. A Forward Look

Living for Jesus means that life has a forward look. Life has a sense of anticipation, a goal, and a direction. So many people don't have a reason for living. They don't know where they came from; they don't know why they are here; they don't know where they are going. They have no purpose. They have no sense of destiny. They think that when it's over it's over. But we are more important than that. God did not make us just to live a meaningless existence for a few years on this earth and then die. We are looking for a city with foundations.

B. An Upward Look

The only foundations in this world that Abraham had were tent pegs driven in the sand. But Abraham knew that out there beyond him, God had promised him a city that had foundations.

God has told us about this wonderful city in the last two chapters of the book of Revelation. It is a city "whose builder and maker is God" (Heb 11:10). The word translated "builder" in the King James version really means "designer." Jesus designed the city. He said, "In my Father's house are many mansions... I go to prepare a place for you" (Jn 14:2). God spoke this world into existence in six days, but our designer has been building the city for almost two thousand years. When we get to Heaven, it's going to be some city!

25

A Tested Faith is a True Faith
Hebrews 11:11-19

God honors us by the trials He allows us to experience. Many years ago I heard W. A. Criswell in Dallas tell a story about a couple at his church who experienced a great trial. They had long prayed that God would give them a child, and they were so thrilled when one was born. But soon it became evident that their baby was hopelessly mentally challenged. Of course, they asked, "Why is our son underdeveloped? We have tried to live for the Lord. We wanted to be the kind of parents God would want us to be. Why did God allow this to happen to us?"

Dr. Criswell replied, "Well, you see, God had a little one who was going to need extra love and care. He searched all over the world for a couple who could adequately look after this hurt child. He picked you because He knew that you would love this youngster enough to take good care of him." God honors us by the greatness of the tests He allows us to experience. Little furnaces are for little faith. Big furnaces are for big faith.

The life of Abraham illustrates faith in God in times of great trial. In Galatians 3:9 God honors Abraham by calling him "faithful Abraham." First Corinthians 4:2 tells us, "It is required in stewards, that a man be found faithful." One of the greatest epitaphs that could ever be assigned to your life or mine is "Found Faithful."

If we are like Abraham, 2 Corinthians 5:7 describes our lives: "We walk by faith, not by sight." Someone translated this verse as follows: "We conduct our lives on the basis of faith and not on the appearance of things."

I. ABRAHAM'S THRILL (11:11-12)

When Abraham left the land of Ur of the Chaldeans, he left on the basis of a promise from God. God said to Abraham, "I'm going to give you offspring that will be so numerous that they will become a multitude of people. The nations of the earth will be blessed through the greatness of your descendants." Well, there was one big problem attached to that promise from God. Abraham and Sarah his wife didn't have any children. But what God did to fulfill His promise to them is one of the most thrilling pages in human history.

A. Human Frailty (11:11-12a)

"Through faith also Sara herself received strength to conceive seed, and was delivered of a child when she was past age." She was past the years when it was normal for a woman to give birth. She was about ninety years old, in fact. From a human perspective there was no way a child could be born to her. When God gave the promise to Sarah, the Scripture says she laughed. But God is able to do what is impossible for us to do. (Then Sarah tried to take things into her own hands and we have the story of Hagar and Ishmael. Their descendants have been a source of trouble for the Jewish people ever since.)

Abraham too was beyond the age to sire a child. He was one hundred years old. Again, human frailty made the promised heir seem like an impossibility. Years passed and the longer they lived, the more impossible their circumstances seemed. Then one night in the tent I can almost imagine Sarah saying, "Abraham, wake up. Go down to the convenience store and get mesome dill pickles. And while you are there, get me some chocolate-covered potato chips." Sarah was going to have a baby. The day came when they heard the first cry of a newborn. Can you imagine Abraham hopping and skipping and kicking up his heels? "Glory to God! Glory to God! We have a son!"

A. Divine Ability (11:12b-c)

If God has made a promise to you, He has obligated Himself to keep it. He will do what He promised in His Word He will do. Sarah "judged him faithful who had promised" (11:11). What is important is not the promise, but the one who makes the promise. If a person making a promise has an unreliable character, we have reason to doubt that promise. A promise is only as good as the character of the promise-giver. God had made a promise to Abraham and Sarah and by faith they had trusted in His ability to do what He said.

In his early years Abraham was called *Abram*. The name *Abram* meant "father of many." I suspect that before God fulfilled His promise, his name was an embarrassment to Abram. We can imagine how awkward it was:

A stranger asks, "What is your name?"

"Abram."

"Oh, father of many. How many children do you have?"

"I don't have any."

Then one day Abram announces to his friends, "I've changed my name."

They whisper to each other, "I don't blame him. He knows people laugh at him because he doesn't have any children."

"Yes, I've changed my name to Abraham [father of a multitude]."

"This old man's gone off his rocker. He's nuts. Father of a multitude!"

In Hebrew there is a difference of only one letter between *Abram* and *Abraham*. That letter is just a breath mark. By changing his name, God was saying to Abram, "I'm going to change your name from 'father of many' to 'father of a multitude,' and I'm going to do it by breathing on you." God's breath on the barren life of Abram meant that the man who could have no child was able to have offspring as numerous as the stars in the sky and the sand on the seashore. Faith is able to bring the power of God into our barren lives. Faith sees the invisible, hears the inaudible, and accomplishes the impossible.

IL ABRAHAM'S TESTIMONY (11:13-16)

Hebrews11:13 begins with a plural pronoun: "These all died in faith." The writer was talking not just about Abraham, but about all of his offspring: Isaac, Jacob, and right on down the line.

A. Apparent Failure (11:13a)

When you look at the next phrase in verse 13, you see apparent failure: "Not having received the promises." In other words, God had made promises to Abraham that had not been fulfilled at the time of his death. God promised Abraham not only that He would give him a seed, but also that He would give him a land. God reiterated that promise to Isaac and Jacob. However, they too died before the promise was fulfilled. Yet they died in faith, still trusting God. It is important for us as believers not only to live by faith, but also to die by faith, believing the promises of God.

B. Appealing Future (11:13b-16)

"These all died in faith, not having received the promises, but having seen them afar off" (11:13). Abraham and his descendants looked out into the future by faith and were certain of the sureness of God's promises. They "were persuaded of them, and embraced them."

That word embraced literally means "greeted or welcomed." The original word was sometimes used to describe what a man on a ship coming close to shore would do; he would wave to his friends awaiting his arrival. At other times this word was used to describe what a returning wanderer would do; as his home appeared on the horizon, he would greet that home with joy. As God's people face the future we should say, "Hello, Promise. Hello, Heaven. Hello, Jesus." Are you embracing God's promises for the future?

Before Abraham and his descendants died, they had this testimony: They "confessed that they were strangers and pilgrims on the earth"

(11:13b). A stranger is someone who is away from home. A pilgrim is on a journey. That is the Bible's description of God's children in this world. This world is not our home. We really don't belong down here. A Christian is not a citizen of this world who is trying to make it to Heaven. A Christian is a citizen of Heaven passing through this world. That's why we ought not to get too attached to this old world. "They that say such things declare plainly that they seek a country" (11:14). The Living Bible says, "They were looking forward to their real home in heaven." That was the testimony of the Old Testament saints.

"If they had been mindful of that country from whence they came out, they might have had opportunity to have returned" (11:15). If they had wanted to, Abraham and the others could have gone back to where they had come from. It is possible for a believer to turn back to this world and live a worldly Christian life. But this verse is basically saying, Why would you want to do that? We need to remember what it was like back there —all the sin, shame, and sorrow.

Hebrews 11:16 says, "But now they desire a better country," a heavenly country. Earthly Canaan was just a picture of heavenly Canaan. They desired this better land, this heavenly land.

Because the Old Testament saints lived by faith, because they had a testimony on earth that they didn't belong here, that Heaven was their home, "God is not ashamed to be called their God" (11:16). That is a remarkable statement. God calls Himself the Father of Abraham, Isaac, and Jacob. He identifies Himself with them. He is not ashamed to call them His people. I wonder if God is proud to be known as our God. Romans 2:24 shakes me up every time I think of it. Paul was dealing with the inconsistent lives of those who named the name of the Lord Jesus Christ. He said, "The name of God is blasphemed among the Gentiles through you." How important it is for us to have a consistent testimony for Jesus. I don't want Him to be ashamed to call us His people.

III. ABRAHAM'S TEST (11:17-19)

Everything was going just great for Abraham. Little Isaac was growing up right there in front of his eyes. I can almost see Abraham's pleasure and joy. I can almost hear him saying, "O God, that's your promised son. Every time I look at that boy I remember your promise that you're going to make of us an innumerable seed." Then one day God came to Abraham and asked him to offer a sacrifice.

A. A Mysterious Offering (11:17-18)

"By faith Abraham, when he was tried" (11:17). That's a strange statement. James said that God tempts no man. Yet Genesis 22 says that God tempted Abraham. The Bible seems to be contradicting itself, but just remember the devil *tempts* us to bring out the worst in us; God *tests* us to bring out the best in us.

Can you imagine what Abraham went through when he was tried? God said, "Abraham, take thy son, thy only son, and offer him for a burnt offering on a mountain I will show thee." Abraham must have been stunned. Put yourself in his place. Here's a man who's been living for the Lord. He left the land of Ur to be a stranger and a pilgrim. Isaac was a miraculous answer to prayer. Then God says, "Take him up and sacrifice him on the altar."

I have a feeling that Abraham's world absolutely collapsed. The bottom fell out; the roof caved in; the walls crumbled. God's directive was hard to accept not only because of his great love for his son, but also because of the mysterious contradiction between the promise of God and the command of God. Sometimes we too go through trials that seem to be contradictory. On the one hand we have the love of God; on the other, the providence of God. They don't seem to match.

The Bible lays a curtain over what Abraham went through that night as he agonized in his heart over that apparent contradiction. Yet when the sun rose, he woke that boy up and they headed to mount Moriah.

I can almost see Abraham as he puts wood on his son's back. They start climbing that mountain and he says to his servants, "You stay here. We're going to worship; then Isaac and I will come back." He is still holding on to the promise. As they head up the mountain, the inevitable question comes: "Father, here's the wood, but where's the lamb for the offering?" In a great statement of faith Abraham says, "God will provide himself a lamb" (Gn 22:8). He takes Isaac and puts him on the altar. I can almost see the tears running down his face.

B, A Miraculous Outcome (11:19)

As Abraham and his son were coming up one side of the mountain, God was coming up the other side with a lamb. When Abraham raised that knife to plunge it into his son's heart, God said, "Abraham, look over there in the thicket." Abraham looked and saw a thorn-crowned lamb. God said, "Offer it,"

When he put that lamb on the altar and the fire was lit and the smoke ascended, I can see Abraham on his knees and hear him saying, "Oh God, I didn't know how you were going to do it, but I knew you were going to work out a way." "Accounting [calculating] that God was able" (11:19). What a statement. God is able.

"Can He help me with a wayward child?"

"Can He help me with this health problem?"

"Can He help me as I face death?"

Ephesians 3:20 says, "Unto him that is able to do exceeding abundantly above all that we ask or think." God is able.

Abraham counted on God being "able to raise him up, even from the dead; from whence also he received him in a figure" (11:19). God's solution to the trial that Abraham faced was resurrection. The solution to our own mysterious trials is resurrection and immortality. One of these days we're going to be resurrected and we're going to sit down in God's great school in Heaven. Then God will show us the whole picture. We're going to understand.

JERRY VINES

26

Dying in Faith Hebrews 11:20-22

The key ingredient in the lives of the individuals named in Hebrews 11 is faith. The Scripture says that all these people lived by faith, and they also died by faith (11:13).

Knowing the Lord Jesus as Savior touches every dimension of life. It touches the past because in Jesus the guilt and burden of past sin have been put away. It touches the present because it gives the potential to live for the Lord day by day. It touches the future because if we are saved, if we are under the blood of the Lord Jesus Christ, we have a wonderful future.

All of us have a future, whether we are lost or saved. We need to make sure we have a happy future. A little boy was taken by his parents to a pet shop to pick out a puppy. He looked at all of the puppy dogs and saw one with his tail wagging. "Daddy," he said, "I want the one with the happy ending." I want a future with a happy ending. Don't you? The only way you can have a happy ending is to know Jesus as your personal Savior.

Whether we are saved or lost, when we look at the future we see one disturbing matter: the reality of death. "It is appointed unto men once to die, but after this the judgment" (9:27). Unless the Lord Jesus Christ comes, that statement applies to every born-again believer as well as to lost people. Death is an appointment that every person sooner or later must face.

There are really only two ways anyone can die. He can die in his sins, or he can die in Christ. The Bible says that it is possible to die in faith. I believe that when the moment of death comes for the Christian, God will give him dying grace. Dying grace is what changes death from gloom to glory for the believer. "Precious in the sight of the Lord is the death of his saints" (Ps 116:15). Christians die with the grace of God surrounding them. With faith they reach out to claim the future God has in store for them.

One day when people were being very critical of the early Methodists, John Wesley said, "But they die well." If you are a child of God, I believe you will be able to die well. Wouldn't it be wonderful if your death could be a testimony to the grace of God and to what faith is able to do?

The lives of Isaac, Jacob, and Joseph were different, but they had one thing in common: the way they faced their deaths.

I. ISAAC: LONGING FAITH (11:20)

Isaac died with longing faith. "By faith Isaac blessed Jacob and Esau concerning things to come" (11:20). When Isaac came to die, he was still looking with confidence to the future.

What do we know about the life of Isaac? First, Isaac lived longer than Jacob and Joseph. Second, less is said about Isaac than about them. Just one short sentence in Hebrews and a chapter or so in Genesis are given to the life of Isaac.

A. A Common Man

Isaac was just an ordinary man. As someone has put it, Isaac was the ordinary son of a great father and the ordinary father of a great son. He was overshadowed by his father Abraham and his son Jacob. All we know about Isaac is that he was a well-digger. All along the way Isaac was digging wells of blessing so that other people could follow him and be refreshed.

We don't see much evidence of faith in the home life of Isaac. Nonetheless there must have been faith in the promises of God. Like his parents, for years he and his wife Rebekah didn't have a child. Surely they prayed and trusted God to give them an heir. Then God gave them twin sons, a double blessing.

If you don't have twins, in my opinion you don't know what living is. God gave us twins. Have you ever seen a mother or father trying to feed twins? It's a sight to behold, one in this highchair and one in that highchair. One starts yelling, and you pop food in his mouth; and then the other one starts yelling, and you pop food in her mouth. Double your pleasure, double your fun.

Isaac was doubly blessed, but his home life was full of deception and disruption. Isaac showed favoritism to his son Esau. Perhaps he saw in Esau the kind of man he himself had wanted to be. Esau was an outdoorsman, rugged and athletic, and maybe Isaac projected his own desires into the life of that boy. At little boys' ballgames, we sometimes encounter the sad spectacle of a father who is trying to live his athletic career through the life of his son. We would do well just to trust God and by faith let Him make our children what He wants them to be and not what we want them to be.

There is evidence that Isaac was very materialistic. It's a sad state of affairs if you have nothing but material things to leave to your children. It would be far better to leave them little materially but make them rich in the things of God. If you can pass faith on to your children, you're leaving them a great legacy.

Yet somehow below the materialistic surface there had to be faith in God in Isaac's life. Somehow, in spite of all the blunders he made, underneath was a vital, living link with Heaven that was based on faith. His faith was not prominent or obvious, yet we read that Isaac was a man who was able to die with faith.

B. A Confident Man

As Isaac approached the end of his life, his faith began to flower. What was formerly in seed form, and very small, somehow blossomed in the closing years of his life. I've seen that happen in the lives of Christians.

Years ago there was a man who was never really active in our church. He was a good man, but he didn't give evidence of the Lord in his life until he was diagnosed as having terminal cancer. Then a marvelous transformation began to take place in his life. The closer he got to death, the more his faith and confidence grew. Despite excruciating pain, he had great faith in God. Church members would visit him, not so much to be a blessing to him as to receive a blessing. Somehow his little faith greatly increased in those last days, and he died longing for Heaven. He died getting ready to go into the gates of glory.

You and I ought to leave testimonies for Jesus when we come to die. We ought to die with the promises of God blazing out there in front of us. We ought to die with longing faith as Isaac did.

II. JACOB: LEANING FAITH (11:21)

What kind of faith did Jacob have when he came to die? "By faith Jacob, when he was a dying, blessed both the sons of Joseph; and worshipped, leaning upon the top of his staff." He died leaning.

A. His Living

Jacob was a rascal, a con man, always trying to pull a deal, trying to bargain with God. If God hadn't saved Jacob, there's no telling what he would have been. He was a sight even after God saved him. But God started working on him to make him what he ought to be. If you are saved, God is not going to stop working on you until He gets you all the way into glory. The Bible says, "Being confident of this very thing, that he which hath begun a good work in you will perform it until the day of Jesus Christ" (Phil 1:6). He's working on us to make us more and more like the Lord Jesus.

As God was dealing with Jacob, there were times when his faith soared. There were other times when his faith tottered. We can identify with Jacob, since there are times when our faith is really strong and then there are other times when our faith is shaky and weak.

Although God was working in his life, Jacob was scheming and bargaining with God until he finally got in a wrestling match with the Lord. Jacob wouldn't give up; he wouldn't give in, so finally God touched him. The next morning Jacob came walking toward the sunrise limping. God had changed him.

B. His Leaving (11:21)

The most magnificent point of Jacob's life—the point chosen by the Holy Spirit to be recorded in the book of Hebrews—was not his living but his dying. Jacob was down in Egypt where his son Joseph had preceded him. When Jacob knew he was dying, he sent for Joseph who came with his two little sons, Jacob's citified grandboys. Their father was the prime minister of Egypt. They probably had everything they wanted. What in the world could an old country granddad from up there in Canaan's land leave to two grandboys? There those boys were, and the Bible says that Jacob died worshiping, leaning on his staff.

So what did he leave those boys as he was dying? Number one, he left them a testimony. In the book of Genesis, we read that the name of the Lord was on Jacob's lips. Jacob left them a testimony that he loved God. Number two, Jacob left them a treasure, his staff, a reminder that he was a pilgrim, just passin' through. We can imagine that after Jacob spoke his last words to his sons, that staff fell from his hands, he smiled up into the face of God, and he was gone into glory.

How do you want to die? I have seen some lost people die; they didn't have the staff of confidence in God in their lives and they faced the terrible horror of death without God. I'd like to die as Jacob did. We ought so to live that when we come to die we can sing, "I'm leaning on the everlasting arms."

One way God gets us ready to go to Heaven is the population shift. If we live long enough, we'll have more relatives and friends in Heaven than we have on earth, so we won't mind so much leaving here to go over there.

II. JOSEPH: LIBERATING FAITH (11:22)

"By faith Joseph, when he died, made mention of the departing [the exodus] of the children of Israel; and gave commandment concerning his bones." It's amazing that Joseph had any faith at all. He was betrayed by his brothers. He lived all his life in a strange land. He was lied about, mistreated, abused, and forgotten. Yet the Bible keeps saying, "And God was with him."

The vicissitudes that Joseph experienced might have made him bitter; instead, they made him better. It's not what happens that matters. What matters is whether our difficulties make us bitter or better. Joseph demonstrated a remarkable faith in God. The greatest evidence of his faith is found at his deathbed. Joseph died with liberating faith.

A. A Promised Exodus

Joseph died believing in the promised exodus. God had promised the Israelites that He would lead them out of that land of Egypt. He said He was going to carry them back into the promised land. So when Joseph reached the end of his life, he died believing the promise of God. He said, "God is going to liberate you. God is going to set you free." That's a good way to die —believing the promises of God.

Jesus died with words from the Scriptures on His lips. He said, "Father, into thy hands I commend my spirit" (Lu 23:46); He was quoting Psalm 31:5. We ought to spend time in the Bible every day feeding the words of God into our memory banks. Joseph died with the promised exodus on his tongue.

B. A Personal Exodus

Joseph said, "When you get ready to go, don't leave my bones down here." The Egyptian people may have wanted to put the embalmed body of Joseph in a royal tomb, since he was one of their national heroes, the man who had saved them during the famine. But Joseph had given a commandment concerning his bones. He left a memorial body. It reminded the Israelites that God had made a promise that one day He was going to liberate them from the land of Egypt. When the time for the exodus came, the Israelites got those old bones of Joseph and that coffin, and they carried them up to Shechem.

Jesus has left us a memorial body. When we partake of the Lord's supper, we celebrate a memorial body. It points us to the past, to what Jesus did when He died for our sins, and it points us to the future. "As often as ye eat this bread, and drink this cup, ye do shew the Lord's death till he come" (1 Cor 11:26). One of these days He's going to come for us. God is not going to leave our bones in this world. He will "change our vile body, that it may be fashioned like unto his glorious body" (Phil 3:21). We will have resurrection bodies. One of these days Jesus is going to take us out of this world, and He's going to carry us to the promised land. We will go out with a liberating faith.

JERRY VINES

27

Moses: Seeing the Invisible God
Hebrews 11:23-27

Moses, the man through whom God gave His people the law, is an illustration of the coming of the Savior who would bring in grace and truth (Jn 1:17). Hebrews gives a thumbnail sketch of Moses' great life of faith. The secret of greatness in anyone's life is dependence on God. There is no greatness in us, but greatness comes if we learn to live our lives by faith in God. We see that beautifully pictured in the life of Moses.

I. PARENTAL FAITH (11:23)

Hebrews 11:23 does not refer to the faith of Moses, but to the faith of Moses' parents. The story of Amram and Jochebed can be found in Exodus 2. There we read about the circumstances surrounding the birth of their son. It was not an easy time. Pharaoh had given a command that all of the firstborn sons of Israel were to be thrown into the Nile, crocodile-infested waters known as the river of death. Today you and I bring up children in dangerous times, in a world that is a river of pornography, a flood of alcohol, and an overwhelming storm of drug abuse.

A. Care

Unwilling for their child to die, Moses' parents hid him for three months. It would be hard to keep a baby quiet for that long. No doubt soldiers were listening for the sounds of newborns. I wonder if one day one of the parents remembered how Noah had built an ark to the saving of himself and his household. At any rate, when it was becoming more and more difficult to hide Moses, his parents made a little ark for their baby and put it in the Nile.

That is a beautiful picture of what we need to do for our children. We cannot protect our children from the world altogether. Sooner or later, they've got to go out on their own. All we can do is to try and get them in the ark of safety as we send them out.

Hebrews 11:23 says that Moses was a "proper child." Acts 7:20 calls him "exceeding fair." There was something unusual about this baby, something striking. Now most parents think their babies are beautiful, but with reference to Moses, there was some indication to his parents that God had His hands on him in a special way.

Of course, all babies are precious to the Lord, and we have a tremendous responsibility to bring them into an atmosphere of faith where God is honored, Jesus is loved, and the Bible is taught. Some parents leave their children to the mercy of the world. They allow their youngsters to watch television five hours a day and don't give them five minutes a day of Bible reading and prayer. Then these parents wonder why their children grow up to be pagans. We must work at the task of bringing up our boys and girls if we expect them to survive in the kind of world we are living in.

B. Courage

Hebrews 11:23 says, "They were not afraid of the king's commandment." There is something about becoming a parent that can produce courage in a person's life. I remember when our firstborn came along. The responsibility that was now mine hit me with striking solemnity. I was answerable to God for the kind of father I would be. You and I cannot create faith in our boys and girls, but we can create an atmosphere of faith so that when they come to the age of understanding, they can invite the Lord Jesus into their hearts.

Moses had a tremendous advantage, a head start. He was brought into the world by parents who had faith in God and committed him to the Lord when he was a baby.

II. PERSONAL FAITH (11:24-26)

When Moses' parents put him in that little boat, Pharaoh's daughter came—and about that time God must have pinched baby Moses and he cried. Her heart was touched, and she decided to adopt this little Hebrew boy. His mother was allowed to nurse him for a certain period of time, and then Pharaoh's daughter took him to the palace and brought him up as her son. Some people believe that Moses was in line to succeed Pharaoh, to be king of all the land of Egypt, which at that time was the most cultured, advanced, wealthy country on the face of the earth.

A. Confession (11:24)

But Hebrews 11:24 says that Moses, "when he was come to years, refused to be called the son of Pharaoh's daughter." That was his confession of faith —his own faith, not his parents' faith. Moses had been given all the advantages of Egyptian royalty. He was in an atmosphere of tremendous wealth. He was probably driving a crocodile Mercedes for all we know. An atmosphere of prosperity is a difficult place to nurture faith, so Moses' confession is impressive.

Materialism can be an enemy to the things of the Spirit. People can get so interested in material things that they fail to understand that truly lasting values are spiritual. Young people sometimes get the idea that if they can just get educated, get jobs that will pay them plenty of money, buy houses and expensive cars and gadgets and trinkets and toys, they will be happy. If they focus on those goals, however, when they come to the end of their lives, they will look back on a wasted, meaningless existence. There is more to life than material things, however. Houses, cars, televisions, and VCRs won't make you happy, although they may make you comfortable. God never intended for a round world to fit a triangle heart. Only a triune God can satisfy that vacuum in the human heart. The man who devotes himself to filling his pockets, allows his heart to go empty.

All through those growing-up years, although Moses was raised in a materialistic atmosphere, he knew who he was. He knew where he came from and who his true mother was. He remembered what she had taught him.

Moses was exposed to an atheistic, humanistic culture and educational system. There was a university of Heliopolis in Egypt. Ten thousand students from all over the world swarmed into that school. It was the Harvard of the ancient world. And Acts 7:22 says that Moses was trained in all the wisdom of the Egyptians.

What did they teach him? They taught him their theory of evolution. We might think that evolution is something recent, that it originated with Darwin. But there have been theories of evolution throughout the centuries. The Egyptians would have taught Moses that human beings came from a worm that crawled out of the Nile. That was their theory of the origin of life.

But Moses knew better than that. He knew that "in the beginning God created the heaven and the earth" (Gn 1:1). God's account of the creation of the world was given through Moses. Yet in the first two chapters of Genesis, nothing even remotely resembles the theories of the university of Heliopolis. Where did Moses get his information about the existence of the universe and its creation? God revealed it to him. Moses was given all the educational and material advantages of Egypt.

Yet when he grew up, Moses decided to turn away from his princely status. (Can you imagine the shock that must have gone through Egypt?) We ought so to nurture our boys and girls that when they come to maturity they will make unashamed confession that they belong to the Lord Jesus Christ. We ought to teach our children who they are and where they came from. They need to know that they are not some higher form of animal, but a creation of God; they need to know that in eternity they will come face to face with the God of this universe.

Sunday school teachers may go home feeling that they're not doing a bit of good. But I've got news for them. They are doing a lot more than they think they are. When I was a fifteen-year-old, they couldn't keep a teacher for our class. We ran them all off. But then they put a man in our Sunday school class who loved Jesus and loved boys and knew that boys would be boys. Some things that man said lodged in my heart. I have not forgotten them to this day.

Parents, keep putting the Word of the Lord into your children. Keep standing for Jesus. Don't let your children go the way of this world. Don't get discouraged. Hang in there. All of those things you've been teaching your children will come to fruition one of these days and they will be a magnificent testimony.

B. Choice (11:25)

Moses made a choice. "Choosing rather to suffer affliction with the people of God, than to enjoy the pleasures of sin for a season." The word *choosing* there means "calculating, giving careful thought." Napoleon said that in a battle there is always a crisis period, ten or fifteen minutes when decisions are made that will ultimately decide the outcome of the battle. Life is like that. There are some crisis points when decisions are made that will have great impact on the course of one's life.

Moses came to that moment of decision, and he made his choice. He moved out of the finery of the palace of Egypt to one of the little huts inhabited by the humble people of God. It's better to be a pauper for Jesus than a millionaire for the devil. The pleasures of sin are only for a season. Anyone who chooses not to suffer affliction with the people of God is a fool; he is choosing temporary pleasure instead of eternal pleasure.

C. Calculation (11:26)

Moses compared Heaven and Hell, and he chose Heaven. "Esteeming the reproach of Christ greater riches than the treasures in Egypt: for he had respect unto the recompense of the reward." Moses looked away from the treasures of Egypt. He was wise because he looked at his life not on the basis of things he could see, but on the basis of things out there beyond. Moses compared the temporary pleasures of this life with the eternal riches of the Lord Jesus Christ, and he chose Christ. Every person comes to that moment of decision: Will I choose the treasures and temporary pleasures of this world, or will I choose eternal life?

III. PURPOSEFUL FAITH (11:27)

"By faith he forsook Egypt, not fearing the wrath of the king." The day came when Moses led the children of Israel out of Egypt toward the promised land. He started on a purposeful journey. His life became an adventure.

A. Venture

Moses turned his back on Egypt and ventured forth. He did not fear the wrath of the king because he had a purpose in his life. Moses was one of the Old Testament saints who confessed that they were strangers and pilgrims on this earth. Do you know the difference between a pilgrim and a tramp? A tramp just wanders around not knowing where he is going. A pilgrim just passes through, and he knows where he is going.

B. Vision

What kept Moses going? "He endured, as seeing him who is invisible." He looked at this world's dangers and they held no fear for him because he saw the invisible. He kept his eyes on the Lord and kept moving forward toward the promised land.

28

Faith is Forever the Victory
Hebrews 11:28-31

The eleventh chapter of Hebrews shows how faith works in the lives of real people. When we are saved, we are to start living our lives on a different basis. We are now to live on the basis of faith. "This is the victory that overcometh the world, even our faith" (1 Jn 5:4). You and I cannot live in our own strength; the problems and difficulties of life are too severe. We have to depend on God daily.

The little phrase *by faith* keeps recurring in Hebrews 11. By faith Abraham did this. By faith Jacob did that. By faith Moses did this. By faith the children of Israel did that. The chapter shows what faith can do in the lives of individuals and in the life of an entire nation.

I. FAITH BRINGS US *OUT:* CALVARY (11:28)

"Through faith he kept the passover, and the sprinkling of blood, lest he that destroyed the firstborn should touch them." By faith Moses observed the first Passover. Exodus 12 gives the historical account of Passover. The children of Israel were in the land of Egypt, and God sent Moses to Pharaoh with the message, "Let my people go." When Pharaoh refused, God sent a series of plagues to Egypt. The tenth plague was to be the death of all the firstborn in the land. However, God instituted a special ceremony—the Passover feast—to help His people in this crisis. As part of the Passover observance, a lamb was to be slain and the blood applied to the door frame of each Hebrew home. The death angel would see the blood and pass over those homes, leaving their firstborn unscathed. That Old Testament experience illustrates the power of the blood of Jesus Christ to cleanse us from our sins.

The blood of the Passover lamb had to be shed and sprinkled.

A. Shed

The Israelites were to take "every man *a* lamb, according to the house of their fathers, *a* lamb for an house" (Ex 12:3, italics added). In Exodus 12:3-5, there is a progression of thought: verse 3 refers to *a* lamb; verse 4 refers more specifically to *the* lamb; and verse 5 refers more personally to *your* lamb. All through the centuries lambs were offered on Jewish altars, but when John the Baptist saw the Lord Jesus Christ coming to the river Jordan he said, "Behold *the* Lamb of God, which taketh away the sin of the world" (Jn 1:29, italics added). Jesus is *the* Savior, and you need Him to be *your* Savior.

The lamb in Exodus 12:3 was to be a substitute. The slaying of the lamb that night took the place of the death of the firstborn. That is the meaning of the cross. Jesus Christ died on that cross not for His sins, but for our sins. Jesus is our substitute. Jesus took our place.

The Passover lamb had to be "without blemish" (Ex 12:5). That flawless lamb reminds us that Jesus had to be sinless to be our substitute. If Jesus had sinned, He would have been dying for His own sins. But the Bible says that although He was tempted, He did not sin. When Jesus died, all our sins were laid on Him. "God commendeth his love toward us, in that, while we were yet sinners, Christ died for us" (Rm 5:8).

Exodus 12:6 tells us the lamb had to be slaughtered. It was not enough for Jesus to live a perfect life; it was necessary that His blood be shed. The fact that His life was exemplary contains in and of itself no salvation. The lamb had to be slain. "Christ our passover is sacrificed for us" (1 Cor 5:7).

B. Sprinkled

It was the sprinkling of the blood over the doorposts of the homes of the children of Israel that protected them when the death angel passed over (Ex 12:7). "When I see the blood, I will pass over you" (Ex 12:13). The blood of the lamb had to be applied. Only those living where the blood was applied were saved when the death angel passed over.

I do not understand it, but in some mystical way, when by faith we invite Jesus Christ into our lives, the blood of Jesus is applied to our hearts, our lives, our consciences. We are covered by the blood of Jesus and "there is therefore now no condemnation to them which are in Christ Jesus" (Rm 8:1). Faith in the blood of the Passover lamb brought the children of Israel out. Faith in Jesus Christ brings us out of sin and death.

II. FAITH BRINGS US *THROUGH:* BRAVERY (11:29)

Faith also brings us through, as illustrated in the account of the children of Israel passing through the Red Sea. After being in bondage for years, they were on their way to the promised land. Then they came to a dead end. Right in front of them was the Red Sea.

Meanwhile back at the palace, Pharaoh began to have second thoughts about letting them go. The Israelites were his slaves doing all the work building his treasured cities. Pharaoh had given them permission to leave the land and now he was without a labor force. So, just like in an old cowboy western, Pharaoh went after them. The Israelites looked in front of them and there was the Red Sea. They looked behind them and there was Pharaoh.

A. Brave Saints

Hebrews 11:29 is a picture of brave saints. Becoming a Christian does not remove the difficulties of life. We all need to learn the lesson that we can trust God to bring us through the difficulties.

What do you do when the waters of danger and difficulty are swirling around you? In Exodus 14 we read what God told Moses to tell the people to do: Be still. I don't know about you, but the last thing I want to do when I have difficulties is to be still. In fact, what I usually want to do is run. I want to get just as far from that situation as I can. But God said, "Stand still, and see the salvation of the Lord" (Ex 14:13).

You and I panic, but God doesn't panic. There are no panics in Heaven, only plans. God knew all the time what He was doing. He said, "Okay, Moses. Take that rod and pass it over the Red Sea." When Moses did that, God sent an east wind and the waters of the Red Sea parted right in front of their eyes. God said to the children of Israel, "Go forward." They took that step into the Red Sea, with the waters on each side of them, and walked though on dry ground.

We all have times when we don't know what to do. We feel trapped in circumstances; there's nowhere to move. However, God is going to part the waters for us. Just be patient. Talk to the Lord and put your confidence in Him. He's got a plan He's working out and just when you think you're going under, you'll go through. It's exciting when God parts the waters.

B. Brazen Sinners

The Egyptians, Scripture says, tried to follow the Israelites through the Red Sea. But the same waters that delivered the Israelites drowned those brazen Egyptians. These waters remind us of the death, burial, and resurrection of Jesus. Because of Jesus there is victory through the storms and waters of life's difficulties for the believer. But the waters do not open up for those who do not put their faith in the Lord Jesus Christ. Unbelief meets the waters and experiences only destruction.

III. FAITH BRINGS US *IN*: VICTORY (11:30-31)

After the children of Israel wandered in the wilderness for about forty years, they crossed the river Jordan and entered Canaan, the promised land. The first thing they encountered in the promised land was a formidable obstacle—the city of Jericho. Obstacles often stand in the way of new Christians, but faith can give them victory over opposition.

Jericho was a magnificent stronghold. The walls of Jericho were impregnable, insurmountable. What were the children of Israel going to do? God said, "Here's what I want you to do. I want you to get in a long line. I want the priests to carry rams' horns (trumpets), and I want you to walk around the walls of Jericho once a day for six days. I want the priests to blow the horns, but don't you folks say a word."

"What was that, Lord? Are you sure that's what you want us to do? It doesn't look like it will do too much good."

Can you imagine what the people of Jericho thought as they stood on the walls of their city and looked down at that bunch? Can you imagine anything sillier than grown people walking around a wall and blowing trumpets? But they obeyed God. Faith is doing what God says to do.

A. Collapse of a Stronghold (11:30)

On the seventh day God said, "Go around the wall six times and don't make a sound, but the seventh time shout when the priests blow the trumpets." The children of Israel shouted, the walls of Jericho came tumbling down, and God's people went in and took the stronghold. That's what faith does. Faith brings us in.

Second Corinthians 10:4 says, "The weapons of our warfare are not carnal, but mighty through God to the pulling down of strong holds." Because of this victory over Jericho, Canaan is a picture of the believer's life of overcoming faith.

B. Conversion of a Sinner (11:31)

Today we brag about things that ought to make us ashamed. The harlot Rahab would probably be the heroine of a TV series or the subject of a bestseller. Rahab was a Gentile, an outcast, a prostitute, a woman under condemnation, living in a city under condemnation. But Rahab had heard what God did at the Red Sea and believed it. She demonstrated her faith by hiding the spies. Because of that, God spared her life when Jericho fell. He took her from the house of shame to the hall of fame. Rahab is included in the family tree of the Lord Jesus Christ (Mt 1:5). That's what Jesus can do for a sinner.

JERRY VINES

29

Always Striving to be Faithful
Hebrews 11:32-40

The motto of the United States Marines is *Semper Fidelis,* "Always Faithful." It should be said of God's people that we are always faithful. "Moreover it is required in stewards, that a man be found faithful" (1 Cor 4:2). That motto could be put as a heading over Hebrews 11 because there we are given a roll call of heroes of the faith—people who in a variety of circumstances, in spite of their weaknesses and failures, learned what it is to live by faith in God.

Through verse 31, Hebrews 11 is a survey of Old Testament characters who lived their lives trusting in God. Then verse 32 just says, "And what shall I more say? for the time would fail me to tell of . . ." The rest of the chapter is just a summary, so, I too will just summarize.

The main point of Hebrews 11:32-40 is that the life of faith is possible to all believers. Regardless of how weak you think you are, it is possible to live your life by daily dependence on God. The life of faith is not a luxury that only some believers can experience. It is a necessity for all of God's people. We need faith to conquer, faith to continue, and faith to conclude.

I. FAITH TO CONQUER (11:32-35)

In Hebrews 11:32-35 are statements about people who had faith to overcome or conquer. Some are referred to by name and others by fame.

A. By Name (11:32)

The writer named six people and summarized the Old Testament period of the judges, kings, and prophets. These six were ordinary people, weak in many ways, yet they learned the secret of living their lives by dependence on God.

One of these characters is Gideon. His life is an illustration of faith that conquers, faith that overcomes. Gideon was a weak, fearful man. He was afraid because the Midianites had invaded the land and were threatening to overcome the people of God.

When we first meet Gideon in the Bible, he is hiding down in the winepress, threshing grain. I don't know if you understand anything about threshing grain or not, but I want to tell you that you don't do it down in the winepress. The winepress is down in the valley. You thresh grain up on the mountaintop where the wind blows. When you throw the grain up in the air, the wind blows the chaff away.

Gideon was throwing the grain up and it was coming down on his head. He didn't exactly look like a hero of the faith. The Lord came to this weak, scared man and said, "The Lord is with thee, thou mighty man of valour" (Jud 6:12).Gideon probably looked around to see whom the Lord was talking to. The Lord said that He was going to win a great victory through him. Then Gideon began to apologize and complain. In fact he said, "Where are the miracles?" Here the Lord was, appearing to him in the form of an angel and Gideon said, "Where are the miracles?" We are all like that sometimes, aren't we? Sometimes God does something right before our eyes and we wonder, "Where is God?"

The Lord said to Gideon, "I'm going to win a great victory for you, and you're going to overcome the Midianites." After being assured that God was with him, Gideon gathered an army of 32,000 men. But the Lord said, "Gideon, that's too many." They were outnumbered about ten to one, yet God said, "Too many. Gideon, tell any soldiers who are afraid to go on home; we don't need them." So 22,000 took off.

Then the Lord came to him a second time and said, "Gideon, you still have too big a crowd." God told him to take all the soldiers down to the stream for a drink of water. Some of them got down on their hands and knees to drink directly from the stream, totally unprepared if the enemy should come while they drank. Others recognized that they should always be prepared for the enemy, so they scooped up the water with their hands. Another 9,700 were sent home. Only 300 were left.

Next morning God said, "Gideon, I'm going to use that little handful of men to win a great victory over the Midianites." What was God doing? He was teaching Gideon what you and I have to learn. Victory is not won by our strength, but by the strength and power of God. God uses the Christian who, though weak in himself, understands that by faith he can claim the power of a great God.

Gideon and his little army surrounded the army of the Midianites. Each of Gideon's men had a pitcher in one hand and a trumpet in the other. There were lamps inside the pitchers. At the signal the Israelites broke the pitchers, held the lamps up, blew the trumpets, and shouted, "The sword of the Lord, and of Gideon" (Jud 7:20) and when they did, God gave them a great victory. Like Gideon and his men, you and I need to depend on God for victory instead of drawing on our own resources.

B. By Fame (11:33-35)

Except for the six people mentioned in verse 32, the names of those who learned to conquer by faith aren't given, but we can guess who they are. Hebrews 11:33 begins, "Who through faith subdued king¬ doms." We can be sure one of those unnamed heroes is Moses, who brought the nation of Egypt to its knees by faith.

The passage continues, "Who through faith . . . wrought righteousness [lived upright lives], obtained promises, stopped the mouths of lions." That could have been said about Daniel. "Who through faith . . . Quenched the violence of fire." This is obviously a reference to the three Hebrew children who walked into the king's fiery furnace. Because they trusted God to lead them through and to lead them out, they emerged without a hair singed.

"Who through faith . . . escaped the edge of the sword." Maybe that was David fleeing from the sword of Saul. "Who through faith . . . waxed valiant in fight, turned to flight the armies of the aliens." That's probably Joshua.

"Women received their dead raised to life again." Remember the woman of Shunem whose son had died? Elisha, the man of God, asked, "Is it well with thee? is it well with thy husband? is it well with the child?" Of course, it wasn't well. Her child was dead. Yet in a great statement of faith in God she said, "It is well" (2 Ki 4:26).

"Others were tortured, not accepting deliverance." The Greek word translated "tortured" means "to stretch out and to beat with rods." In Bible days sometimes people would be stretched over torture racks and beaten with sticks. So, the reference here is to God's people who encountered great hardship. Yet the Bible says they refused to surrender their faith in God for temporary deliverance, "that they might obtain a better resurrection" (v. 35).

The point of these illustrations is to show us that faith enables us to conquer. "This is the victory that overcometh the world, even our faith" (1 Jn 5:4).

IL FAITH TO CONTINUE (11:36-38)

We have been thinking about the victories of faith. Now we discover the perplexities of faith.

A. The Woe of Endurance (11:36-37)

The faithful people in Hebrews 11:36-38 don't look like winners; they look like losers. Instead of victory, their lives seem to be full of perplexity. Instead of a faith that escapes, theirs was a faith that has to endure.

"Cruel mockings"—they were sarcastically attacked. "Scourgings"— they were beaten. "Bonds and imprisonment"— they were thrown into jail. "Sawn asunder"—there's a tradition that the prophet Ezekiel was sawed in two with a wooden saw.

"They wandered about in sheepskins and goatskins; being destitute" —they suffered need. "Afflicted"—they were under unbelievable pressure. "Tormented"—they were treated evilly by others. These quotes from Hebrews 11:36-37 don't sound like the language of victory, but they are realistic descriptions of the life of faith.

We need faith not only to conquer but also to continue when there are difficulties. We need faith to hang on when things don't seem to be working out. Some teach that faith always helps us remove obstacles, whatever they are; if we have enough faith, we can be delivered from any trials that come our way. People with that point of view have problems with a passage like this.

B. The Worth of Endurance (11:38)

Notice the contrast in Hebrews 11:34 and 37. Some people escaped the edge of the sword. Other people were slain with the sword. Did the latter group not have enough faith?

Sometimes preachers want to make us think that if we have enough faith we can be healthy, wealthy, and wise. But that won't harmonize with the teachings of the New Testament. I believe with all my heart that God heals people; any time someone is healed, God does the healing. All healing comes from God, but sometimes God doesn't choose to heal. God is not a cosmic bellboy who sits around waiting for us to tell Him what to do. God is the Sovereign of this universe, and He knows what is best for our lives.

Some people are preaching today that if you give your life to Jesus, He'll make you a celebrity. The truth is, if you give your life to Jesus, you may never be heard of again. You may end up on some foreign mission field telling people in a jungle about the Lord Jesus Christ.

Well, are we going to give up and quit because we're not healthy, wealthy, and famous? No. We need faith to continue. We need to remember that sometimes God chooses to deliver us in response to faith, but other times He chooses not to deliver us. Sometimes God will lead us through a difficulty, and other times He'll leave us in a difficulty. Sometimes it takes more faith to endure than to overcome.

It's the easiest thing in the world to have faith in God when everything's going your way. It's great to live with God when your family is in good health. But what are you going to do when a loved one doesn't get well? You pray, pray, pray, but instead of getting better he gets worse? Are you going to throw your faith overboard?

You'll never know what the strength of your faith is until it's put to the test. Faith never really reveals its character, its caliber, in the sunshine. It's the rainy day and the shadows and darkness that show whether you have the faith that continues. 1 want to be true to the Lord regardless of what happens.

Look at the people in Hebrews 11:36-37. They didn't get in anybody's *Who's Who*. But verse 38 says the world was not worthy of them. This world looks at God's people and thinks they are unworthy. The uppity-ups may think that you don't count. You haven't been to their schools. You're not part of their social circles. You may not count down here, but if you love Jesus Christ you count up there. This world learns too late who its real heroes are.

So if this world doesn't appreciate you, that's all right—because God does. Continue on. If you don't have much of this world's goods, that's all right—because you have treasures laid up for you in Heaven. Continue on.

III. FAITH TO CONCLUDE (11:39-40)

A. The Promise (11:39)

"And these all, having obtained a good report through faith, received not the promise." Although they did not receive the promise, they continued. They had faith that concludes. Someone said, "A faith that falters before the finish had a fatal flaw from the first."

Not one Old Testament character saw the consummation of his faith before he died. The Old Testament saints experienced the fulfillment of many of the great promises of God, but not *The* promise. God had told them, "I'm going to send a Savior," but every one of these people died before the promise came.

B. The Perfection (11:40)

"God having provided some better thing for us." We're right back to the beginning of the book of Hebrews where the emphasis was that what we have in Christ is better. The Old Testament saints were saved by faith looking forward to Christ. You and I are saved by faith looking backward to Christ. They were saved by what Christ would do. We are saved by what Christ has done. They died holding on to the promise that God would send them a Savior. We can face death because we put our confidence and faith in things we cannot see. Since we have given our lives to Jesus, we have a reason to live and we will have a hope in the hour of death.

JERRY VINES

30

Ready...Set...Go for the Gold!
Hebrews 12:1-3

The first three verses of Hebrews 12 are really the climax of Hebrews 11. Chapter and verse divisions were added many years after the text of the New Testament was given. The purpose of such divisions was to enable readers to find a particular passage quickly. Often these man-made divisions help us, but other times they obscure the fact that a certain chapter or verse relates to what precedes it. One way to pick up such a connection is the word *wherefore*. Every time we see a *wherefore* in the Bible, we must ask ourselves what the *wherefore* is there for. It will always point to something previously said.

The successful Christian life is described with many figures of speech and various images in the New Testament. For instance, Christian living is compared to being a soldier. "Endure hardness, as a good soldier of Jesus Christ" (2 Ti 2:3). Christian living is also described as being part of a family. We read about being born again, being born into God's family; we are encouraged to grow and mature into full stature as children of God. Elsewhere Christians are compared to a flock of sheep and the Lord Jesus is called the Good Shepherd. We are to follow Him and be obedient just as sheep follow their shepherd. In Hebrews 12:1 Christians are compared to runners in a race: "Let us run with patience the race that is set before us." The apostle Paul used that same figure of speech in 1 Corinthians 9:24-26 and Philippians 3:13-14. We are to run to obtain the prize, to strive for Christlikeness.

The great theme of Hebrews is to encourage us to go on to maturity. Hebrews 6:1 specifically states, "Let us go on unto perfection." All through this letter the call keeps coming: Let's not be satisfied with where we are; let's move on; let's get on with the business of living the Christian life to the fullest extent.

I. OUR ENCOURAGEMENT (12:1a)

Great encouragement is given to us in this pursuit of maturity: "Wherefore seeing we also are compassed about with so great a cloud of witnesses." Here we have a picture of a stadium like the ones packed to capacity with crowds who come to view the greatest athletes in the world compete in the Olympics. They work very hard, and their goal is to win the gold medal. They are going for the gold.

In this verse the "cloud of witnesses" refers to the spectators who have come to watch the race. The spectators are the saints who have already gone on before. Some of these spectators are listed in Hebrews 11. They are the great heroes and spiritual athletes of the Lord who competed successfully in the game of life.

A. Their Experience

Those witnesses are encouragers to us who come along after them. They encourage us because of their experience of living successfully for the Lord. If they could do it, we can do it. I like to read the biographies of great Christians and see what God did in their lives because it encourages me. If other people who were just ordinary, mundane, down-to-earth people could live for Jesus and have successful Christian lives, then I can too. The roll call of the faithful in Hebrews 11 has the same effect. The faith of those heroes is intended to be a motivating factor for us. There is a wonderful difference between running the race for Jesus and running in the Olympics. In an Olympic event only one person can get the gold. But in the Christian life, every one of us can get the gold. Every one of us can be a winner for the Lord Jesus Christ.

B. Their Expertise

Let's suppose that you are going to run a race and the stadium is filled to capacity. You look up in that stadium and you see Joe Blow. Joe Blow is out of shape; he has never run a race in his life; he has a good bit of weight on him; and he is out there yelling, "Come on, you can do it! You can do it!" Sitting next to Joe Blow is the great Olympic runner, Carl Lewis. Carl knows what's involved, what it takes to be a winner, and he's up there in the stands personally encouraging you. There would be a lot more encouragement in seeing Carl Lewis cheering for you than in seeing Joe Blow.

Similarly in our Christian lives those who have been successful in living for the Lord are the most influential. I don't want my life to be a discouragement to others. I want my life to be an encouragement.

We are circled about with a great cloud of witnesses, but they are not just ordinary spectators in the stands. And these Old Testament believers are not merely sitting up there watching us. They are also witnesses *to* us. They are saying, "You can do it! You can win! You can be successful!"

II. OUR ENLISTMENT (12:1b)

Twice in Hebrews 12:1 the writer said, "Let us." "Let us lay aside every weight, and the sin which doth so easily beset us, and let us run with patience the race that is set before us." With that little phrase the writer was enlisting us. He was saying, "I want you to get involved in the race. I want you to become a participant in successfully living the Christian life." You can just wander through the Christian life or you can join the race and be everything God wants you to be. There's a negative and a positive side to running the race.

A. The Negative Side (12:1b)

"Let us lay aside every weight, and the sin which doth so easily beset us." If you are going to win the race for Jesus, you've got to be able to lay aside the things that encumber you. The word translated *weight* was used by medical writers in Bible times to refer to excess body weight. You have to lay aside excess weight.

A friend of mine told his doctor, "I've got back trouble." The doctor examined him and said, "No, you don't have back trouble; you have front trouble. You have excess weight up front, and if you lose it, your back will feel better."

Olympic runners have very little body fat. Every muscle is fine-tuned; they are sleek and thin, in absolutely perfect condition. Successful athletes have to diet and exercise off the extra weight that encumbers them. And a great deal of exertion and sacrifice are required if you are going to live successfully for the Lord Jesus Christ.

What keeps us as Christians from being what we ought to be? Self. Self encumbers us from living for the Lord Jesus. That's why Jesus said you ought to deny yourself. John the Baptist, one of the great athletes for Jesus, once said about Him, "He must increase, and I must decrease." This is the ME generation. We are narcissistic; we are self-centered; we live for ourselves; we talk about ourselves. For example, too many people contemplating divorce forget about their children; they just think, *How is this going to affect me?*

The writer of Hebrews may have been talking about self, but he may also have been talking about anything that would hinder us from running the race successfully for Jesus. The things that encumber us are not necessarily bad. Good things that have gotten out of proportion can encumber us.

I enjoy a good banana split. In fact, I try to have one a week. But if I were getting ready for the Olympics, I would have to lay that enjoyment aside because I couldn't gain the excess weight that a banana split would add to my body and expect to compete successfully.

Some people like to fish. A member of my church once told me, "The reason two-thirds of the earth is water and one-third land is because the Lord expects us to fish about two-thirds of the time." Some men feel that way. But if you let fishing come in the way of living for Jesus, then that's a weight you ought to lay aside.

I always look forward to football season. There's nothing wrong with football unless you let it come between you and Jesus. If you miss church on Sunday because of football, and you read sports magazines more than the Word of God, then your sports-addiction is a weight that you need to lay aside.

We also need to lay aside things that entangle us, "the sin which doth so easily beset us." (Some Bible commentators believe that "the sin" is the sin of unbelief. Of course, that is an entangling sin.) The writer wanted us to picture a runner laying aside a long, flowing robe. We don't see Olympic track stars running in overcoats. They may be wearing all kinds of paraphernalia before they compete, but when it comes time to run, athletes lay aside every bit of excess clothing. They'll be as thinly clad as possible.

As Christians we still have the tendency to sin. It can be a surprise to a new Christian when he realizes how easy it still is for him to sin. The Bible says if you come to the Lord, He will forgive you of your sins, so you come forward and accept Jesus as your personal Savior. Then you discover that sin still does so easily beset us; it is still possible to do what we ought not to do.

Sin is a tragedy whether it is committed by a lost person or a saved person, but I think it's a bigger tragedy when a saved person sins. Lost people sometimes don't know any better. For example, they may use bad language without being aware of what they are saying; it's the only vocabulary they have. They're just talking the way they normally talk. That's their nature. But a saved person has a new nature. When he sins, it hurts his testimony. It keeps him from competing successfully for the Lord Jesus.

B. The Positive Side (12:1b)

"Let us run with patience the race that is set before us." The Lord has a plan for your life, a race that is set before you. There are probably seven or eight lanes on a track, and every runner is assigned a specific lane. When the gun fires and the race begins, the runner is to stay in his lane. God has a great plan for your life. Why take anything that is second best when you can have God's best?

Each young person ought to pray for the mate God wants to send him. He ought to ask the Lord what job He wants him to do. If He wants him to be a businessman, he should run his business for Jesus. If He wants him to be a teacher, he should teach school for Jesus. It doesn't matter what he does as long as he does what God wants him to do and gives it his very best.

Our tendency is to get our eyes on the other runners in the race. We want to see how everybody else is doing. We're pretty good at checking out all the others. But Jesus says, "Don't worry about the other runners in the race. You keep your eyes on Me." "Let us run with patience." *Patience* here means "endurance." The Christian race is not a dash; it's a marathon. Some new converts head out in a mad dash and then somewhere along the way they fizzle out. Paul must have had them in mind when he said, "Ye did run well; who did hinder you?" (Ga 5:7)

We're in a distance run, so let us run with endurance and not stop until we hit the tape at the finish line.

III. OUR ENABLEMENT (12:2-3)

A divine enablement is provided to make it possible for us to run the Christian life successfully.

A. Looking to Jesus (12:2)

"Looking unto Jesus." We have a divine enabler, the Lord Jesus Christ, and we are to keep our eyes on Him. You can't win a race if you're looking back. If you want to be a loser in the Christian life, get your eyes off Jesus. The Bible says we are to look unto Jesus—the author (the one who started the race) and the finisher (the one who has completed the race). He gets us in the race and starts us off. Then when we come down to the end of the track, guess who's going to be there to greet us. Jesus. I like that.

B. Learning from Jesus (12:2-3)

We can learn from Jesus' example of endurance. "Who for the joy that was set before him endured the cross, despising the shame." Nothing was more despicable than death by crucifixion. Why was Jesus willing to die that kind of death? The Bible says He was willing to endure the shame because of the joy that was set before Him. Jesus saw that by His death He would have the joy of seeing you and me coming to know Him. Jesus had us in mind when He died. The thief on the cross said, "Lord, remember me when thou comest into thy kingdom." Jesus replied, "To day shalt thou be with me in paradise" (Lu 23:42-43). That was the joy that was set before Him.

Hebrews 12:3 says, "Consider him." Set your mind on Him. Contemplate Him. Think of Him who "endured such contradiction of sinners against himself, lest ye be wearied and faint in your minds." The next time you are criticized, remember Him. The next time you are mistreated, consider Him. The next time you are lied about, think of Him. If anyone ever had a right to give up, be bitter, and quit in the race of life, it was the Lord Jesus Christ. But He didn't falter or fail. The Lord Jesus Christ went straight to the goal, to the cross.

So when you and I are tempted to quit in the Christian life, we must consider Him and not give up. One of these days we are going to be like Paul. He said, "I have fought a good fight, I have finished my course, I have kept the faith: Henceforth there is laid up for me a crown of righteousness, which the Lord, the righteous judge, shall give me at that day" (2 Ti 4:7-8). One of these days you and I are going to hit the tape and the great God of Heaven is going to call us up and give us the gold.

JERRY VINES

31

God's Loving Chastisement
Hebrews 12:4-13

A lot of people share a misconception. They look on God only as a God of love. Certainly it is true that God is a God of love, but He is also a holy God. The Bible makes clear that our holy God considers sin a serious matter, not only in the life of a lost person, but also in the life of a believer.

Numbers 32:23 says, "Be sure your sin will find you out." Somewhere along the way, your sin is going to catch up with you—in your body, in your emotions, or both. The primary reference in this verse in Numbers was to the children of Israel, God's chosen people; God does not ignore in His children what He deals with in an unsaved world.

Amos 3:2 indicates that God is especially interested in the matter of sin in the lives of believers: "You only have I known of all of the families of the earth: therefore I will punish you for all your iniquities." Hebrews 12:4, whatever else it may mean, certainly means that sin in the life of a Christian is such a serious, damaging matter that he ought to fight against it—resist it even to the point of shedding blood.

According to the Bible, judgment is threefold for believers. One judgment is past. Two thousand years ago God judged us as sinners in the person of His Son, the Lord Jesus Christ. "There is therefore now no condemnation [no judgment] to them which are in Christ Jesus" (Rm 8:1). Our judgment as sinners has already taken place.

The Bible also teaches that in the future God is going to judge us as servants. When we are saved, we are called on to serve the Lord Jesus Christ. Servants are accountable to their master for the caliber of their service. So one day there is going to be a judgment seat of Christ (2 Cor 5:10). You and I are heading for an examination day.

There is also a present judgment; God deals with us right now as sons (1 Cor 11:30-32). When we sin as believers, as members of the family of God, as God's children, the Bible teaches we are to judge ourselves. We are to deal with that sin based on 1 John 1:9. The moment we do something we ought not to do, we ought to go to God and ask Him to forgive us and cleanse us.

But suppose we don't do that. Suppose we let sin linger in our hearts. Then what does the Bible say? "But when we are judged [if we do not judge ourselves], we are chastened of the Lord, that we should not be condemned with the world" (1 Cor 11:32). When we do not deal with our sins, God will deal with them by chastising us. Chastisement is what Hebrews 12:4-13 is about. Let us consider three statements from these verses.

I. A FORGOTTEN TRUTH (12:5-6)

Statement number one: Chastisement is a forgotten truth. Hebrews 12:5 says, "Ye have forgotten the exhortation [from Proverbs 3:11-12]." The Old Testament had already taught the Hebrews about chastisement, but they had a tendency to forget it.

People don't seem to understand what kind of God God is. A lot of people look on God as an indulgent father who turns His head when they sin, but that's not true. God is not up there in Heaven saying, "It's all right; this time I'll just let him get by." No. God deals with sin in the lives of His children.

I never could get by with anything as a boy. Every time I did something wrong I got caught. One of the rules my dad had was that you didn't play ball on Sunday, but I remember sneaking away from home to play ball one Sunday. The first ball was hit and instead of fielding it with my glove, I tried to field it with my right thumb. That thumb swelled to about twice its size. I had to go home with the evidence of my disobedience. And I was chastised.

Some form of the word *chastisement* is used eight times in Hebrews 12:4-13: chastening, chasteneth, chastisement, corrected. The word means the whole training and educating of a child. In other words, chastisement involves all of that discipline and correction that are essential to help a child grow and become everything that he is intended to be.

A. Interested in Us (12:5)

When God chastens us, it means that He is interested in us. Paraphrased, Hebrews12:5 says, "My son, don't despise it [don't think lightly of it, and also don't lose heart] when the Lord rebukes you." The writer was warning of two extremes. Some Christians don't take chastisement seriously. Other Christians faint under it; they get depressed.

B. Involved with Us (12:6)

When we are chastened, it means that God has a stake in our lives. When a person is chastised by the Lord, it may mean that He is trying to protect him.

When our children were little, we had to warn them not to touch anything hot. They didn't know that heat would hurt them, so when they reached out to put their hands on a hot iron, we said no and pulled their hands back. When they tried again, we were a little more forceful. And when they kept insisting, we gave them a few slaps on their hands. They cried, but we knew we were protecting them from something that could hurt them.

Sometimes when God chastises us, He is trying to protect us from something far worse. Which would be worse, to lose your business or your family? You say, "Of course,1 would rather lose my business than lose my family." God might allow someone to lose his business because some business-related activities, if continued, could result in his losing his family.

Sometimes God chastises us to educate us. "For whom the Lord loveth he chasteneth, and scourgeth every son whom he receiveth." Discipline is an evidence that the parent loves the child. Children left undisciplined have reason to question whether or not they are really loved by their parents. Children have a natural desire for their parents to be involved in their lives. Yet some parents don't seem to care whether their children pass or fail.

When I taught school, if a teacher sent a letter home with a student, the parents jumped right on it. Today that doesn't always happen. So many parents are so interested in their own selfish affairs they don't really care how their children turn out. They don't really love their children; they love themselves. It is tragic to see children brought up like that. Loving parents try to be alert to what is going on in their children's lives. Their concern is proof that they love them. When God has to deal with us in discipline and correction, He is doing it as evidence of His love.

Three words show us the process that God uses in His discipline: *rebuked, chasteneth,* and *scourgeth.* The first step God uses in dealing with us is rebuke. In Revelation 3:19 the Lord is talking to us, the church, giving an important principle in the matter of discipline: "As many as I love, I rebuke and chasten." How does God rebuke? Second Timothy 4:2 tells preachers to preach the Word; the Word rebukes. Sometimes the preacher speaks just as if he knows everything that is going on in your life. You sit there wondering, *Whoever told him about me?* I know it's true because I've had it happen to me. God rebukes His children by the Word. Sometimes in your daily devotions you're reading along, having a pleasant morning, and all of a sudden God rebukes you with a statement from His Word.

Children are different. Some children only need a word of rebuke. Some children only need a look. Simon Peter was like them. When he denied the Lord and went back to using bad language, cursing around the fire, the rooster crowed; it was God's messenger to his soul to remind him he had sinned. He looked toward the Lord Jesus, and he saw that the Lord was looking at him. Just a look of love from the Savior broke the heart of Simon Peter and he went out and wept bitterly. I want to be like Peter. I don't want to be one of God's hard-headed children. When I get that rebuke from the Lord, I want to repent, get right with Him, and rid my life of that sin.

But sometimes God's children are hard-headed, so God has to rebuke *and* chasten. How does God chasten? I think He uses circumstances, like sickness. I don't think that every time you're sick, God is chastening you. That's not true. When the disciples asked, "Who did sin, this man, or his parents, that he was born blind?" Jesus answered, "Neither hath this man sinned, nor his parents: but that the works of God should be made manifest in him" (Jn 9:2-3). But some sickness *is* the chastening of the Lord. If you let sin stay in your life, it will make you sick. For example, an ulcer could be your body's way of reminding you that you are worrying about something God told you not to worry about.

God can use other circumstances to chasten you. For example, a girl may lose a boyfriend. Perhaps God knew that boyfriend was going to drag her down, so He took him out of her life. Jonah was chastened by circumstances. God told him to go to Nineveh and Jonah said, "Not on your life." Instead Jonah went down to Joppa and a boat was going right where he wanted to go and he had just enough money to get there. Jonah said, "Boy, I'm in the will of God."

Isn't it amazing how Christians can talk themselves into believing that the sin they are committing is in the will of God? If you are doing anything that His Word says is wrong—I don't care how favorable circumstances seem—God is not pleased. Jonah got in that boat, and the boat put out to sea, and the Lord hurled a storm on the sea. Jonah was thrown overboard and he hit bottom with seaweed wrapped around his head. God was chastising him.

If you let sin stay in your life, you're going to end up at the bottom of some sea in dire circumstances too, and you're going to be crying out to God to rescue you because you wouldn't listen to His rebuke. If you don't obey what God says in His Word, God will have to send a storm into your circumstances.

Scourging is the most severe discipline. God rebuked David, but he didn't pay attention. God chastised him, but he failed to respond. So God had to scourge him. David lost his baby son, his family members caused him heartache, and the latter days of his life were filled with turmoil because he was under the scourging of the Lord. It is a serious matter when we fail to deal with sin in our lives.

II. A FAMILY TRUTH (12:7-10)

Statement number two: Chastisement is a family truth.

A. How It Is Expressed (12:7-8)

"If ye endure chastening, God dealeth with you as with sons; for what son is he whom the father chasteneth not?" One reason I know I am saved is that when I sin, the heavenly Father chastens me. God will chasten His children. If you are reading this and saying, "Now that's not true. I've got sin in my life, and I'm enjoying it; I'm getting by with it; God's not chastening me," then Hebrews 12:8 is for you: "But if ye be without chastisement, whereof all are partakers, then are ye bastards, and not sons." If you are sinning and getting by with it, you have never been saved; you are not God's child.

B. How It Is Explained (12:9-10)

"We have had fathers of our flesh [our earthly fathers] which corrected us, and we gave them reverence . . . For they verily for a few days chastened us after their own pleasure." Parents make mistakes, but we have to learn to forgive them and not go through life holding those mistakes against them. Usually, parents do the best they can under the circumstances. And when children grow up they talk fondly about the way their parents disciplined them. The chastening wasn't pleasant at the time, but the children brag about it later; they give their parents reverence. If we revere our earthly parents, what about our heavenly Father? Shouldn't we subject ourselves to Him and live?

III. A FRUITFUL TRUTH (12:11-13)

Statement number three: Chastisement is a fruitful truth.

A. Grow Up (12:11)

Hebrews 12:11 begins, "No chastening for the present seemeth to be joyous, but grievous." When chastening is happening it's not fun. We don't say, "Hallelujah! It hurts." The verse continues, "Nevertheless afterward it yieldeth the peaceable fruit of righteousness unto them which are exercised thereby." When you exercise, you sweat and strain. Your muscles get sore. But after the workout is over, you feel good because you know the exercise has done you good. Chastisement has the same effect. You feel good when it's over.

Chastisement helps us grow up. A restless little child can push you and push you until finally you have to give him a spanking. But then after the spanking there is peace and calm. When we are mature Christians, we will bear spiritual fruit such as peace.

B. Go On (12:12-13)

Hebrews 12:12-13 reads like a coach issuing orders: Lift up your hands and knees. The writer was telling us believers to shape up. We should respond to God's discipline and become everything we ought to become so that our lives will be examples and testimonies to the lost.

We should go on and stay in our path. We are challenged to win the race for the Lord Jesus, and not be a hindrance to the unsaved.

JERRY VINES

32

Missing the Grace of God
Hebrews 12:14-17

All the way through Hebrews, emphasis is placed on the importance of believers' being everything they can be by the grace of God. Hebrews 6:1 says, "Let us go on unto perfection." The Bible is not saying we can arrive at sinlessness in our lives, but it is saying we are called to go on to full maturity in the Lord.

Hebrews 12:14-17 is the last in a series of five exhortation or warning passages that challenge us to grow to maturity. The challenge is expressed in 12:15: "Looking diligently lest any man fail of the grace of God."

The writer was not suggesting that it is possible for a believer to be saved and then to be lost again. That would be contrary to what we know the Bible teaches. We must never interpret Bible doctrine by overturning a clear passage of Scripture with an obscure one. We must never let something that is difficult to understand counteract things that are easy and simple to understand. So here the reference is not to losing salvation, but to missing out on everything salvation can mean daily.

The verb translated *fail* means "come short of, fail to reach a goal." The same verb is used in Romans 3:23: "All have sinned, and come short of the glory of God." Hebrews 12:15 warns us that believers can come short of the grace of God.

We are saved by grace. Nothing we can do saves us. We are saved by the sheer favor of God in giving us His Son, Jesus Christ. "By grace are ye saved through faith; and that not of yourselves: it is the gift of God: Not of works, lest any man should boast" (Eph 2:8-9). For us who have been saved by the grace of God, there is the potential in that grace of God to provide us with every power, every opportunity, every strength necessary to grow to full maturity in the Lord Jesus Christ. The apostle Paul said, "By the grace of God I am what I am" (1 Cor 15:10). He was saying, "I am saved by the grace of God and anything good in my life is due to the working of God's grace."

I want to be all I can be for the Lord. Wouldn't it be a tragedy to come to the end of life and look back on the years and see all kinds of missed opportunities we had to grow in the Lord? The writer of Hebrews was warning, "Do not fail to be everything that grace can make you."

I. DIRECTIONS OF OUR LIVES (12:14)

To avoid failure, we are warned to give careful attention to the direction of our lives. What is your life's direction? What are you pursuing? Hebrews 12:14 instructs us to follow peace and holiness. That word *follow* means "pursue." A strong word indicates intensity. We are to give total attention and concentration to our pursuit of the right direction.

A. Harmony

"Follow peace with all men [that's our manward responsibility], and holiness [our godward responsibility], without which no man shall see the Lord." My human relationships ought to be guided in the direction of peace. I am to live in peace with other people. It should be my desire as a believer to be a source of peace and never to be a source of conflict. The Lord Jesus said in the sermon on the mount, "Blessed are the peacemakers: for they shall be called the children of God" (Mt 5:9). We should be peacemakers, not peacebreakers.

You can't have peace with other people if there is not peace in your own heart. Philippians 4:7 says, "And the peace of God, which passeth all understanding, shall keep your hearts and minds through Christ Jesus." When you have peace in your heart, the peace that God gives, you can be a peacemaker and you can more readily live in peace with other people. If you have a war going on in your own heart, it's going to be difficult for you to get along with people.

We believers ought to strive to get along with people. There is never any excuse for us to be rude, unkind, or tactless in our relationships with others. I have been in the presence of Christians who have not been peaceful in their attitudes, in restaurants for example. I have seen Christians be very rude to their waitress. There is no excuse for that. We always ought to be kind in our dealings with those who serve and wait on us. We are a testimony for Jesus that way.

It is not always easy to have peace in our relationships with other people. Some people make it very difficult for anyone to get along with them. That's why Romans 12:18 says, "If it be possible, as much as lieth in you, live peaceably with all men." There are some people with whom it is not possible to live in peace. When I run into people like that, I put as much distance between myself and them as I can. I don't want to have unnecessary conflict.

B. Holiness

In our godward relationship we are to pursue holiness. The word *holiness* scares a lot of people. No one wants to be accused of being too holy. Yet Hebrews 12:14 says we are to follow holiness, "without which no man shall see the Lord." The Bible teaches that God is holy (Lev 11:44; 19:2). An unholy person cannot come into the presence of a holy God. Jesus said in the sermon on the mount, "Blessed are the pure in heart: for they shall see God" (Mt 5:8).

But no one is pure in heart. God must make us holy. That's what salvation is all about. The wonder of the gospel is that a holy God sent His holy Son to make a holy sacrifice at Calvary; Christ shed His holy blood for unholy sinners like you and me. At salvation God imparted His holiness to me so that now I am by position holy in the Lord. I'm not holy in myself, but I am holy in what Jesus Christ has done for me.

The word *saint* means "a holy one." If you are saved, you're a saint—even if your husband or wife finds that thought incredible. In other words, God sees us through the shed blood of the Lord Jesus and our position is therefore holy in Him.

But the first part of Hebrews 12:14 is not talking about our *positional* holiness. It's talking about our *practical* holiness. We are to live holy lives. The word *holy* means several things. It means "complete." Holiness is to the soul what health is to the body. It also means "different." A believer is to be different. It also means "like God." "But as he which hath called you is holy, so be ye holy in all manner of conversation [everyday living]; Because it is written, Be ye holy; for I am holy" (1 Pe 1:15-16). In every detail of our lives, we should strive to be like God.

Zechariah 14:20 speaks of the day when "Holiness unto the Lord" will be engraved on the bells on the bridles of the horses. With every movement of the horses, those bells are going to be ringing a message of the Lord's holiness. That's the way it ought to be in our daily lives right now. Holiness is God's standard for our lives; we are to grow up in the image of the Lord. We believers are to remind people of the heavenly Father.

II. DISPOSITIONS OF OUR LIVES (12:15)

We are also warned to mature as Christians "lest any root of bitterness springing up trouble you, and thereby many be defiled [stained or soiled]." (Also see Prv 14:10 and Rm 3:14.) Bitterness is a matter of one's disposition. Have you ever met anyone whose mouth spews out bitterness? There is never anything pleasant, never any sweetness in that person's talk. Poison comes from his or her lips. The Bible says, "Let all bitterness ... be put away from you" (Eph 4:31). A root of bitterness means just a beginning of bitterness. Bitterness in your heart will grow and ruin your life.

A. Ourselves

What happens to us is not the important thing. Basically, we don't have control over the things that happen to us, but we do have control over how we respond to what happens. The fact is, bad things happen. How we respond will make us either bitter or better. We make the decision.

Let's suppose that someone does you wrong. You believe in the Lord, you are treating people right, you are trying to do right, and yet someone does you wrong. Let's even suppose that the "someone" is a Christian. It may be that the devil has set out to wreck you. If you are saved, the devil can't take away your salvation, but he certainly can make you miserable. He can ruin your testimony and rob you of victory and joy in the Lord. The devil may not have been able to make you commit adultery, or make you drink liquor, or make you dishonest in your business. But another Christian does you wrong, and you carelessly harbor a little root of bitterness. The devil tells you that you are justified in being bitter because a Christian has done something wrong to you. So you justify a wrong disposition. You allow seeds of bitterness to take root in your life and then that root of bitterness starts to grow. If you allow that root of bitterness to continue to grow, it will ruin you.

You might ask, What about the other person? Well, God will take care of him. It's not your job to deal with the sin in the lives of other believers.

B. Others

What is the result of a bitter disposition? "Thereby many [are] defiled." Other people are affected. One of the blessings of a big church is that it is difficult for bitter Christians to spread their poison the way they can in a small church. If you want to see a bad situation, go to a small church somewhere with a bitter Christian in the congregation. Such a person may even be a deacon or Sunday school teacher. Whenever you run into him he says, "I don't like the color of the carpet in this classroom. The teacher talks too long. The choir number wasn't any good today."

A Christian who has bitterness in his heart tastes like rotten eggs or sulfur water. Have you ever tasted that? I did when I was seven years old. I lived in St. Petersburg right across from a fountain of youth. I saw people going over there with big jugs and I thought, "Boy, I bet that tastes like soda, chocolate milkshakes, and Kool Aid all mixed into one!" So, one day I got up enough courage to go over there. I couldn't wait to get my mouth under that spout where the water was coming out. I didn't know it was sulfur water. It was the most bitter-tasting stuff I'd ever had.

None of us will ever become what God wants us to be as long as roots of bitterness are springing into fruits of bitterness in our lives. We must let God pull up those roots and sow the seeds of grace so that our lives will be like gardens of roses, sweet and fragrant.

III. DECISIONS OF OUR LIVES (12:16-17)

Finally we are warned to seek God's will in making decisions "lest there be any fornicator, or profane person" (12:16). The decisions we make have a great deal to do with whether the grace of God will work in our lives the way it should.

In this warning the writer of Hebrews used the Old Testament character Esau as an illustration. Esau was the twin brother of Jacob and the son of Isaac and Rebekah. You probably would have liked Esau because he was a gregarious, outgoing, rugged kind of individual, yet the Bible calls him a fornicator. He was an evil man. He was described as *profane* because he had no place for God in his life. Today we would use the word *secular* instead. Secularism allows no place for God. We are living in a secular society; there is progressively less and less room for God in it.

A. The Birthright Esau Sold (12:16)

One day Esau had been hunting and he came in absolutely famished. Jacob had a bowl of stew cooking. Esau told Jacob to give him part of that stew and Jacob said, "All right, if you'll sell me your birthright."

Esau replied, "What good is a birthright if I'm starving to death?" In Old Testament days a birthright carried with it not only temporal but also spiritual benefits. Esau was a godless man and made his decision based on present gratification rather than future satisfaction. He sold his birthright for one bowl of stew.

Jesus says, "What shall it profit a man, if he shall gain the whole world?" (Mk 8:36) All this world has to offer is one bowl of stew.

B. The Blessing Esau Sought (12:17)

Afterward Esau sought the blessing, but it was too late. Hebrews 12:17 says, "He found no place of repentance, though he sought it carefully with tears." I believe Esau was trying to get his father Isaac to change his mind. But the tears of adulthood don't undo the foolish choices of youth. That's why it is important to make right decisions throughout your life. When Esau came to the end of his life, he discovered he had been pursuing things that had no eternal value.

33

Where We Have Now Come
Hebrews 12:18-24

I received the Lord Jesus as my personal Savior when I was nine years old. It happened this way. A friend of mine came by the house and told me he had been thinking about giving his life to the Lord. That got me interested in giving my life to the Lord too. So, I went with him that Sunday night to church, and we talked to the pastor for a little while. He explained to us God's simple plan of salvation.

Obviously, I did not have an adult understanding of what it meant to be saved. But I realized that I was a sinner, that Jesus had died on the cross for my sins, and that if I would ask the Lord to come into my heart and be my personal Savior, I would be saved.

That night in the evening service I was sitting on the second row. When the preacher stood to preach—and he preached with compassion, with tears rolling down his cheeks—the Holy Spirit of God dealt with my heart. I saw that I was a sinner. I understood more clearly than ever before that Jesus loved me enough to die for me. So, when the invitation hymn was given, I got up, walked down the aisle, and gave my hand to the preacher and my heart to Jesus.

That night there was no way I could understand everything that had happened to me. Today I'm over eighty years old, and I still don't understand everything that happened. Not until I get to Heaven will I really understand everything that transpired when I passed out of death into life, when I moved from darkness into light, when I came out of the kingdom of Satan into the kingdom of God's dear Son. But all these years, I have been growing in my understanding of what it means to be saved and where I have come.

Hebrews 12:18 says, "For ye [those who are saved] are not come unto the mount that might be touched," and Hebrews 12:22 says, "But ye are come unto mount Sion." These two verses give us a tremendous contrast. Two mountains are compared here: mount Sinai, a physical mountain; and mount Zion, the spiritual destination of those who have been born again.

On mount Sinai Moses received the ten commandments from God (Ex 19-20). Hebrews 12:18-21 describes mount Sinai on that occasion. It was a place of fearful sights. The Israelites saw blackness, darkness, and tempest. In other words, there were awesome, frightening, physical manifestations that day when God gave the law. Mount Sinai was also a place of fearful sounds. The people heard a trumpet that grew louder and louder. And that mountain was a place of fearful speech. The people heard a voice that they didn't want to listen to. The scene was so terrible that Moses said, "I exceedingly fear and quake" (Heb 12:21).

Moses had been brought up in the majesty, grandeur, and splendor of the Egyptian empire. He had witnessed the miracles of God in the plagues, as God prepared the children of Israel to leave the land of Egypt and go into the promised land. Moses was not a man who had never seen manmade wonders or manifestations of the power of God. But when the Lord gave the ten commandments on mount Sinai that day, it was frightening even to Moses. Mount Sinai was an awesome display of the holiness of God.

When human beings experience the presence of God, they are stunned. When anyone really has an encounter with God, he is not light and flippant about it. When Isaiah saw the Lord, his response was, "Woe is me! for I am undone; because I am a man of unclean lips" (Is 6:5). To see the holiness and splendor of God is frightening.

The day that the law was given was one of the most frightening days of history. Israel began to understand just what kind of God it was with whom they had to deal. In their own strength and goodness, they were totally unprepared to stand in the presence of the holy God. God's holiness was vividly illustrated that day on mount Sinai. The mountain began to shake, and the people at the foot of the mountain also began to shake because they were in the presence of a holy God. A lot of people want to drag the Lord Jesus down to their level so that they will have a God who is no greater than they are; but Hebrews 7:26 describes the Lord Jesus as "holy, harmless, undefiled, separate from sinners."

The law of God reminds us that sinners have no way to approach a holy God. If we are honest, we must admit that we have broken every one of the ten commandments. Jesus showed that we break the ten commandments not only in act but also in attitude and thought. Not one of us can say that we have perfectly kept the laws of God.

The ten commandments are like a mirror. In them we see ourselves as we are. If you have dirt on your face, the mirror can show you that the dirt is there, but it can't remove the dirt. The law of God shows us our sin, but it has no power to remove that sin.

The law of God is also like a yardstick. A yardstick can measure your height, but it has no power to increase your height. The law of God measures us, but it has no power to make us more than we are. None of us has any hope of Heaven apart from the Lord Jesus Christ.

Spiritually speaking, if we are at the foot of mount Sinai, the holy law of God condemns us. But if we have been saved, we have arrived at mount Zion. In Hebrews 12:22 mount Zion refers to Heaven. That night I was saved, when my pastor took my hand. He would have been correct if he had greeted me with these words: "Welcome to Heaven." My eternity began the moment I received Jesus as my Savior. Hebrews 12:22-24 is a beautiful passage on Heaven. In some ways this passage is more meaningful than the descriptions of Heaven in the book of Revelation.

There doesn't seem to be much interest in Heaven today. So many people have it so good down here that they don't see any reason to be interested in something over there. As we grow older, however, we are going to get more and more interested in Heaven. Along the way we will lose precious loved ones. Some who are dear to us will be taken from earth to Heaven. Once we have loved ones in Heaven —a child or mother or father—Heaven means more to us than it used to mean. As we grow older, we are likely to lose our health. Our physical bodies are going to break down. So, Heaven is going to get sweeter the longer we live in this world.

There will come a time when material things are going to mean less and less to us. A man in a home for the elderly has a million dollars in the bank, but all his money can't buy his health back. There are things that money can buy, but there are things money can't buy. Money can buy a house, but it can't buy a home. Money can't buy happiness. Money can't buy love. Material things are going to become less satisfying, and we will become more and more interested in Heaven.

I. HEAVEN'S LOCATION (12:22a)

Have you ever wondered about the location of Heaven? Heaven is a place, a real, literal place. How do I know? Because Jesus said so. "Let not your heart be troubled: ye believe in God, believe also in me. In my Father's house are many mansions: if it were not so, I would have told you. I go to prepare a place for you" (Jn 14:1-2). Heaven is as real as Jacksonville, Florida, New Orleans, Louisiana, or my home in North Georgia.

A. God's Protection

"Ye are come unto mount Sion." Mount Zion was one of the mountains in the city of Jerusalem. In fact, the city of Jerusalem was built on a series of mountains. The temple was located on mount Moriah. The Lord Jesus went back to Heaven from the mount of Olives.

Mount Zion was the stronghold of King David, the site where he built his fortress. It was the strongest point in the city. To refer to Heaven as mount Zion is to remind us that Heaven is going to be the place of God's protection, a safe place. There is very little safety in this world. But when we get to Heaven, we won't need locks on our doors, and we will be able to cruise up and down the streets of glory without worrying about running into a drunk driver.

B. God's Presence

"Ye are come . . . unto the city of the living God." It is not only our city but God's city. Heaven is the place of God's presence. God is going to be there.

C. God's Permanence

Earthly Jerusalem was not a permanent place. It was often ransacked by enemies, and the inhabitants were captured and taken to distant lands, far away from the city in Judea. But if we know the heavenly Father, if we come into the heavenly Jerusalem, our move into Heaven is our last move. I don't know what my street address or zip code will be, but when I get there, I won't have to move again.

Have you had to move lately? I hope I never have to move again. If you and your wife can move furniture and not get a divorce, then your marriage is pretty solid! Yes, it's a terrible experience to have to move. But our move into Heaven is going to be a glorious move because we will never have to move out.

II. HEAVEN'S POPULATION (12:22b-23)

Heaven is going to be a populated place. Who will be there?

A. The Servants of God (12:22b)

The servants of God are going to be there: "Ye are come . . .. to an innumerable company of angels, To the general assembly." That phrase *general assembly* probably refers to a festive gathering. If the angels in Heaven rejoice over sinners repenting (Lu 15:10), what a celebration there will be when myriad angels are up there and all of the redeemed of God are up there too!

Angels are real. Jesus talked about angels. Referring to little children He said, "In heaven their angels do always behold the face of my Father" (Mt 18:10). I believe that angels also have a special interest in the redeemed and the whole salvation process. Angels have never known what it is to be saved, so the Bible says that the angels learn about the manifold wisdom of God in the church.

Won't it be interesting if when you arrive in Heaven an angel walks up to you and says, "I'm your guardian angel; I was placed in charge of you. I'm so glad you made it up here because you sure gave me a hard time."

B. The Saints of God (12:23)

The saints of God will be there: "And the church of the firstborn, which are written in heaven." Elsewhere Jesus is referred to as the firstborn, but here the redeemed are called the firstborn. In Jesus Christ, all that He is we are. The Bible says we shall be like Him. We are heirs of God, joint-heirs with Jesus Christ. So here the firstborn are the twice born.

The names of the saints have been inscribed in the Lamb's book of life. Is your name there? Having your name on a church roll is not enough. You need to have your name written down where it counts —in Heaven. You may not be listed in *Who's Who,* but if you are saved your name is written in Heaven.

It will be a glorious time when that last person to be recorded in the Lamb's book of life is saved, the church of the firstborn is caught up to meet the Lord in the air, and all God's saints gather in Heaven. You'll meet all your loved ones who have been saved. All your friends who have already gone to Heaven will be there.

The Old Testament saints will be in Heaven too: "The spirits of just men made perfect." I've got a lot of questions I would like to ask Abraham, Jonah, and David. We'll have some great conversations when we meet the redeemed of all the ages.

III. HEAVEN'S JUBILATION (12:24)

The best part of all is, "Ye are come... to Jesus." One of these days, what we now see by faith, we will see by sight. Seeing Christ will be reason for jubilation. First Peter 1:8 says, "Whom having not seen, ye love." But on the authority of Hebrews 12:24, 1can say there will come a time when we will come to Jesus Himself.

A. Christ's Continual Work

Christ's continual work there is to be "the mediator of the new covenant." By His intercessory prayer He constantly makes our salvation valid.

B. Christ's Completed Work

Christ's completed work is the shedding of His blood. "Ye are come ... to the blood of sprinkling, that speaketh better things than that of Abel." Abel was slain by his brother Cain. When Cain killed Abel, we are told that Abel's blood cried out for vengeance (Ge 4:10). Abel's blood was shed because of a murder, so it cried out for judgment. In Heaven we will be reminded that the only basis for our getting into Heaven is the shed blood of Jesus that was applied to our hearts. When we get to Heaven, we will understand it's all because of Jesus. There is peace, cleansing, and power in the blood of Jesus Christ. And that blood of Jesus Christ will have the power to maintain our salvation for eternity. First John 1:7 says, "The blood of Jesus Christ his Son cleanseth [present tense] us from all sin."

JERRY VINES

34

Things Unshakable That Remain
Hebrews 12:25-29

In his best-selling book *Cosmos,* Professor Carl Sagan of Cornell University stated his view of the universe in the opening sentence: "The Cosmos is all that is or ever was or ever will be." Sagan was saying that the universe came into existence by chance. He differs with those of us who believe Genesis 1:1: "In the beginning God created the heaven and the earth." Our formula for creation is: nothing + God = everything. Sagan's formula is: nothing + chance = everything.

What we believe about the origin of the universe has a lot to do with what we believe will be the destiny of the universe. If we believe that this world is all there is and that it will last forever and ever, then we are more likely to put the foundation of our lives on this physical universe and material things. But if we do not believe that this world is eternal, if we believe that it will one day pass away, then we will seek to find a more solid foundation for our lives.

Hebrews 12:25-29 is unsettling for those who have rested their lives on foundations that will ultimately be shaken. If you are living for this world, if this is the only world you expect to live in, then these verses have some very bad news for you.

I. THE LORD SPEAKING (12:25)

Hebrews 12:25 refers to the Lord speaking: "See that ye refuse not him that speaketh." For people who do not believe in a Creator, such a statement seems irrelevant. For others who believe in a Creator but think He is no longer interested in His creation, such a statement has no impact. But for those who believe in a Creator who is vitally interested in His creation and has spoken to the world, such a statement is highly significant.

The book of Hebrews begins, "God, who at sundry times and in divers manners spake in time past unto the fathers by the prophets, Hath in these last days spoken unto us by his Son" (1:1- 2). The opening affirmation of the epistle is: God has spoken. We Christians believe that there is a God who is great enough and big enough to have created the whole universe, and that God has also spoken to His world.

A. In Old Testament Times

Hebrews 12:25 says that God spoke on earth. The verse is probably referring to God's giving the ten commandments to Moses on mount Sinai. At different times God has spoken to men in different ways. In Old Testament times God sometimes spoke with a direct voice. At other times He spoke through visions or dreams. Those people were accountable for what they did with the revelation they received. If they refused to heed the voice of God, there was no escape.

B. In New Testament Times

God has also spoken to us in New Testament times. When Jesus came into the world, He was God in human flesh: "In the beginning was the Word, and the Word was with God, and the Word was God" (Jn 1:1). A word is a vehicle of thought. By means of words I let you know what is in my mind and in my heart. I communicate my heart and mind by the thoughts I express in my words. The Bible says that God has communicated to us in the person of His Son. If you want to know what God is like, look at Jesus Christ. If you want to know what God thinks about a subject or what He would do in a particular situation, observe the Lord Jesus as revealed in the pages of the written Word of God.

If those who heard God in Old Testament times could not escape responsibility, how much more sobering it is that those of us who have the New Testament revelation are not going to escape. You and I have a responsibility to deal with the Word of God and with God's revelation of Himself in Jesus. We cannot be neutral about the Lord Jesus Christ. Jesus says, "He that is not with me is against me" (Lu 11:23).

If a policeman has something to say, we pay close attention because of his position. When the president of the United States speaks, we listen with keen interest because of his position. When God speaks, we are responsible to listen to Him because He is the Creator, sustainer, and finisher of this universe. Hebrews 12:25 says, "See that ye refuse not him that speaketh."

II. THE UNIVERSE SHAKING (12:26-27)

In Hebrews 12:26-27 we foresee a universe in convulsion and upheaval. The voice that shook the earth at mount Sinai promises that one day this whole universe is going to be shaken to its foundations.

A. The Promise (12:26)

The writer of Hebrews was quoting from Haggai 2:6 when he said, "Yet once more I shake not the earth only, but also heaven." The day will come when all physical things are going to experience the shaking of God. The Bible predicts in several places that God is going to shake this universe; for an example see Revelation 6:12-14: "And, lo, there was a great earthquake; and the sun became black as sackcloth of hair, and the moon became as blood; And the stars of heaven fell unto the earth, even as a fig tree casteth her untimely figs, when she is shaken of a mighty wind. And the heaven departed as a scroll when it is rolled together; and every mountain and island were moved out of their places."

If you are building your life on things that are temporary, earthly, and passing, what are you going to do when all that you have depended on is removed? Second Peter 3:10,12 warns: "But the day of the Lord will come as a thief in the night; in the which the heavens shall pass away with a great noise, and the elements shall melt with fervent heat, the earth also and the works that are therein shall be burned up. . . . the heavens being on fire shall be dissolved."

In the day that the universe crumbles, the value of things will be properly understood. If you don't have your life founded in the Lord Jesus Christ, you are going to be in slim pickings when the promised shaking comes to pass.

B. The Purpose (12:27)

Hebrews 12:27 says, "And this word, Yet once more, signifieth the removing of those things that are shaken, as of things that are made." Everything that is made, every physical thing, is going to be shaken. Magnificent tall buildings that look as if they are going to be here forever are one day going to come tumbling down just like Jericho's walls.

What is the purpose of this future shaking? The answer is given in the last part of Hebrews 12:27: "That those things which cannot be shaken may remain." In that day everyone will see which things are solid and substantial. Those things that are shaken will be removed. Material foundations will disappear. What remains will be spiritual.

If we live long enough in this world, we will have experiences that are going to shake us. So we need to be sure we have put our lives on a foundation that cannot be shaken by the troubles, trials, and perplexities of this world.

What things cannot be shaken?

First, the throne of God cannot be shaken. God's throne is secure while the kingdoms of this world come and go. They are like a house of cards; they will fall. They are like sand castles; they will be washed away. Sometimes as we observe ruthless dictators march across human history, we get the idea that the parade will never end. But the Bible says, "He that sitteth in the heavens shall laugh" (Ps 2:4) and "Thy throne, O God, is for ever and ever" (Ps 45:6).

Second, the Word of God cannot be shaken. Christians are currently engaged in a great struggle over the nature of Scripture. Is the Bible the Word of God, or does it merely contain the word of God? Is all the

Bible inspired or not? I believe that it is. Don't ever get the idea that those of us who have been engaged in the struggle for the Bible are anxious for the future of the Bible, that we are afraid the Bible is going to be shaken. I take the view of Charles Haddon Spurgeon. Back in his day they were attacking the Bible, and someone asked, "Mr. Spurgeon, aren't you going to defend the Bible?" He laughed. "Defend the Bible? You might as well defend a lion. Let it loose and it will defend itself."

Early Christians struggled over the nature of Christ—who is Jesus? That struggle was resolved when the church came to realize that He is the God-man, all God and all man. Later Christians struggled over the nature of salvation. That struggle was resolved in the days of the Reformation when Martin Luther reminded Christendom that "the just shall live by faith" (Rm 1:17). We are saved by the grace of God through faith, plus nothing and minus nothing.

Now Christians are struggling over the nature of Scripture, but I am not implying that the Bible is going to be shaken by the attacks that are lodged against it. The problem is, confidence in the Bible can be shaken in the minds and hearts of individuals. When people have lost their confidence in the Word, they have no foundation of authority upon which to build their lives.

Psalm 119:89 tells us what God says about His Bible: "For ever, O Lord, thy word is settled in heaven." God's Word cannot be shaken. Let hostile men beat their hammer against the anvil of God's Word; the anvil will remain secure. We need to build our lives on the Bible. We need to rest our faith in the authority of Scripture as it reveals the Lord Jesus Christ as our Savior.

Third, the church of God cannot be shaken. Jesus said in Matthew 16:18, "Upon this rock I will build my church; and the gates of hell shall not prevail against it." (1 believe He was talking about Himself. Peter was a little pebble; Christ is the rock.) No one is going to destroy the church. Somebody asks, "Do you think the church is on the way down?" No way. The church is on the way up. The Lord is going to come one of these days for His church, and it's going to be alive and well when He comes. I'm not worried about the future of the church. It has a foundation that cannot be shaken.

Fourth, the Son of God cannot be shaken. We don't have to worry about the future of the Lord Jesus Christ. Not even the blasphemous movie *The Last Temptation of Christ* can detract from Him. Hebrews 13:8 says, "Jesus Christ the same yesterday, and to day, and for ever." We can build our lives on Jesus. He is a foundation that will never be shaken.

If you are building your life on the throne of God, the Word of God, the church of God, and the Son of God, then Jesus' words in John 10:28 apply to you: "1give unto them eternal life; and they shall never perish." You too will never be shaken.

III. THE CHRISTIAN SERVING (12:28-29)

The Obligation (12:28)

Based on the fact that we have a kingdom that cannot be shaken, "let us have grace, whereby we may serve God acceptably with reverence and godly fear." Christians have an obligation to serve.

How can we serve God effectively? By grace. We are saved by grace, but we must also serve God by grace. Paul said, "But by the grace of God I am what I am: and his grace which was bestowed upon me was not in vain; but I laboured more abundantly than they all: yet not I, but the grace of God which was with me" (1 Cor 15:10).

By grace we can serve God "acceptably with reverence and godly fear"—we can serve with a wholesome respect for a holy God. By grace someone who used to curse the name of Jesus can stand up in Sunday school class and give a testimony. By grace a musician who used to sing for the devil can sing for the Lord. We should always be conscious of the amazing grace that saved us, and we should always remember it is grace that enables us to serve God acceptably and with godly fear.

A. The Examination (12:29)

We serve with "godly fear" because we are dealing with a God of burning holiness. "Our God is a consuming fire," One of these days you and I are going to stand before this God, and our service is going to be examined. Our works are going to be made manifest; the fire will try everyone's works (1 Cor 3:13). When we believers stand before God, everything we have done will be reviewed.

Hebrews 12:29 also has a message for the lost. Jesus says that those who have rejected Him will one day hear the Lord say, "Depart from me, ye cursed, into everlasting fire" (Mt 25:41). We don't like to hear such a statement, but it's right there in God's Word. The only way we can come to this God who is a consuming fire is to come to the cross, where the fire of God's holy wrath was poured out against our Lord Jesus Christ. In His sacrifice on Calvary, Jesus endured the fire of God's wrath so that you and I might be saved.

JERRY VINES

35

We Can Build a Better Life
Hebrews 13:1-8,17,24

If I had an opportunity to sit down with you for a little while and talk to you one on one, I have a feeling you would say to me that you desire to experience a better life. You may not put it in the words of Simon Peter in 1 Peter 3:10, but I think you would agree with him that you want to love life and see good days. Not many people would say that their goal in life was to be as miserable as possible. Everyone is interested in the good life, and just about everyone wants to have a better life.

Few people really experience abundant, overflowing life. In the book of Ecclesiastes, King Solomon told us about all the things he tried to do to have a better life. But right in the middle of it all he said, "I hated life."

There are only three possible ways to live your life. Number one, you can endure your life—just go through it and endure it. Number two, you can try to escape life—by suicide, drugs, or alcohol. Number three, you can decide to enjoy life. Hebrews 13 gives practical directions to help us enjoy life.

A great Christian prayed, "Dear Lord, help us to be deeply spiritual but intensely practical." We see those two emphases in the book of Hebrews: the deeply spiritual and the intensely practical.

I. SOCIAL LIFE (13:1-3)

The first directions concern social life —our relationships with other people, whether family or strangers. We do not live in a vacuum. No man is an island. "For none of us liveth to himself, and no man dieth to himself" (Rm 14:7).

A. Siblings in the Lord (13:1)

Love ought to characterize every area of our social lives. We must love our siblings, our Christian brothers and sisters. "Let brotherly love continue." The idea keeps recurring in the Bible. "Seeing ye have purified your souls in obeying the truth through the Spirit unto unfeigned love of the brethren, see that ye love one another with a pure heart fervently" (1 Pe 1:22). "Beloved, let us love one another: for love is of God" (1Jn 4:7). "Beloved, if God so loved us, we ought also to love one another. No man hath seen God at any time. If we love one another, God dwelleth in us, and his love is perfected in us" (1 Jn 4:11-12). "If a man say, I love God, and hateth his brother, he is a liar: for he that loveth not his brother whom he hath seen, how can he love God whom he hath not seen?" (1 Jn 4:20)

It's easier for us to talk about loving others than to do it. God's children aren't always so lovable. To dwell above with saints we love, That will indeed be glory. To live below with saints we know, Well, that's another story. But if we ask the Lord, He will help us to have a genuine, Christlike love for our brothers and sisters in the Lord.

A. Strangers (13:2)

Christians are also to love strangers. "Be not forgetful to entertain strangers." In Bible times the inns where people stayed were not known for their cleanliness or safety, so traveling preachers and believers going from place to place to spread the gospel of the Lord Jesus would stay in the homes of other Christians. The Bible commands that we are to entertain and be open to those in the family of God whom we may not know. Christian believers are to have an attitude of love toward strangers in their midst.

You never know what some stranger is going to mean in your life. "For thereby some have entertained angels unawares." Think of someone who is a great blessing to you or is one of your dearest friends. When you first met that person, he was a stranger.

Abraham entertained angels unawares. It was about time for his afternoon nap. Abraham looked up and saw three men he had never seen before. Nonetheless, he invited all of them to lunch. It turned out that two of those men were angels and the other was the Lord Himself. Imagine it: the Lord was sitting in the home of Abraham eating a meal. Jesus said, "I was a stranger, and ye took me in" (Mt 25:35). We never know how the Lord may come to us.

B. Sufferers (13:3)

We are not to forget those believers who have been imprisoned for their faith. "Remember them that are in bonds, as bound with them." Christians should also love "them which suffer adversity, as being yourselves also in the body."

Some of God's people are suffering great adversities these days. One person may have lost his job, and he doesn't know what he is going to do. Another person may have a son or daughter going through a divorce. Someone else may have experienced a stunning tragedy that has left him shell-shocked. Many hearts are hurting. We need to love our brothers in Christ who are suffering.

In 1 Corinthians 12 Paul used the example of the physical body to show how we are all bound together in the family of God. When one part of the body hurts, the rest of the body hurts too. If you hit your finger with a hammer, your eyes begin to get teary, your face twists, your mouth yells, and your whole body feels the pain. The Bible says that when one member is honored we are all honored, and when one member suffers we all suffer. I wouldn't want to go through the heartaches and sufferings of this world if I didn't have a church family around me that loved me and helped me in times of sorrow.

II. MARITAL LIFE (13:4)

Hebrews 13:4 gives directions to safeguard marital life: "Marriage is honourable in all, and the bed undefiled: but whoremongers and adulterers God will judge." The word for *honorable* here could be translated "precious." The same word is used to describe the *precious* blood of Jesus. The same word is used to talk about the *precious* stones in the foundation of our home in the new Jerusalem. And the same word is used in 1 Corinthians 3:12 where the Bible says we are to build our lives with gold and silver and *precious* stones. So, the writer was saying that marriage is to be highly esteemed. We are living in a society where the institution of marriage is belittled, but God says marriage is precious.

A. The Purity of Sex

"And the bed undefiled" —the word rendered *bed* there could be translated "sexual intercourse." The Bible places sexual experience within the confines of the marriage relationship. God says that sex is not wrong; it is unspotted and untainted when it is kept within the context of marriage. If you want to have a better life, decide to do what God says about keeping sex within marriage.

B. The Perversion of Sex

Sex within marriage is beautiful, fulfilling, and creative; sex outside marriage is ugly, destructive, and damning. Sex is a gift from God, but to those who put it before marriage or take it outside marriage He says, "But whoremongers and adulterers God will judge."

In the sixties a sexual revolution began in America. We were told we had entered into a new age of sexual freedom and expression. We were encouraged to throw off the old restraints and enjoy a better life. That was now more than half a century ago. Are we any better off?

Premarital pregnancies are at a record level. "Hooking up" is common place. Rape is almost epidemic. STDs are like a plague on our society. Family life is going to pieces; homes are being shattered. Children are being brought up in abusive situations. Are we better off?

God will judge whoremongers and adulterers. God judges sexual immorality physically, emotionally, and spiritually. No one can violate

God's laws with impunity. But you will never go wrong going God's way. You will have a better life if you follow His directions for marriage.

III. FINANCIAL LIFE (13:5-6)

Hebrews 13:5-6 gives directions concerning financial life. We must pay attention to finances in order to survive. We don't live in a world where other people take care of us. Young people soon discover that. I told my youngest child, then in college, "Enjoy it, because the day you graduate it's all over."

We are directed to be content, not covetous. "Let your conversation be without covetousness; and be content with such things as ye have: for he hath said, I will never leave thee, nor forsake thee" (13:5). The writer of Hebrews was telling his readers not to love silver. Now there is nothing inherently wrong with silver. First Timothy 6:17 says that God gives "us richly all things to enjoy." There is nothing wrong with money, but "the *love* of money is the root of all evil" (1 Ti 6:10, italics added).

We must understand what money can and cannot do. Money can buy almost everything except happiness. Money is a passport to almost everywhere except Heaven. We must keep that in mind if we want to live better lives.

A, Contentment (13:5)

Paul said, "Not that I speak in respect of want: for I have learned, in whatsoever state I am, therewith to be content" (Phil 4:11). The word *content* means "self-contained." It was originally used to describe a country that had within its boundaries everything it needed to sustain the life of its people without any imports. We can be content because in Christ we have everything we need, and He will never leave us or forsake us. We can put our trust in Him.

B. Courage (13:6)

Because the Lord is trustworthy, we can be brave. Hebrews 13:6 says, "The Lord is my helper, and I will not fear what man shall do unto me." The writer was quoting from Psalm 118:6. A helper is one who runs to the call of danger—like a mother runs when she hears the cry of her child. Since we can trust the Lord to help us, we can have courage.

Psalm 118:8 says, "It is better to trust in the Lord than to put confidence in man." What man are you going to trust? Your boss? You may think he is great today, but one month from now he may fire you. Are you going to put your trust in your banker? He may embezzle your money. Are you going to put your trust in the president? Republican or Democrat, he may turn out to be a liar.

Trusting the Lord is important to your financial life. Depend on the Lord. Ask Him to lead you in your investments and expenditures. "But seek ye first the kingdom of God, and his righteousness; and all these things shall be added unto you" (Mt 6:33). God will meet your financial needs.

IV. SPIRITUAL LIFE (13:7,8,17,24)

Hebrews 13 also provides directions for spiritual life. If your spiritual life is not healthy, you will not be able to handle the social, marital, and financial aspects of life effectively. Your relationship to the Savior and your relationship to church leaders reveal the health of your spiritual life.

A. Your Leaders (13:7,17,24)

We are given instructions regarding our church leaders. Hebrews 13:7 says, "Remember them which have the rule over you." The writer did not mean that these leaders are dictators. One who has "the rule over you" is one who leads or directs you. The expression is used two other times in Hebrews 13: "Obey them that have the rule over you" (13:17); and "Salute all them that have the rule over you" (13:24). In these three verses are three directives concerning your relationship with the spiritual leaders in your church: remember them, respond to them, respect them.

The writer was saying that God has given us spiritual leaders. They may not always be right, but they are accountable to God to find out

God's will and direction concerning the congregation, so we should obey them.

Spiritual leaders have two important responsibilities. One is to speak the Word of God, and the other is to live out the Word of God through their lives. If your preacher doesn't preach the Word of God, then go to a church where the Word is preached. You also need to go to a church where there is personal integrity on the part of the preacher. Hebrews 13:7 says, "Whose faith follow, considering the end of their conversation." A preacher's doctrine should produce a Christlike life. If your preacher is not living right, something is wrong with his doctrine.

A lot of misinformation has been circulated about how a church should determine its direction and activities. Some people think that a church is a democracy where the people run things, but that's not true. I know some churches where the people do run things; they run the preacher and everything else. But the church was not intended to be a democracy. The church is not a monarchy either, where the preacher runs everything. Nor is the church an anarchy, where everyone does as he pleases.

None of those forms of government is correct. A church is a theocracy. God is supposed to run the church. How does God do that? By the leadership of godly individuals and *the fellowship* of all in the congregation. Hebrews 13:17 says, "Submit yourselves." Show me a church that will follow the direction of the leaders as they are led by the Holy Spirit, and I will show you a church that will grow and be a blessing.

B. Your Savior (13:8)

If you really want to build a good life, you need to build it on Jesus Christ. "Jesus Christ the same yesterday, and to day, and for ever."

> Yesterday He helped me;
> Today He did the same.
> How long will this continue?
> Forever, praise His name!

He is the same Jesus He was in the past. Think about when He came: His virgin birth, His virtuous life, His vicarious death, His victorious resurrection. He is the same today. Think about the Christ of the present, who comes into our hearts in answer to believing faith and lives to be real in our lives day by day. Finally think about the Christ of forever. Unto the ages, Jesus Christ is the same!

36

It Just Keeps Getting Better!
Hebrews 13:9-16

Everything we have in Jesus is far better than anything other religious systems offer. Jesus is the only way to God. He said, "I am the way, the truth, and the life: no man cometh unto the Father, but by me" (Jn 14:6). Jesus is not just *a* way to God, but *the* way to God. "Neither is there salvation in any other: for there is none other name under heaven given among men, whereby we must be saved" (Acts 4:12).

All through the book of Hebrews we have been following the theme that Jesus Christ is better. Hebrews 13:9-16 shows us one more time how much better the Lord Jesus Christ is.

I. A BETTER SYSTEM (13:9-10)

The system of grace is better than the system of law. The first people who read this epistle had recently come out of the old system. Since new believers then and now are susceptible to being carried away with false teachings, the writer of Hebrews warned against strange or alien doctrines.

In our day liberal theologians cause young believers to doubt their faith. The liberals offer a Bible full of holes instead of a whole Bible. They worship a stained Christ instead of a sinless Christ.

The admonition in Hebrews is clear. We are not to allow our minds to get carried away with teachings contrary to Scripture. Check everything you hear by the Word of God. See if the doctrine agrees with the Bible. Never allow yourself to be drawn away by any point of view that minimizes the Lord Jesus.

A. Grace Stabilizes Us (13:9)

What is the best way to keep your mind right? Keep your heart right. That's why Hebrews 13:9 says, "It is a good thing that the heart be established with grace." Some people try to live the Christian life based on ceremony and law. They have the idea that if they keep enough rules and participate in enough rituals, they will gain favor with God. But none of the ceremonies of Judaism was sufficient to stabilize the hearts of the Hebrews and make them strong in the Lord. The writer was referring to the ineffectiveness of the Jewish ceremonies when he wrote, "Not with meats, which have not profited them that have been occupied therein."

So, we are to have our hearts established, made firm, stabilized, not with rituals but with grace. Under grace, God works on the inside making us what we ought to be; under law, we work on the outside trying to make ourselves what we ought to be. Under grace you do not have to try to live the Christian life in your own ability and strength. Christ, in the person of the Holy Spirit, has come to live in your life, and based on the indwelling grace of God, you can live the way the Lord wants you to live.

B. Grace Satisfies Us (13:10)

"We have an altar, whereof they have no right to eat." Those who have not left that old religious system cannot participate in the spiritual benefits of the new altar. What did the writer mean when he said, "We have an altar"? I don't believe he was referring to a literal altar in any earthly location. Our altar is Christ. What Jesus did in His sacrifice at Calvary makes it possible for us to meet God. In Old Testament times God would meet man at an altar based on a sacrifice. When the priest laid the sacrifice on the altar, the fire of God came down, the glory cloud came down, and God met man at that literal, physical altar. Now our meeting place with God is not a place but a person.

We have an altar, and you and I have the privilege of eating at that altar. When Jesus was institutionalizing the Lord's supper He said in essence, "This cup is my blood; drink it. This bread is my flesh; eat it." We remember that figure of speech every time we gather around the Lord's table. But you and I can draw our nourishment from Jesus Christ daily. We are not only saved by the sacrifice of Jesus Christ, we are also sustained by that sacrifice. The Lord Jesus Christ daily gives us strength, spiritual nourishment, to help us live by His grace and be what He wants us to be. Grace satisfies us.

II. A BETTER SACRIFICE (13:11-14)

A. An Illustration (13:11)

Hebrews 13:11 says, "For the bodies of those beasts, whose blood is brought into the sanctuary by the high priest for sin, are burned without the camp." The writer was referring to the sacrifice, the sin offering, made on the day of atonement. On that day the blood of the sacrificial victim was brought by the high priest into the sanctuary, into the holy of holies. But in Leviticus 16:27 we are told that the body of the sacrificial animal was taken outside the camp and was completely burned.

The body of the victim was not to be used as nourishment. The worshipers did not feast on the body. In fact, Leviticus 4 details how every part of that animal was to be thoroughly burned. Why? The sin offering made on the day of atonement was a reminder of the seriousness of sin and the severity of the judgment of God. That sacrifice on the day of atonement illustrated that sin had to be thoroughly and totally dealt with.

B. An Application (13:12)

Jesus perfectly fulfilled that Old Testament type. "Wherefore Jesus also, that he might sanctify the people with his own blood, suffered without the gate." Christ was crucified outside the city of Jerusalem. He suffered outside the gate.

Outside the gate of Jerusalem, He prayed until His perspiration became like drops of blood. Outside men mocked Him and reviled His holy name. Outside He cried, "My God, my God, why hast thou forsaken me?" (Mt 27:46) May we never forget what Jesus did when He went outside the gate to be the sacrifice for our sins. Jesus went outside the gate of glory to come to this wicked world. He went outside the robe of royalty to be the servant who would become our Savior.

C. An Exhortation (13:13-14)

"Let us go forth therefore unto him without the camp, bearing his reproach" (13:13). The Jews of that day were called to come outside their religious system to receive what Jesus did for them. If you want to meet God, you must go outside the camp of all religious systems. Hebrews 13:13 is a call to separation. God's people are called to bear His reproach, His shame. There is a reproach attached to giving your life to the Lord Jesus Christ.

In London, England, Charles Haddon Spurgeon was the preacher at the Metropolitan Tabernacle, which seated five thousand back in the 1800s. It had no sound system like we have today. Spurgeon must have had quite a voice if all five thousand people could hear him. So many people came to the services that the leaders had to start issuing admission tickets. Spurgeon pleaded with his members not to come on Sunday night so lost people could get seats.

Some of the intelligentsia and wealthy were drawn by the ministry of this man and actually joined his congregation. But others didn't, because in those days in London, to affiliate with Metropolitan Tabernacle where Spurgeon preached had a measure of opprobrium attached to it. It is the same today. If you attach yourself to a church where the Bible is preached, Christ is magnified, and a holy life is the standard, you face the reproach of this godless world. You can escape reproach and be a part of the upper crust if you belong to some society church where they serve wine and cheese at their receptions, listen to lifeless lectures, and have worldly lifestyles. But the call of the Bible is to come outside the camp, where Jesus is, and to bear reproach for His name.

The world may look down on you and call you a fundamentalist. Every time I pick up a newspaper and see myself called a fundamentalist, I want to set the record straight. I don't know what is meant by *fundamentalist*. In today's media that label attaches itself to all the Jim Joneses and Ayatollahs of the world. If *fundamentalist* means that I believe in all the fundamentals in the Bible, I plead guilty as charged. But if *fundamentalist* means that I am a narrow-minded, anti-intellectual, extreme right-winger who needs to clean the dirt out from under his fingernails, I am not guilty.

Some of you reading this book need to come outside the camp. You are undercover attenders of a gospel-preaching church. You sneak in, hoping no one you know will see you. You may escape reproach, but you're a fool if you stay inside the city, inside the camp, inside the gate, to live your life for this old world "for here we have no continuing city, but we seek one to come" (13:14). Our prospects are not earthward, but heavenward.

> This world is not my home;
> I'm just a-passin' through.
> My treasures are laid up
> Somewhere beyond the blue.
> The angels beckon me
> From heaven's open door.
> And I can't feel at home
> In this world anymore.

I would rather know what I know in my heart and have the peace of Jesus I have in my soul today, bearing the reproach of this godless world, than to have anything it offers. One of these days I'm going to the new Jerusalem. The gates of that city are pearl; the streets are paved with gold; the music is led by the angelic choirs of Heaven; and the worship and praise of Jesus are the focal point of activity. If you'll come outside the camp to Jesus, you'll go up with Him to the new Jerusalem.

III. A BETTER SERVICE (13:15-16)

The priests in the Old Testament had service responsibilities. They served the Lord in the temple by offering sacrifices up to God. In these New Testament times if you have been saved, you are a priest and have service responsibilities. You can serve the Lord by offering spiritual sacrifices. "Ye also, as lively stones, are built up a spiritual house, a holy priesthood, to offer up spiritual sacrifices, acceptable to God by Jesus Christ" (1 Pe 2:5).

A. A Godward Aspect of Service (13:15)

Many different sacrifices are mentioned in the Bible. For example, Romans 12:1 says, "I beseech you therefore, brethren, by the mercies of God, that ye present your bodies a living sacrifice, holy, acceptable unto God, which is your reasonable service." The first sacrifice you ought to offer to the Lord as a believer-priest is your body. Every morning of my life I pray these words:

> O Lord, this day, as best I know how, I offer these hands to You. I offer these ears to You. I offer these eyes to You. These feet are Yours. These lips are for You. Don't let me do anything with these hands You wouldn't want me to do. Don't let me hear anything with these ears You wouldn't have me hear. Don't let me see with these eyes anything You wouldn't have me see. Don't let me go anywhere with these feet You wouldn't have me go. Don't let me speak with these lips anything You wouldn't have me speak.

As a believer-priest, I have a responsibility to lay my entire self on the altar every day of my life.

Philippians 4:18 mentions another sacrifice. There Paul made reference to the offering given him by the believers at Philippi: "But I have all, and abound: I am full, having received of Epaphroditus the things which were sent from you, an odour of a sweet smell, a sacrifice acceptable, well pleasing to God." Their gift was a sacrifice that pleased God. That realization puts a different perspective on giving. Giving is an act of worship. When the offering plate is passed, you as a believer-priest have an opportunity to place an offering envelope in the collection plate. When you do, you are saying to God, "This is just another sacrifice that I am offering up to you."

Winning souls to the Lord is another kind of sacrifice. When Paul toured the Roman empire, he didn't go as a sightseer but as a soulwinner. He had a ministry to win Gentiles to Jesus. Look at how he described his ministry: "That I should be the minister of Jesus Christ to the Gentiles, ministering the gospel of God, that the offering up of the Gentiles might be acceptable, being sanctified by the Holy Ghost" (Rm 15:16). Paul pictured himself as a believer-priest winning someone to the Lord, laying that soul on the altar, and saying, "Lord, I won this one for you." An outlook like Paul's could change your soulwinning activity.

There is also the sacrifice of praise. Hebrews 13:15 says, "By him therefore let us offer the sacrifice of praise to God continually, that is, the fruit of our lips giving thanks to his name." The growth of fruit must be natural. You can't force fruit to grow. (Some people's praise is artificial, manufactured. It's just like a plastic apple.) But if there is genuine gratitude in the heart, there is a natural welling up that will ultimately express itself in the fruit of the lips giving thanks to the Lord. One of the best ways to praise God is to use the lips to tell someone about Jesus. I have a lot more confidence in the person who is using his lips to tell a soul about Jesus than in the person who uses his lips to holler "Praise the Lord" all the time.

We are to give thanks *in* everything (1 Thes 5:18; Eph 5:20). A lot of us can give thanks *in* all things, but it's a little harder to give thanks *for* all things. Sometimes we don't really understand what God is doing and we need to learn to trust that through it all God is at work. We should praise Him when we understand and also when we don't.

B. A Manward Aspect of Service (13:16)

Lip service must be accompanied by life service. Hebrews 13:16 says, "To do good and to communicate forget not: for with such sacrifices God is well pleased." We are to give loving service to other people; we are to be good neighbors and share with the needy. When we give such life service as offerings to God, He will be pleased with the sacrifices.

When the Lord Jesus walked on this earth, Heaven opened and the Father said, "This is my beloved Son, in whom I am well pleased" (Mt 3:17). If you live your life to serve Jesus, the heavens probably won't open up now for you, but one of these days they will. You will be caught up and taken to the judgment seat, and the Lord will say, "This is one of My sons, and I am well pleased."

37

Pay Attention to This Letter
Hebrews 13:18-23,25

The closing words of the Epistle to the Hebrews summarize what has been said and give us a further word of encouragement. Hebrews 13:22 says, "1 beseech you, brethren suffer the word of exhortation: for I have written a letter unto you in few words." The writer was appealing to his readers to give this difficult letter a fair hearing. This verse is a reminder to us to pay attention to the Word of God and to what God has to say in its pages.

I. CLOSING ADMONITION (13:18-19)

The closing admonition is "Pray for us" (13:18). That request is found frequently in the New Testament. All of us need the prayers of other people. Every pastor desperately needs the prayers of his congregation. If you and I really understood the forces that are active in the spirit world, unseen by human eyes, we would know the importance of prayer. God honors the prayers of humble, simple, praying people, but prayer is no simple activity.

Have you ever thought about the attention you draw when you begin to pray? You draw the attention of the devil. When you begin to pray, the devil will do anything he can to keep you from continuing.

He knows that if he can keep you from praying, he can stop the lifeline of spiritual power into your life. When you begin to pray, the devil will send wandering thoughts into your mind. I don't know about you, but when I get ready to pray, everything I need to do comes to my mind. I have to work to concentrate on praying.

You also draw the attention of the God of Heaven when you pray. God must see that the sun comes up at just the right time every day. He must keep this earth circling in its orbit. He must watch every sparrow that falls. God has a lot to do. Yet when you kneel down and say, "Our heavenly Father," He says to the angels, "Shhhh. One of My children down there has something to tell Me, and I'm going to give him My best attention."

A. Spiritual Matters (13:18)

We are to pray for spiritual blessings. We should pray that our hearts will be right and that we will live honorably. As Hebrews 13:18 says, "We trust we have a good conscience, in all things willing to live honestly." It's a wonderful thing to have a clear conscience, to know deep down in your heart that you have done, as best as you know how, what God would have you to do. It's a wonderful thing to be able to go to bed at night and know that there is nothing between your soul and the Savior.

We need to pray for one another because the devil doesn't want us to have that honorable kind of life. He wants to bring temptations, trials, and difficulties into our lives to keep us from being the kind of believers that God wants us to be.

B. Personal Matters (13:19)

We are also to pray for personal blessings. The writer of Hebrews did. Hebrews 13:19 says, "I beseech you the rather to do this [to pray for us], that I may be restored to you the sooner." We don't know what circumstances prompted this request, but the writer was asking for prayer that his circumstances be changed.

That request was very specific. We ought to be specific when we pray. Too often we are general in our praying. When we pray in general terms, we cannot expect specific answers. If you could ask God for one thing today, what would it be? Which particular lost person are you praying for God to save? It's wonderful to pray, "God save the lost," and we do pray that way. But we need to get specific and name names.

I have heard it said that when we pray, God doesn't change things; God changes us. I do believe that God changes us when we pray. I know He has changed me. Prayer does change people. But God also changes things. Prayer changes circumstances. Do you want proof? The Old Testament prophet Elijah came out of nowhere and went back into nowhere. He came suddenly on the scene and then quickly passed off the scene. Yet Elijah had such power with God in prayer that he was able to lock the windows of heaven so that it didn't rain for many months. Then in answer to his prayers, the windows of heaven were unlocked and the rain came.

Prayer can change circumstances in your life too. Sometimes when a person gets married, he thinks his job is to change his mate. But you can't change your mate. Some of you have been trying for thirty years and haven't succeeded. But if your wife or husband needs changing, God can do it. The best thing you can do is to talk to God about the situation. It may be that it's you who needs changing, so when you pray, God may change you.

Whatever the circumstances may be, God's people need to pray. "Pray for us" is a simple little admonition, but there is spiritual dynamite in it.

II, CLOSING BENEDICTION (13:20-21)

In Hebrews 13:20-21 is one of the great benedictions of the Bible. This closing blessing states all the major themes of the book of Hebrews and everything God intends to do in the life of a believer.

A. His Peace (13:20)

The benediction begins, "Now the God of peace." That's one of the favorite phrases of the apostle Paul and because it is used here, some people continue to believe that Paul is the author of the book of Hebrews.

In the garden of Eden, man declared war on God. Yes, when Adam and Eve disobeyed God and ate the forbidden fruit, they declared war on God. Sin is rebellion against a holy God. All through the ages, human beings have been at war with God, fighting Him, battling Him. So God had to do something to reconcile them to Himself, to bring about peace again. The wonderful thing is, God takes the initiative. It is always God who makes the first step. So, the Bible says that God sent His Son, the Lord Jesus.

When Jesus was born the heavenly host said, "On earth peace, good will toward men" (Lu 2:14). The Lord Jesus came to be a peacemaker. When He went to the cross of Calvary and shed His precious blood, He made peace between God and man. The only way we can have peace with God is to meet Him at the cross. Colossians 1:20 says, "Having made peace through the blood of his cross." In other words, the peace treaty between man and God was signed by our Lord Jesus Christ. No one has personal peace until he comes to the God of peace. Nor will there be international peace in this world until the Prince of Peace comes back.

B. His Provision (13:20)

The benediction continues, "That brought again from the dead our Lord Jesus, that great shepherd of the sheep, through the blood of the everlasting covenant." Isn't that a beautiful figure of speech for Jesus? David called Jesus the shepherd in Psalm 23: "The Lord is my shepherd; I shall not want." And Psalm 100:3 compares us to sheep: "We are his people, and the sheep of his pasture."

When the Bible compares us to sheep, don't think it is a compliment. "All we like sheep have gone astray" (Isa 53:6). Growing up, I was not around sheep, so all I thought of was little white fluffy animals. "Mary had a little lamb; its fleece was white as snow." But sheep are dirty and dumb. They are also absolutely defenseless. So if we are like sheep, we need a shepherd; and we have one.

What kind of shepherd is Jesus? Jesus calls Himself the good shepherd: "I am the good shepherd: the good shepherd giveth his life for the sheep" (Jn 10:11). Hebrews calls Jesus the great shepherd who not only died for us, but also lives for us. Peter called Jesus the chief shepherd who one of these days will appear for us (1 Pe 5:4). So, Jesus provides for us. He takes care of our past as the good shepherd, our present as the great shepherd, and our future as the chief shepherd. We have a shepherd who loves us and leads us and is coming again for us.

C. His Purpose (13:21)

There is more to the benediction: May the God of peace "make you perfect in every good work to do his will, working in you that which is well pleasing in his sight, through Jesus Christ." Verse 20 tells what God does *for* us; verse 21 tells what God does *in* us. God wants to make us perfect.

Almost without exception, when the word *perfect* is used in relationship to the believer, it does not refer to that ultimate perfection which will be his when he stands in the presence of God. Rather, the word refers to full maturity in the Lord. The word translated *make perfect* in Hebrews 13:21 means "bring together what has been broken." A doctor would use this word when speaking of restoring a broken bone.

The word translated *make perfect* could also be interpreted "equip." A soldier would use it when speaking of supplying an army. To paraphrase, "May the God of peace equip you in every good work to do His will." God is the one who can enable you to do what He has told you to do. God tells you what He wants you to do, but He doesn't stop there. He says, "I am going to equip you to do what I have told you to do."

Have you ever thought about what a motley crew those first disciples were? I wouldn't have chosen most of them if I had been doing the picking.

There was Simon Peter who was known to curse when he was under pressure. James and John were known to have asked God to rain down fire on people. Thomas was a doubter who wouldn't believe unless he had irrefutable proof. Yet the Lord Jesus gave those disciples the great commission. He told them to go into all the world and preach the gospel. They must have felt a tremendous sense of inadequacy when they heard their assignment. But Jesus assured them, "Lo, I am with you alway, even unto the end of the world" (Mt 28:20). He was saying, "I'm going to enable you to do what I have commanded you to do."

The secret to victorious Christian living is that God gives us the power to do what He has commanded us to do. God works in us. Paul said, "It is God which worketh in you both to will and to do of his good pleasure" (Phil 2:13).

How does God equip us? How does God work in our lives? One way God works is by means of the Bible, the Word of God. Second Timothy 3:16-17 tells us that the Word of God equips the people of God that we might be "thoroughly furnished unto all good works." As we read the Word of God, He shows us His will.

Another way God equips us is by means of prayer. In 2 Thessalonians 3:1 Paul wrote, "Pray for us, that the word of the Lord may have free course, and be glorified."

God also works through other Christians. "Brethren, if a man be overtaken in a fault, ye which are spiritual, restore such an one in the spirit of meekness; considering thyself, lest thou also be tempted" (Ga 6:1).

Then too God works in us by means of suffering. "After that ye have suffered a while, [He will] make you perfect, stablish, strengthen, settle you" (1 Pe 5:10). Sometimes we are not equipped to be all that we ought to be in the Christian life until we have suffered —until we have had some heartaches, burdens, problems.

So, God works in various ways to accomplish His purpose, to bring us to full maturity. The closing benediction of Hebrews reminds us of this goal. Every day of our lives we ought to pray, "O Lord, equip me to do Your will. Work in me that which is well-pleasing in Your sight. Amen."

III. CLOSING EXHORTATION (13:22-23,25)

A. An Appeal (13:22)

In Hebrews 13:22 the writer asked his readers to pay attention to his words: "And I beseech you, brethren, suffer the word of exhortation: for I have written a letter unto you in few words." Relatively speaking, when you consider all the great doctrines mentioned in Hebrews, his words *are* few. Actually, one can read this book in less than an hour, but the content is infinitely important.

B. An Encouragement (13:23)

Before the writer closed his letter, he referred to Timothy. This reference is an encouragement to be interested in the welfare of our brothers and sisters in the Lord. We are part of the family of God. When others hurt, we hurt. When they have a burden, we have a burden. When they have a problem, we have a problem.

Hebrews 13:23 says, "Know ye that our brother Timothy is set at liberty." That verse may suggest that Paul did not write the epistle, because he almost always spoke of Timothy as his son. The point is, though, that Timothy had been released. The Hebrews were concerned about what happened to Timothy, and we should be concerned about our fellow Christians.

It is reassuring that Timothy's name is given. That reminds us of the wonderful fact that God knows us by name. You are not just a number to the God of this universe. God has your name on His heart. When an Old Testament priest went into the presence of God, he wore a breastplate over his heart. On the breastplate were the names of all of the children of Israel by tribe. Therefore, the priest went into the presence of God with the names of the people on his heart. Isn't it great to know we have a great high priest in Heaven and that our names are on His heart? Don't ever think you are a nobody, that no one cares for you. God cares for you and knows you by name.

C. A Conclusion (13:25)

The closing exhortation is "Grace be with you all." *Grace* and *glory* are the two great words of our faith. *Grace* is the word that talks about how the Christian life begins. *Glory* is the word that talks about how the Christian life ends (13:21). Grace is the root; glory is the fruit. Grace and glory are the two arms of God's rich embrace of the soul. Psalm 84:11 says, "The Lord will give grace and glory: no good thing will he withhold from them that walk uprightly."

The theme of grace runs all through the epistle. Hebrews 2:9 tells us that Jesus by the grace of God tasted death for every man. Hebrews 4:16 says that the place where we meet God is the throne of grace. Hebrews 10:29 warns us. that we are not to despise the Spirit of grace. Hebrews 13:9 says that our hearts are to be established with grace.

It is the grace of God that we need. "Grace be with you all. Amen."

ABOUT THE AUTHOR

JERRY VINES

Dr. Jerry Vines is a native of Carrollton, Georgia. He was educated at Mercer University (B.A.), New Orleans Theological Seminary (B.D.), Luther Rice Seminary (Th.D.), and Southwestern Baptist Theological Seminary (PhD). He was elected President of the Alabama Pastors' Conference in 1976, President of the Southern Baptist Pastors' Conference for 1976 -1977. He also served two terms as President of the Southern Baptist Convention from 1988 – 1989.

Dr. Vines accepted the call to be pastor at First Baptist Church, Jacksonville, Florida, in July 1982 and retired from the pastorate in February of 2006.

Dr. Vines' interests include Alabama football. It's a year-round passion! He also enjoys spending his free time in the Smoky Mountains with his family, especially his grandchildren! While there, it is a tradition for him to frequent The Old Mill restaurant for breakfast in Pigeon Forge, Tennessee.

He and his wife, Janet, have four children: two daughters, Joy and Jodi, and two sons, Jim and Jon. He and Mrs. Vines also have seven grandchildren: Brittney, Ashlyn, Jay, Caroline, Catherine, Jack and Carson. Son in law Tim Williams and daughter in law Leslie Vines.

For more books and resources by Dr. Jerry Vines, visit the webstore at jerryvines.com

www.ingramcontent.com/pod-product-compliance
Lightning Source LLC
Chambersburg PA
CBHW030513080526
44586CB00011B/172